The exodus of more than 250,000 Soviet Jews during the 1970s has opened a window for the authors of this volume to gain significant new insights into the essentially closed society and political decision-making process of the Soviet Union. Divided into two parts, the book first analyzes the nature and development of Soviet anti-Semitism as well as examining the effects of world pressure from 1971 to 1980 on the Soviet government's decision to allow Soviet Jews to emigrate. It then offers useful cross-cultural comparisons of the emigration experience, with a specific focus on Soviet-Jewish resettlement in Israel and the United States.

Related titles in Duke Press Policy Studies

Afghanistan and the Soviet Union
Henry S. Bradsher

NATO under Attack
Why the Western Alliance Can Fight Outnumbered and Win in Central Europe without Nuclear Weapons
F. W. von Mellenthin *and* R. H. S. Stolfi *with* E. Sobik

Alcohol in the USSR
A Statistical Study
Vladimir G. Treml

The Political Reliability of the Warsaw Pact Armies
The Southern Tier
Ivan Volgyes

Soviet Jewry in the Decisive Decade, 1971-80

Edited by
Robert O. Freedman

Duke Press Policy Studies
Duke University Press   Durham, North Carolina   1984

© 1984, Duke University Press, all rights reserved

Printed in the United States of America
on acid-free paper

Library of Congress Cataloging in Publication Data
Main entry under title:

Soviet Jewry in the Decisive Decade, 1971–1980.

(Duke Press policy studies)
Bibliography: p.
Includes index.
1. Jews—Soviet Union—History—1971–   —Addresses, essays, lectures. 2. Antisemitism—Soviet Union—Addresses, essays, lectures. 3. Soviet Union—Ethnic relations—Addresses, essays, lectures. 4. Jews, Russian—Israel—Addresses, essays, lectures. 5. Jews, Russian—United States—Addresses, essays, lectures.
I. Freedman, Robert Owen. II. Series.
DS135.R92S657   1984   305.8′924047   83-20592
ISBN 0-8223-0544-5

This book is dedicated to M. Budd Kolker (beloved brother of Fabian Kolker) who died in December 1981. The memory of M. Budd Kolker will always be an inspiration to those throughout the world who struggle for human rights, Jewish values, and social justice.

Contents

List of Tables and Figures   ix

Preface   xi

Introduction   xiii

1. Soviet-Jewish Emigration, 1971–80: An Overview   *Jerome M. Gilison*   3

2. The Jews in the Soviet Union: Emigration and Its Difficulties   *Jerry Goodman*   17

3. Brezhnev and Soviet Anti-Semitism   *William Korey*   29

4. Soviet Jewry and Soviet-American Relations: A Historical Analysis   *Robert O. Freedman*   38

5. The Welcome Home: Absorption of Soviet Jews in Israel   *Theodore Friedgut*   68

6. A New Soviet Jewry Plan   *Fabian Kolker*   79

7. Soviet-Jewish Immigrants to the United States: Profile, Problems, Prospects   *Zvi Gitelman*   89

8. Aspects of Integrating Soviet-Jewish Immigrants in America: Attitudes of American Jewry Toward the Recent Immigration   *Stephen C. Feinstein*   99

9. Adaptation and Acculturation of Soviet Jews in the United States: A Preliminary Analysis   *Ilya I. Levkov*   109

Epilogue   144

Annex 1: Jewish Emigration from the USSR, 1965–81   149

Annex 2: Soviet-American Trade and Soviet-Jewish Emigration, 1969–80   150

Notes   151

Bibliography   161

Index   165

Tables and Figures

Tables

2.1. Emigration from the USSR since 1967   22
5.1. Comparison of areas of life in Israel with life in the USSR   77
7.1. Geographic origin of Soviet-Jewish immigration from 1974–June 30, 1979   90
9.1. Ages of the emigrants   110
9.2. Amount of the emigrants' salary and the number of people working under their supervision   111
9.3. Reasons given for emigration, by national sample and cities   117
9.4. Number of evenings per week spent by the emigrants with friends   119
9.5. Role of Jewish organizations in assisting the emigrants' absorption into American life   121
9.6. Comparison of the emigrants' perceptions of status in the United States and the USSR   123
9.7. Length of the emigrants' leisure time spent with their parents   126
9.8. Acquaintance of the emigrants with Jewish history and customs   134
9.9. Interest of the emigrants in books and courses   134
9.10. Possibilities of combining a deep Jewish religious conviction with contemporary values   135
9.11. Soviet Jews' self-perception of their intellectual levels   140
9.12. Overall perceptions by Soviet Jews of their American counterparts   141

Figures

1.1. Annual rate of Soviet Jewish emigration to Israel and the United States   8
1.2. Trends in age distribution of Soviet emigration to the United States 1972–80   15

Preface

It is rare in human history when the exodus of a people from its native land attracts as much worldwide attention as did the departure of the quarter-million Jews who left the Soviet Union from 1971 through 1980. Jews and non-Jews, American congressmen and senators, secretaries of state and presidents, Israeli prime ministers, and Soviet politburo members have all been involved in the process that has enabled these Soviet Jews to find new homes in the West. Nonetheless, the Soviet-Jewish exodus has not been without its difficulties both for Soviet Jews seeking to leave the USSR and for the emigrants trying to begin life again in their new country. It is the purpose of this book, which analyzes the first decade of the Soviet-Jewish exodus, to examine these dual problems: the emigration process itself, and the process of resettlement in both Israel and the United States.

The book had its origins in a conference held at the Baltimore Hebrew College on May 3, 1981. This was the third in a series of conferences dealing with the problems of Soviet-Jewish emigration and resettlement that have been sponsored by the Center for the Study of Soviet Jewish Emigration and Resettlement of the Baltimore Hebrew College. The first, in 1976, analyzed the "mental baggage" that Soviet Jews brought with them to the United States; the second, in 1980, examined the problems inherent in the resettlement process. The planners of the third conference felt that sufficient time had passed to enable a number of highly qualified scholars to look at the Soviet Jewry movement, in all of its aspects of emigration and resettlement, from the prism of a decade of historical experience.

Many individuals and organizations are deserving of praise for their assistance in this project. First and foremost, I would like to thank Dr. Leivy Smolar, President of the Baltimore Hebrew College, who has given his wholehearted support for the series of conferences on Soviet Jewry held at the college. Second, I would like to thank Stephen Solender, Executive Vice President of the Associated Jewish Charities and Welfare Fund of Baltimore, who has strongly supported the college's research on Soviet Jewry. Third, I would like to thank Stanley Sollins, Executive Director of the Baltimore Jewish Community Relations Council, and his staff for their assistance in cosponsoring the conference.

A special expression of gratitude is due Fabian Kolker, who together with his brother, M. Budd Kolker, established the Kolker Foundation for the Study of Soviet Jewry and the Contemporary Middle East at the Baltimore Hebrew College. Their generous support has enabled the college to expand its research efforts in these two major areas of modern Jewish history. Unfortunately, in the period between the holding of the conference and the publication of this book,

M. Budd Kolker passed away. It is to his memory therefore that this book is dedicated.

Baltimore, Maryland   Robert O. Freedman

Introduction

Understanding Soviet society and the motivations of Soviet leaders has long been a most difficult task, both for statesmen and for academic analysts. The essentially closed nature of Soviet society and the hidden mechanisms of Soviet decision making have proved to be formidable obstacles in the way of those who seek to understand the USSR. Nonetheless, the exodus of more than 250,000 Soviet Jews over the last decade has opened up a window that enables outside observers to learn a significant amount about Soviet society. It is now possible, for the first time since World War II, to survey a relatively large number of former Soviet citizens so as to obtain new insights into Soviet society. Second, the very emigration process itself has enabled close observers to gain a new feeling for the operation of Soviet foreign policy decision making. Finally, in the last decade much has been revealed about the nature of Soviet anti-Semitism, a phenomenon closely tied to the Soviet leadership's domestic and foreign policies.

Thus, the Soviet-Jewish emigration movement, as analyzed in this book, offers a significant opening into understanding the workings of Soviet society and government in the decade of the 1970s.

While the emigration movement as a whole offers new insights into Soviet society, the resettlement process of Soviet Jews in America and Israel provides useful cross-cultural comparisons of the absorption process, particularly for students of international migration and resettlement, and for those social workers charged with the responsiblity of helping to resettle Soviet Jews. The Sovet-Jewish experience, given the large sample of émigrés and the open nature of both Israeli and American societies, provides an excellent laboratory for analyzing the resettlement process and, in particular, for learning which resettlement techniques are more successful than others and which parts of the émigrés' mental baggage from his country of origin are the most difficult to discard.

The book, consequently, falls into two sections. The first deals with the politics and process of the emigration movement, the second with the process of resettlement in Israel and the United States. In the opening chapter Jerome Gilison presents an overview of the central developments of Soviet Jewry during the period from 1971 through 1980. He deals with the growing Soviet anti-Semitism that helped spark the exodus, the international conditions that made the exodus possible, the types of Jews who have decided to leave, the plight of Jews who have been unable to obtain exit visas, and the increasing preference of exiting Soviet Jews for the United States rather than Israel.

Jewish emigration peaked in 1979, dropping precipitously in 1980. The reasons for this development are dealt with by Jerry Goodman, who presents an in-depth analysis of the emigration process and offers a series of possible explanations for the decreasing tendency of emigrating Soviet Jews to settle in

Israel. After noting that virtually one-third of the entire Jewish population of the Soviet Union has at one time or another requested an exit visa, Goodman discusses the increasingly severe problem of "refuseniks"—those Jews who have been refused permission to leave the USSR. He highlights the case of Viktor Brailovsky, who, before his arrest, served as editor of the Jewish samizdat publication, *Jews in the USSR*.

Perhaps the primary reason for the Soviet-Jewish exodus has been the growth in anti-Semitism in the Soviet Union over the last decade. Soviet anti-Semitism, which is often disguised by an anti-Zionist label, is analyzed by William Korey, who suggests that the rise in anti-Semitism may be linked to the post-Brezhnev succession struggle. Korey states that Brezhnev himself, along with a number of his politburo colleagues, has been accused by Russian anti-Semites of being "Kremlin Zionists." Korey suggests that this rise in anti-Semitism may well have been the reason for Brezhnev's denunciation of anti-Semitism as a "nationalistic aberration" during his speech to the Twenty-sixth Congress of the Communist Party of the Soviet Union in February 1981, although the Soviet leader was also to denounce Zionism in similar terms. Korey concludes that despite Brezhnev's speech, anti-Semitism, whether clothed as anti-Zionism or not, will continue to pervade Soviet life.

One of the most hotly debated questions about the exodus of Soviet Jews in the 1970s is the motivation of Soviet leaders in allowing so many Jews to leave. Without inside information about Kremlin debates on this topic, it is impossible to be totally certain of the answer. However, Robert Freedman suggests that the primary cause has been a desire to gain benefits from the West, particularly from the United States, and that the number of Soviet Jews allowed to leave the USSR during any one year of the 1970s can serve as a barometer of the state of Soviet-American relations during that period. Freedman suggests that Soviet desires for new strategic arms agreements and American grain and technology, along with the Soviet hope of keeping the United States and China from joining together in an anti-Soviet alliance, have been central to the Soviet calculation to relax emigration policy during the past decade. Consequently, it was not accidental that the number of Soviet Jews allowed to leave the Soviet Union dropped precipitously following the Soviet invasion of Afghanistan when President Carter imposed a partial grain embargo on the USSR, withheld high technology exports to the USSR, and withdrew the SALT II agreement from Senate consideration.

The absorption process for Soviet Jews choosing to go to Israel in the 1970s was different in a number of respects from the absorption process in the United States, as pointed out by Theodore Friedgut in his study of Soviet-Jewish emigration to Israel. In contrast to the situation in the United States, absorption machinery was already in place in Israel as a result of previous Jewish emigrations, and, given the country's relatively small population, the influx of large numbers of Soviet-Jewish immigrants had a much greater impact on Israeli society than on American society. By 1973 what Friedgut describes as a "critical mass" of 80,000 Soviet Jews had arrived in Israel. By this time many of the difficulties in the absorption process had been worked out, and the existing Soviet-Jewish community was able to help newly arrived Soviet Jews adjust to Israeli life, both economically and culturally. Friedgut concludes that despite a number of serious initial difficulties, the absorption process of Soviet Jewry within Israel has been a major success and points to a very low re-emigration rate as evidence for this conclusion.

The "dropout" phenomenon, touched on by nearly every one of the contributors, has become a matter of bitter debate between Israel and diaspora Jewish communities, particularly the American-Jewish community. While many American Jews have asserted that the central issue for Soviet Jews is to emigrate to a place where they will have the chance to live as Jews, Israeli Jews, and especially the Jewish Agency officials, have complained that exiting Soviet Jews have been "bribed" to come to the United States and have demanded that they go to Israel. Taking a middle road in this debate is Fabian Kolker, an American activist in the cause of Soviet Jewry. Kolker suggests a plan whereby Israel, rather than Italy, would become the transit stop for exiting Soviet Jews after Vienna. After living a year in Israel, the émigrés would be given the opportunity to emigrate to the United States if they still wished to do so.

While Israel was the destination chosen by the first major group of Soviet Jews to leave the USSR, the United States has been increasingly popular with subsequent groups. Zvi Gitelman examines the Soviet Jews who have come to the United States and concludes that they differ from those who previously went to Israel in terms of their area of origin in the Soviet Union. Those who came from areas only recently conquered, such as the Baltic Republics, or from areas less Russified or more religious, such as the Georgian Republic and Soviet Central Asia, tended to go to Israel. Those now coming to the United States are from the heartland of the Soviet Union, particularly the main cities: Moscow, Leningrad, and Kiev. Gitelman concludes, on the basis of existing studies and his own observations, that, on the whole, immigrants from this group are far more skilled than any other immigrant group in United States history; that, nonetheless, many have experienced downward occupational mobility; that the immigrants are younger as a group than are Soviet Jews remaining in the USSR; and that they see the problem of finding suitable employment and mastery of the English language as their two most serious problems. As a whole, Gitelman finds the standard of living of Soviet Jews goes up when they emigrate to the United States, and he notes a positive identification with American-Jewish culture among the new immigrants. Gitelman also notes that the new immigrants, in addition to enriching American society with their talents, particularly in the artistic area, are helping to create a new Russian subculture in the United States.

As new Soviet-Jewish immigrants were settling into American life, what were American Jews thinking about them? This is the question addressed by Stephen Feinstein's study of the St. Paul, Minnesota, Jewish community and its attitudes toward Soviet-Jewish immigrants. In his research Feinstein finds that native residents of St. Paul were the least helpful and friendly toward the newcomers, while those born out of state or in another country were the most friendly. In addition, a correlation was discovered between old age and frequent contact with Soviet Jews, and between membership in Jewish organizations and awareness of Soviet-Jewish issues. Feinstein's study has a number of important implications for the resettlement process in the United States, and it would be most useful to compare the findings of the St. Paul study with similar studies in other American-Jewish communities to determine whether the attitudes of St. Paul Jews toward the new immigrants are unique or whether they represent Jewish attitudes throughout the country.

While Feinstein has examined American-Jewish attitudes toward Soviet Jews, Ilya Levkov, himself a Soviet-Jewish immigrant to the United States, analyzes the attitudes of his fellow immigrants toward American life. After examining the motivations of Soviet Jews for leaving the USSR, Levkov, on the basis of responses to a nationwide survey, analyzes the behavior of Soviet Jews once they arrive in the United States. He discusses their methods of obtaining employment, their buying patterns for such items as automobiles and television sets, their reading habits, the cohesion of their families, and their perceptions of American Jews and of the resettlement process. He concludes that while Soviet Jews in general have made a positive economic integration into American life, their relations with American Jews have been somewhat problematical. He also asserts that on the basis of his survey the basic form of Jewish identification of Soviet Jews in the United States appears to be ethnic and nationalistic, rather than cultural or religious.

In sum, the contributors to this volume have analyzed many aspects of the Soviet-Jewish emigration process, from the often traumatic departure from the USSR to resettlement either in Israel or the United States. While much has been covered here, much remains to be learned about the emigration and resettlement processes. It is hoped that this volume will serve to stimulate further research in both areas.

Soviet Jewry in the Decisive Decade, 1971-80

1. Soviet-Jewish Emigration, 1971-80: An Overview

Jerome M. Gilison

The exodus of one-tenth of the Jewish population of the Soviet Union during the decade of the 1970s is a unique—and totally unexpected—event in Soviet history. The mass emigration of over 250,000 people belonging to one nationality group has no precedent in Soviet practice, past or present, and runs counter to Soviet theory, if not to Soviet law.[1]

Certainly during the Stalin years the exit door was tightly locked. Even those who left the country for a time on "legitimate business," such as fighting against Franco in the Spanish Civil War, were treated as pariahs on their return, and many were shipped off to the Gulag. Stalin's morbid suspicions extended to anyone who had inhaled the subversive atmosphere of the West—even under conditions of war. This attitude—that the West is a place of contamination from which Soviet citizens must be protected—has persisted through the Khrushchev and Brezhnev years to the present.

Although foreign travel is one of the perquisites of elite status in the Soviet social system, the door remains closed to the average Ivan-in-the-street. Undoubtedly, Soviet suspicions concerning the seductiveness of the West have been heightened by the continued defections of prominent members of the artistic, intellectual, and even political elites while on foreign visits. Although there is nothing in the civil or criminal code to prohibit emigration, and although the Soviet Union is signatory to international declarations of the right to free migration,[2] actual Soviet policy concerning emigration essentially defines it as the act of a traitor or a fool. The Soviet Union, after all, is the home of the "builders of Communism"; the country is now in the stage of "developed socialism," and therefore anyone who would voluntarily leave it is, by definition, either misguided or guilty of a traitorous act. Despite government claims of an advanced and happy Soviet society, those who leave are charged with the vice of seeking the relatively easy life of the West rather than submitting to the rigors and self-sacrifice required to achieve the goal of communism.

In the late 1960s any dreams of substantial emigration from the USSR would have been unthinkable. The mass emigration of Soviet Jews that took place in the seventies was the result of the confluence of several developments within Soviet society. During the sixties the regime pursued a course of retrenchment from the hesitant liberalization of the preceding decade. This retrenchment was begun during the last year of Khrushchev's tenure but was implemented with greater determination by his successors. The dismissal of Alexander Tvardovsky and the muzzling of his somewhat adventurous journal, *Novy Mir*, was followed by a succession of trials of dissidents. Starting with the Sinyavsky-Daniel trial (1966), each repressive act by the regime seemed to mobilize its opponents. The rumor network that had traditionally filled the information void left by the official media soon developed into the samizdat network, and more and more people were drawn into oppositional activities, even if only to sign a protest petition or a letter to the authorities. It is still impossible to determine the extent of the network of unauthorized dissent, but there is no doubt that its creative center was within the intelligentsia of the largest urban centers.

Thus, dissent was centered in precisely those locations and social strata where the Jewish population was concentrated. It is therefore not surprising that a rather high proportion of the most prominent figures in the Democratic Movement were Jews. However, these were Jews who were highly assimilated into Russian culture and who, like Larisa Bogoraz, asked themselves agonizing questions:

> Who am I now? . . . Unfortunately, I do not feel like a Jew. I understand that I have an unquestionable genetic tie with Jewry. I also assume that this is reflected in my mentality, in my mode of thinking, and in my behavior . . . (but) I am accustomed to the color, smell, rustle of the Russian landscape, as I am to the Russian language, the rhythm of Russian poetry. I react to everything else as alien.[3]

Ironically, the Jewish dissidents found themselves facing the same dilemma that split the Jewish revolutionaries a century earlier. Then as now, there were highly assimilated Jews who worked for changes within Russia, and other, generally less assimilated Jews who saw their salvation in Zionism. The obvious difference for the Zionists of the late 1960s was the presence of a Jewish state that would warmly welcome them and that was, especially after the Six Day War (1967), seen as an indomitable and dynamic national homeland.

But if things were better for the Zionists at the point of destination, they were certainly more problematical at the point of departure. The Soviet regime, which Jews had helped install fifty years earlier, had become a formidable adversary. The KGB, while not as terrifying as Stalin's NKVD, represented a distinct improvement in repressive efficiency over the tsarist secret police. It applied pressure to both the dissident and Jewish emigration movements, ultimately driving them closer together. Initially, many Jewish nationalists divorced themselves from the struggle of the dissidents. They drew the same conclusions as Jewish activist Edward Kuznetsov in his *Prison Diaries*:

> I think that the essential characteristics of the structure of the regime are to all intents and purposes immutable, and that the particular political culture of the Russian people may be classed as despotic. . . . A Jew with neither any inclination towards the wielding of power, nor with any hope of seeing a radical democratization of an essentially repressive regime in the foreseeable

future . . . [can only choose] to leave the Soviet Union. I consider it not only impossible but unnecessary to fight against the Soviet regime. It fully answers the heartfelt wishes of a significant—but alas not the better—part of the population.[4]

Rather than fight for a hopeless cause, and thereby be implicated in activities that eventually could bring them long periods of residence in prison, labor camps, remote villages, or, worst of all, psychiatric hospitals, they chose the route of emigration—a goal that must have seemed initially almost as hopeless as the prospect of reforming the Soviet regime. The Jewish emigration movement arose out of a complex set of circumstances in which the growing significance of dissident activities, the apparent ineptitude of the Brezhnev regime, and endemic anti-Semitism, spiritless conformity, and demoralization of Soviet society all played a part.

The failure of the Brezhnev regime to sustain popular enthusiasm for its traditional goals created an ideological vacuum into which various nationalisms flowed. Thus, it was not only among the Jews that a renascence of nationalism occurred.

Still, the rebirth of Zionism must be counted one of Soviet history's more remarkable phenomena. The Jewish population, geographically dispersed and deprived of its traditional culture and its religious institutions, was apparently on the road to total assimilation. Only its concentration in urban centers and the anti-Semitism of Soviet life worked to keep Jewish consciousness alive. However, despite continual reminders of their non-Russian status, most Jews, like Larisa Bogoraz, would be hard put to find something specifically "Jewish" in their upbringing. The Jewish nationality inscribed on their internal passports seemed to be nothing more than a convenient means of targeting potential victims of anti-Semitism. Indeed, the regime tried to discredit some of its more prominent critics by making a point of their Jewish identity—even in some cases where they are clearly not Jewish (such as Solzhenitsyn). Jewish identity within Soviet society carries only negative consequences, and survival instincts lead most Jews to adopt a protective coating of Russian culture.

Thus, the rebirth of Jewish national feeling in the late 1960s represented a remarkable reversal of the existing attitudes of self-denial prevalent among Soviet Jews. Its main cause was the victory of Israel in the Six Day War, which was a great spur to Zionist feelings and at the same time created a visible and viable focal point for those feelings. Yet only a handful of Soviet Jews were able to emigrate to Israel in the late 1960s. A variety of obstacles were placed in the way of anyone who applied for an exit visa, and various harassments and penalties were created in order to discourage those who might have been contemplating this momentous step.

The procedure, then as now, was for the Soviet-Jewish aspirant for emigration to request an invitation (*vyzov*) from a family member living in Israel. When the invitation was received the prospective emigrant would then request "references" from his workplace, and with these documents apply to the OVIR (the Soviet emigration office) for an exit visa. This procedure made it necessary for the applicant to reveal emigration plans to co-workers and superiors and run the risk of being dismissed or demoted. Especially in the early days of the emigration movement, and during periods of severe repression, a prospective Jewish emigrant ran the risk of being caught in a state of limbo: unemployed and unemployable because of the desire to leave, and unable to leave due to lack of employment and the necessary references. Of course, a number of other official justifications also were used to deny visas, most notably various reasons of "state security," but in truth the regime did not have to give any explanations at all to disappointed applicants and sometimes refused to do so.

By 1970 a movement whose goal was emigration to Israel had grown and become more daring, but it was being frustrated by the regime's suppression. At this juncture a catalytic event occurred: the Leningrad trial of several Jews (Kuznetsov, Dymshitz, et al.) charged with treason for conspiring to hijack a Soviet plane to Sweden. The conviction of the conspirators was a foregone conclusion, but when two of them were sentenced to the death penalty, the international outcry was so great that the regime was forced to back down. The trial not only focused international attention on the plight of the Jewish emigration movement, it also served to mobilize the movement toward more concerted efforts.

Apparently, about this time, a decision was reached in higher party circles to ease the restrictions on Jewish emigration, for shortly after the end of the Leningrad trial exit visas were issued in much greater numbers. The mass exodus had begun. In the year following the trial more than 12,000 Jews left the country, more than in the previous decade.

Although the number of emigrants increased in the succeeding years, the regime continued to impede the flow by a tactic of random harassment and penalties. The inconsistency of this pattern leads one to suspect that it was not tightly controlled from the center, but was left, in matters of crucial detail, to local authorities. In any case the partially open door to emigration could be closed in the face of anyone who approached it, and this situation quickly led to the growth of a fairly substantial demiclass of refuseniks, or applicants who had been denied permission to emigrate, and who suffered reprisals to varying degrees. Whether or not this was calculated Soviet policy, the result was a dilemma for those Soviet Jews with an inclination to depart. They were forced to play a game of chance with ever-changing odds. The odds varied in relation to the Soviet emigration trends of the moment, the characteristics of the particular applicant, and, apparently, the whims of local officials. The number of Soviet Jews seeking to emigrate depended on a system of informal communication stories of success or failure at OVIR, as well as speculation about subtle shifts in the regime's amorphous emigration policies and in its war against dissidents. Thus, if rumored successes greatly outnumbered failures, longer lines of hopeful applicants appeared at the OVIR offices.

During the early 1970s the first wave of emigrants went to Israel. There was little thought then of any alternative destination. The Yom Kippur War (1973), however, dampened the enthusiasm of many Soviet Jews. The reality of Israel's security problems became clear, as did the protracted nature of the Middle East conflict. It also should be mentioned that the feedback from immigrants in Israel was not always positive as the newcomers went through the painful process of adjustment. Thus, after the initial peak years of 1972 and 1973 (see figure 1.1), there was a downturn in emigration from the USSR to Israel.

These were years of marked cooling in Soviet-American relations. Soviet behavior during the Yom Kippur War in October of 1973 was seen as highly provocative and a violation of the "spirit of detente." These Soviet actions and the sudden imposition of the "head tax"—the requirement that, as a condition of emigration, Soviet Jews compensate the state for the education they had received—caused a negative reaction in the U.S. Congress and resulted in the Stevenson Amendment, which severely restricted the amount of credits available to the Soviet Union. This, in turn, precipitated the angry Soviet rejection of the Jackson-Vanik Amendment, which tied increased trade to free emigration policies, as an "interference in the internal affairs" of the USSR.

The supposition that the Kremlin has viewed Soviet Jews as bargaining chips in political and trade negotiations with the United States is supported by the close correlation of the emigration rate with the ups and downs of Soviet-American relations. As these relations cooled after 1973, the flow of emigrants dropped dramatically to about one-third of the previous years (see figure 1.1). Other factors, as previously mentioned, also played a part in the ebb and flow, but the most crucial factor was the degree of bureaucratic harassment and threat of penalties imposed by the regime. The regime's ability to manipulate the rate of emigration had actually increased over the period because the most highly motivated and desperate Jews—those who would plot to hijack a plane or stage a demonstration—departed in the first wave of emigration, leaving behind many who were more tentative and uncertain candidates for emigration.

The Jewish emigration posed a dilemma for Soviet policy. The exchange of Jews for American grain and computers probably seemed to be a good bargain from Brezhnev's vantage point, but events showed that the deal was not quite so straightforward. Even if it had been, it still would have been dangerous to open the door too wide. Both from the point of view of maintaining social control and preventing brain drain, the regime could not let the door swing fully open, even though it had signed international declarations to this effect. To limit the outflow the regime had to insist on family reunion as the justification for permanent departure, and Israel as the only legitimate destination. This effectively limited the rights of emigration to Jews (and their spouses), although the official position, as given by *Izvestia*, did not make this explicit: "Petitions by individual citizens for permission to resettle in other countries for purposes of reuniting separated families are thoroughly and attentively considered in each case."[5] Nevertheless, it became clear that Jews are in a privileged

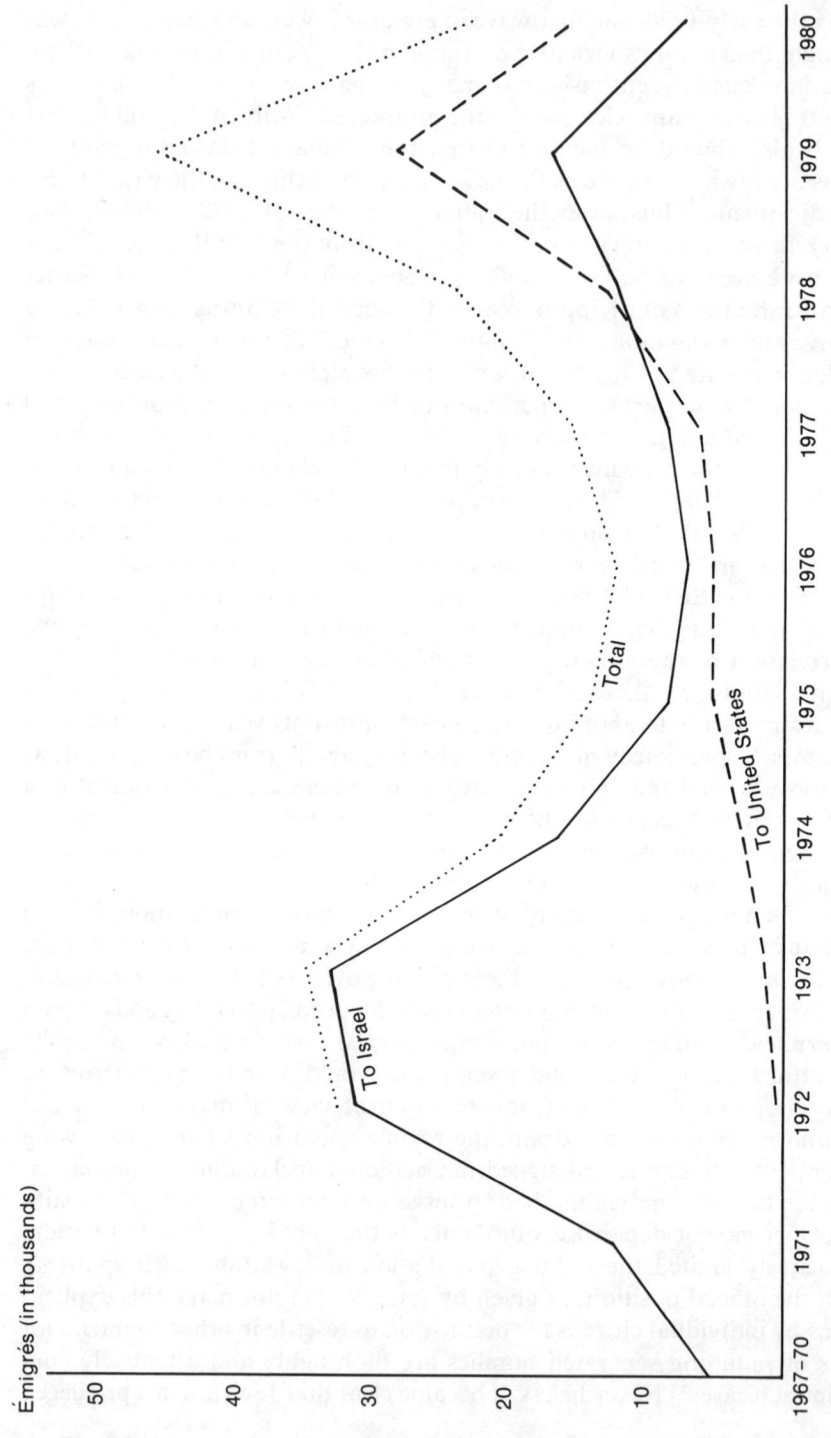

Figure 1.1. Annual rate of Soviet Jewish emigration to Israel and the United States (data from HIAS and Israeli Embassy)

position with regard to the right of emigration. Occasional newspaper accounts of nefarious doings among applicants for emigration make this clear: "This was not a group of lovers of easy money come together by chance. It was a criminal syndicate whose goal, to be reached at any price, was to amass capital both here and abroad, since many of its members planned to emigrate to Israel or to some other Western country."[6] The notion that such Jewish émigrés are essentially traitors to their motherland is clearly insinuated: "They didn't believe that King Solomon's treasures were waiting for them beside the Dead Sea. Therefore, they plundered treasures here, in the country where they were born, raised and lived."[7] To connect Jewish emigration with the dissident movement and thus, one suspects, discredit both movements, non-Jewish dissidents (like the late Andrei Amalrik) were required to list Israel as their intended destination in order to be granted a visa.

Administrative restrictions, however, were not sufficient to prevent large-scale emigration of Soviet Jews, and the regime resorted to arbitrary and seemingly random harassment of individual applicants, with particular attention paid to those connected with dissident activities. The various actions taken by the regime to stem the tide of emigration hardly justify the term "policy." These actions were hesitant and inconsistent, perhaps reflecting a certain degree of ambivalence or disagreement at the highest levels. It also seems that whatever directives were issued were implemented differently in the various republics, indicating that local initiative filled the void left by the absence of a strong directing hand at the center.

From 1975 through 1977 the outflow of Soviet Jews averaged less than 14,000 per year, a considerable drop from the peak period (1972–73), but still considerably greater than had ever been permitted before the beginning of the decade. Despite the adverse conditions of those years, emigration of Soviet Jews was now an established feature of Soviet life with its own special bureaucratic machinery. The strong Zionist impetus seemed to have abated, and at the prevailing emigration rate it would have taken about 150 years for all the Jews to leave—hardly likely and certainly not worrisome to the regime.

However, in 1974 a new development in emigration had become noticeable. About 17 percent of the Jews arriving at the Vienna transit point en route to Israel declared their wish to go to the United States instead. In the previous year only 4 percent of those arriving in Vienna had chosen to continue on to the United States. A new system for handling these *noshrim*, as they came to be called in Israel, had to be devised. After an initial period with the Jewish Agency, which handles transfers to Israel, they were transferred to the Hebrew Immigrant Aid Society (HIAS), a privately financed Jewish-American organization that assists Jewish (and other) immigrants in reaching the United States. HIAS established transit facilities in Rome and Ostia, where the émigrés waited for several weeks or months for the documents necessary for U.S. immigration.

As the new route became established and as more Soviet émigrés successfully traversed it, the direction of flow changed dramatically. By 1978 more than half of the Soviet-Jewish emigrants chose to settle in the United States, although the Soviet government refused to accept any destination other than Israel on their visas.[8] In this way the Soviet government underscored its decision that national repatriation was open only to specific national groups with a national homeland outside the Soviet Union. If open migration to the United States had been permitted, the rationale of national repatriation would have been lost and the Jewish émigrés hardly distinguishable from the stream of ballerinas and concert musicians who had chosen to live in the West, and many Ukrainians and Balts would have sought to emigrate to the United States.

The availability of a more promising destination, and the apparent willingness of Soviet authorities to look the other way when émigrés changed their destination in Vienna, began a new chapter in the saga of Jewish emigration. The possibility of emigration to America coincided with a marked improvement in Soviet-American relations in the late 1970s as President Carter backed off from his insistence on observance of human rights as a precondition of harmonious relations. It also served Soviet interests to have something to pull out of the so-called basket three (the Human Rights section) for the Belgrade conference (1977) on the Helsinki Accord.

If a new destination had been found, it was a new type of Jewish émigré who would seek it. The earlier wave of émigrés was to a large extent motivated by Zionism and came at a time, between the 1967 and 1973 wars, when Israel was a most attractive goal. However, for reasons already suggested, this wave had already ebbed by 1975. While Zionism (and migration to Israel) has continued to be a force to the present day, it ceased to be the dominant factor in Jewish emigration about 1974.

The second wave of Soviet-Jewish emigration in the seventies was more a response to worsening conditions in the Soviet Union than to the allure of any particular alternative. These conditions were of two types: those that pertained to all Soviet subjects in roughly equal measure, and those that pertained specifically to Jews because of their national identity. In the first category were those conditions resulting from the general demoralization, decay, and decrepitude of the Soviet system as a whole. The regime and its aged leadership had lost all sense of social dynamism and had become staunchly conservative, afraid of change, afraid of new ideas, engrossed in protecting the status quo and in rooting out all opposition. It no longer had the will, or even the desire, to inspire its subjects with new social goals. The ideology was still pervasive, but it rang hollow, an empty public ritual. In the absence of meaningful public social goals, most citizens adopted private goals that revolved around careers, positions, influence, and acquisitions. Success in Soviet society in the Brezhnev years thus came to mean playing a deceptive, hypocritical game in which the public and private rules stood in stark contrast. Corruption and cynicism were pervasive and in a sense held the system together by implicating everyone in shared guilt.

It would be overstating the case to suggest that every Soviet citizen agonized over the moral and spiritual vacuum that characterized the Brezhnev years. As in other situations, there are many more who find ways of accommodating themselves to the world as it is than who devote themselves to tilting at windmills. Yet the situation was particularly acute for Soviet Jews under these circumstances for two very substantial reasons. One was the possibiity, not open to other Soviet citizens, of legal escape from the system through emigration. For the non-Jewish citizen the impossibility of emigration combined with the impossibility of opposition has been an overwhelming rationale for playing the game according to the system's rules. By 1977, however, a Jew who was dissatisfied with these conditions, but who had no strong Zionist feelings, could seek the alternative of resettlement in the United States.

The second circumstance that affected the Jewish population in particular was the palpable increase in overt and covert anti-Semitism that took place during the seventies. Until the past decade one might characterize the Soviet regime's stance toward anti-Semitism as one of benign neglect: while officially condemning it (along with all forms of national discrimination), the regime did nothing to eradicate the endemic, widespread, and virulent anti-Semitism inherited from the past. Both Stalin and Khrushchev typified the Soviet bureaucrat who uttered anti-Semitic remarks in private while publicly disavowing such prejudices. The regime also continually attacked Judaism, both as a religion and as a social doctrine, but this stream of invective came under the heading of antireligious propaganda, and most Jews drew the conclusion that they could stay "clean" by avoiding religious observances. Also, anti-Judaism propaganda was issued at a rather low level of authority and did not seem to receive the imprimatur of top leadership.

During the past decade, however, the regime became the sponsor of a strident anti-Semitic propaganda campaign under the cover of "anti-Zionism." This campaign included most of the old themes of classic anti-Semitism: the Zionists' conspiracy for worldwide domination, their nefarious money manipulation schemes, their attempts to infiltrate and capture control of respectable institutions. In Soviet cartoons the Zionists have been depicted with hooked beaks, beady eyes, skullcaps, and taloned claws, hardly distinguishable from the caricatures that once appeared in the Nazi publication *Der Sturmer*.

Indeed, Zionism has been equated with Nazism, and Soviet history books and publications have been distorted to show that Zionists cooperated with the Nazis and that Zionism and Judaism are racist doctrines (or components of a single doctrine) in which the concept of a chosen people is described as a Jewish claim of racial superiority. While the various authors of this anti-Zionist literature differ on the fine points,[9] the reading public does not make fine distinctions and interprets Zionists to mean Jews. In this way government attacks on Zionism, which can be found in Soviet literature going back to Lenin, have taken on new meaning due to the extremity to which the themes are pushed. It is no longer a set of ideas that are attacked, but a set of people who hold them, and by implication that set of people potentially includes all Jews.

Anti-Zionism can serve many purposes of the regime, but it is probably not accidental that the anti-Jewish atmosphere has intensified at a time of a general increase in Russian nationalism, which apparently received the leadership's blessing in the 1970s. It would seem that the regime, lacking fresh inspiration, has fallen back on the old and popular sentiments of nationalism—sentiments that years ago were incorporated into the ideology, but which have received new prominence in recent years. The official propaganda organs have not taken the lead in stirring up these sentiments, and the leadership is undoubtedly aware that national extremists pose a danger to the regime that is no less serious than the opposition of the various tendencies within the "Democratic Movement".[10] Extremists like those who for a short time put together the samizdat journal *Veche* had few kind words for the Communist party or its ideology, which they viewed as alien importations. The fact that the journal and its authors were eventually suppressed indicates that the regime is sensitive to the subversive nature of such viewpoints. Nevertheless, such nationalist spokesmen as the painter Ilya Glazunov were given prominent display, and the regime discreetly supported such widely popular viewpoints.

Historically, nationalist or Slavophile doctrines have been associated with anti-Semitism, and this connection can be observed in recent years as well. The relationship is heightened when the nationalism acquires racial overtones, as in the writings of Vladimir Osipov, the leader of the *Veche* group:

> What is a nation? It is faith, blood and land. Religion and even a certain totality of the rituals constitutes . . . perhaps the most essential part of the spirit of a nation. . . . The amazing distinctiveness of the biological [blood line] cannot be explained without turning to mysticism. In a living national organism there is always some mystery.[11]

From this line of meditation it is not surprising that Osipov draws the conclusion that "one people is petty and thrifty, another is careless and extravagant, a third likes its home and law, a fourth does not even have a word for 'freedom,' a fifth wanders and is crafty."[12]

While Osipov represents an extreme view, the surfacing of such attitudes is a barometer of the general trend toward a national and anti-Jewish climate in the Soviet Union. While the anti-Zionist campaign has brought to the surface much latent anti-Semitism, the fact of Jewish emigration has itself stirred a kind of anti-Jewish backlash. The fact of emigration demonstrates that Jews are guilty of that "cosmopolitanism" that has always been a charge against them. Undoubtedly, popular feelings toward the emigration are varied and complex, but there can be no question that emigration sets the Jewish population apart as a privileged group and feeds the anti-Semitism already existing in the population. Thus, the emigration has made life more difficult for those Jews who stay behind, and this has forced more Jews to conclude that they and their children have no future in the Soviet Union.

It also would seem that the regime has reacted to the emigration by reducing its dependence on Jewish "brain power." It is a well-known fact (often used by Soviet apologists to counter charges of anti-Jewish discrimination) that a disproportionately high percentage of the Jewish population has managed to obtain a higher education and has found skilled, "mental" jobs. Jewish prominence in the professions, arts, and sciences means that a large gap would be left by the wholesale departure of the Jewish intelligentsia from the country. It would seem that the regime has taken steps to guard against this. Admission of Jews to institutions of higher education has been severely curtailed, and stories abound of serious job and promotion discrimination. The Soviet leadership has apparently decided that little of value should be given to people who eventually are likely to contribute their skills to Israel or the United States. Of course, such policies only serve to encourage more emigration.

The emigration of the late seventies can thus be seen as largely a reaction to worsening conditions of Soviet Jews within the country. To a larger extent than before, the emigration was reaching the more assimilated Jews from the Ukrainian and Russian urban centers. Not particularly attracted by the prospect of settling in an Israel surrounded by hostile neighbors and experiencing triple-digit inflation, the majority of emigrants chose to settle in the United States. During the period of highest emigration (1978 and 1979), 58 percent of the emigrants chose the United States, while another 7 percent chose Australia, Canada, and other countries in Europe and Latin America.[13]

While Zionism was clearly waning as a motivation for emigration, many émigrés still chose Israel for a variety of reasons, most importantly to join family and friends already settled there. However, the émigrés of 1978 and 1979 were different Jews. In the aggregate they had less connection to any aspect of the Jewish tradition, be it religious or cultural, than the Jews of any previous migration. Without substantial underpinnings in Jewish tradition, most of the émigrés chose countries other than Israel, but even those who settled in Israel "had naturally less commitment to Israel and less patience with its overburdened and undertrained absorption bureaucracy than did the pioneers of the exodus."[14] By and large, these were people who had reacted in a very practical way to the increasingly difficult situation of Jews in the Soviet Union rather than out of a positive desire to return to Zion. In addition, in many cases the decision to emigrate was precipitated by the emigration of family and close friends, particularly in cities with concentrated Jewish populations.

The second wave of emigration of the 1970s reached a climax in 1979 with a total of 51,320 emigrants, of whom only 34 percent chose to settle in Israel. In 1980 emigration dropped by 44 percent, a decline that followed the cooling of Soviet-American relations after the Soviet invasion of Afghanistan. Reports from cities across the Soviet Union indicated that OVIR officials were raising new obstacles, particularly the requirement that family reunion apply only to "first-degree relatives" and that all members of a family, including the elderly, emigrate together. Various new harassments were introduced locally, and word soon spread that the regime was implementing a new restrictive policy. Emigration policy once again was following the ups and downs of Soviet-American relations.[15]

Interestingly, the recent tightening of the screws by Soviet authorities has eliminated the over-representation of Ukrainian Jews in the emigration to the United States. Although only 39 percent of Soviet Jews live in the Ukraine (1979 Soviet census), this republic produced between 54 and 69 percent of the U.S.-bound emigration from 1972 through 1979. This dropped, however, to 35 percent in 1980, apparently due to particularly severe emigration restrictions in the Ukraine.[16]

Aside from the Ukraine and the Russian Republic (which together account for about 80 percent of the emigration to the United States), Jewish emigrants have come from Moldavia, Byelorussia, Latvia, Georgia, Uzbekistan, and Azerbaidzhan. Each region, of course, has its own distinctive culture, and this means that Jewish émigrés are a diverse group, despite the similarities imposed by the heavy hand of "Soviet culture." In addition, the relationship between Jews and the majority nationality is quite different, for example, in Soviet Georgia (where Jews have traditionally gotten along well with the Georgians) and in Soviet Ukraine (where anti-Semitism has deep roots).

The composition of the emigration to Israel was very different from the emigration to the United States with respect to the union republics from which the emigrants originated. For example, Jews from Soviet Georgia are far more likely to have settled in Israel than in the United States, and, in addition, are more likely to have left the USSR during the first wave of emigration. The contrary is true of Jews from the Ukraine: they are far more likely to have been attracted to the United States and to have departed during the second wave. Thus, 90 percent of Jewish émigrés from Tbilisi (Georgia) settled in Israel, while only 17.3 percent of émigrés from Odessa (Ukraine) settled there. Generally, Jews from the RSFSR, Byelorussian SSR, and Ukrainian SSR are more likely to have settled in the United States, while Jews from any of the other union republics are more likely to have settled in Israel.

As can be seen from figure 1.2, the proportion of elderly Jews emigrating to the United States increased over the 1972–80 period, with a corresponding decline in the proportion of émigrés in the years when they were likely to become employed in the Soviet Union. Some Western observers have suggested that the Soviet authorities are more than willing to rid themselves of Jewish pensioners and have imposed few barriers to their departure, but it is also likely that the elderly have been more reluctant to leave and face the uncertainties of retirement in the West. There also has been a noticeable and steady decline in the percentage of Jewish males emigrating since 1974 (from 52 to 46)—a fact that may be related to the increasing age of the émigré population and the shorter life span of Soviet males.

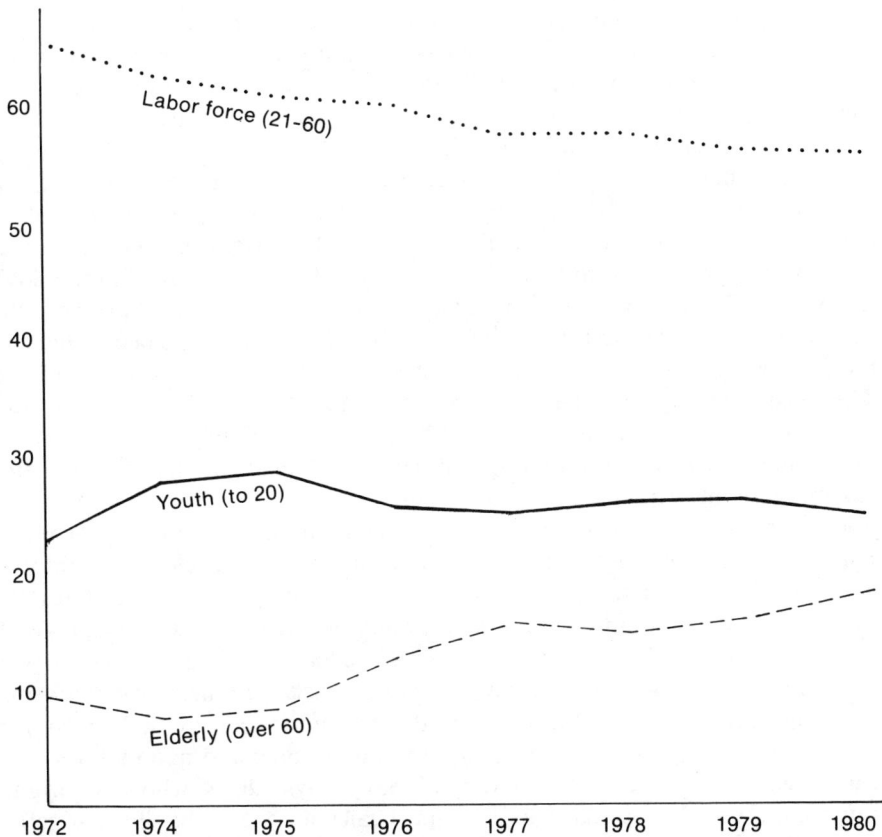

Figure 1.2. Trends in age distribution of Soviet emigration to the United States, 1972-80

Occupational analysis of the recent Jewish immigrant population in the United States shows a remarkably high proportion of professionals, engineers, and technicians, and white-collar and service employees. To use the Soviet terminology, those engaged in mental (*umstvenyi*) labor typically compose more than 80 percent of the annual outflow of émigrés. In fact, since 1975 blue-collar émigrés have steadily declined from 19 to 14 percent of the total. During the same period the proportion of engineers has climbed from 11 to 20 percent. It also should be noted that females have greatly outnumbered males in the professional, white-collar, and service employee categories, while males have dominated the engineering, technical, blue-collar, and transportation categories. Within the total émigré population, females comprise about half of those who were employed in the Soviet Union, reflecting the very high level of female employment in that country.

The high occupational skill levels in this group of emigrants is consonant with the known characteristics of the Soviet-Jewish population, especially its urban concentration and high educational attainment. Yet, as only about one-tenth of the Soviet-Jewish population has emigrated since 1970, many Jews who have attained high status remain in the USSR.

A cost-benefit analysis of emigration is most difficult for those Jews among the Soviet elite. Elite status may help a Jew to avoid the consequences— although not the experience—of anti-Semitism. In any case one can guess that, aside from a growing number of refuseniks, the Jews who remain in the Soviet Union include many relatively high-status individuals who would leave if they had greater assurance that they would not be refused, for these people have the most to lose if they are cast in the Kafkaesque twilight world of the refuseniks. They also probably have the most to lose in terms of status if they are permitted to emigrate. They may have heard of the difficulties of émigré professionals in the United States, where retraining and recertification are often necessary before resuming an interrupted career.

During the course of the past decade the symbiotic relationship of regime policies and the progress of Jewish emigration has become clearly established. The regime has pursued certain policies whose latent or intended result is the increased alienation of the Jewish population from Soviet society. At the same time, and to a varying degree, the regime has restricted emigration, without clearly defining standards or imposing strict administrative uniformity throughout the country. This has permitted the regime considerable freedom to manipulate the emigration in response to international and national pressures. But it also has heightened the anxiety of many Soviet Jews, who see a brighter future for themselves abroad, but who must calculate the probabilities of refusal or harassment on a day-to-day basis, with only rumors to guide them. This is truly a game of Russian roulette, which many of them are unwilling to play.

At the present, Soviet-Jewish emigration has dropped sharply. Even if these numbers decline further, it is well to remember that despite the Siberian chill that has descended on Soviet-American relations, the ponderous machinery of emigration is still functioning. As long as the machinery functions, the leadership can adjust its rate of operation in accord with Soviet international policy interests or as a means to send signals to the West. In the meantime, however, Soviet Jews, both would-be emigrants and those not planning to leave the USSR, are facing an increasingly difficult future.

2. The Jews in the Soviet Union: Emigration and Its Difficulties

Jerry Goodman

Virtually all Americans owe their citizenship to the right to emigrate, Senator Henry M. Jackson recalled several years ago in an address to the National Conference on Soviet Jewry. We are a nation of immigrants, he asserted, which "gives us a responsibility for the right to emigrate."

For Jews in the Soviet Union, emigration remains an elusive and often heartbreaking goal. For more than a decade the attention of Jews and non-Jews, especially in Western nations, has been focused on this subject whose dimensions, regrettably, are as political as they are human. In its earliest phases the emigration of Soviet Jews was viewed as a factor of *aliya*, or emigration to Israel. *Aliya* was essentially linked to a variety of interacting elements, including the desire of the people to live in Israel and their ability or willingness to struggle toward that end, the development of a variety of strategies by Soviet Jews to achieve their goals, international efforts on behalf of Soviet Jews, and public and private pressures exerted on Soviet authorities and Soviet policies. Equally critical was the situation in Israel, including an effective absorption climate that could accommodate many different economic, cultural, social, and spiritual needs. In varying degrees these factors had an impact on *aliya*. At different times these elements also were affected by events within and outside the USSR.

Today, as in the past, what we know about Soviet decision making in regard to emigration is often much less than what we do not know. Contradictory reports from the Soviet Union, publications that carry only parts of the requisite data, rumors, or deliberate misinformation from official sources prevent us from making absolute determinations concerning emigration patterns or basic policies. Many conclusions, therefore, are only as valid as our ability to secure reliable data, whether from publications, speeches by officials, or emigrants. Nevertheless, whether to escape growing anti-Semitism, to build a Jewish life, to strengthen Israel, or to satisfy personal needs, it is evident that Jews continue to seek to leave the Soviet Union, as they have done for more than a decade.

For the nearly two million Jews who remain in the USSR (by official count), however, a paradox has been created. Current Soviet policies in many ways have unleashed pressures that encourage Jews to leave. This impulse has been expressed by an increasing number of Jewish families. At the same time recent practices have made it increasingly difficult for those same Jews to leave. The inevitable results are frustration, despair, and anxiety.

The number of Jews permitted to emigrate from the Soviet Union declined sharply in 1980 compared with 1979. Why? Because Soviet officials relied on increasingly stringent, and apparently arbitrary, rules to curtail emigration. In 1980, 21,471 Jews emigrated via Vienna, a 58 percent decrease from the 51,320 who emigrated in 1979. The trend began in May 1979 when the Soviets began to institute restrictions on the right to apply for emigration. Primarily, they began to question the relationship between persons applying and the persons who invited them.

Emigration remains restricted for all Soviet citizens. Soviet authorities speak of the "reunification of families," usually meaning families torn apart by World War II and its aftermath, and avoid the term "emigration" itself. Jews have been permitted to leave since the late 1960s on the ground that they want to be reunited with relatives, usually in Israel. The Soviet Union requires that would-be Jewish emigrants present an invitation from a relative in Israel.

In September 1980, in a rare public discussion of Soviet policy, an article in the Yiddish monthly *Sovietische Heimland* by Konstantin I. Zotov, a Moscow emigration official, described the emigration policy as "humane." He said anyone who wanted to be reunified with relatives could do so, except for those who faced criminal charges or who were required to settle personal affairs, such as debts. In previous years the closeness of the would-be émigré's relationship was not crucial. However, in 1980 Soviet officials began to issue visas mainly to those who had invitations from first-degree relatives—parents, spouses, siblings, or children. Invitations from more distant relatives were ignored.

Although Soviet bureaucratic procedure assumes that Israel is the destination of virtually all Jewish emigrants, increasing numbers of Jews have preferred to settle elsewhere, mostly in the United States. In 1980, 65 percent of the Jews leaving the Soviet Union, though headed to Israel according to their emigration papers, did not go there.

In addition to the close-relationship requirement adopted by Soviet officials, other harassing restrictions were reported in recent years. Young couples usually have to obtain their parents' permission to leave, but in Minsk such permission was expected even if the emigrating couple were in their forties and their parents in their eighties. There also has been a reduction of office hours in some emigration offices, occasionally to as little as one hour a week. Another spreading practice is to urge the entire family to leave, regardless of personal desires. In some cities if one member has not applied, applicants are told that this is contrary to the principle of family reunification. Each member is thus made responsible for the actions and fate of others. In the Ukraine an applicant may be forced to read a warning against giving up a job or leaving an apartment before getting an answer, and then be forced to sign an affidavit that he or she has done so.

To complicate the situation, there also has been an increase in the percentage of older émigrés, a trend that accelerated in the last quarter of 1980. In Moscow

46 percent of the Jews able to leave in that year were more than 56 years of age, although the annual percentile had been 22 percent to 25 percent.

The precipitous decrease in emigration reflects the introduction of the new demands for an invitation from a close (or first-degree) relative, in addition to increased administrative and bureaucratic obstacles. The application of an insufficient kinship restriction to reject the invitations was first observed in Odessa. By the end of 1979 it had spread to Kharkov and Kiev, then to Kishinev and Tashkent. It has been applied in Leningrad and, to a lesser degree, in cities such as Riga and Moscow. Initial appliations have been rejected if the invitation is signed by a relative other than spouse, parents, children, or siblings. (In Kiev, where two thousand Jews left in September 1979, only parents and children qualified. In the past year fifty to sixty left per month.) The new procedures have caused Odessa, Kiev, and Kharkov to be virtually closed to emigration.

The 1980 rate of exit gradually dropped, almost month by month, and ended with 20,319 individual emigration visas granted, as opposed to 50,343 the previous year, a 60 percent reduction in exits. In the first half of 1980, 14,295 visas were issued, compared with 25,152 during the same period in 1979. But in the second half of 1980, only 6,024 visas were issued, as opposed to 25,191 issued during the same period in 1979. (It should be noted that there is a gap between visas granted and actual arrivals in Vienna, depending upon such factors as departure dates.)

As a result of the increased Soviet restrictions, in the first half of 1980 the number of visas granted was only 56.8 percent of those granted in the same period of 1979, while in the second half the number of visas reached only 23.9 percent of those granted in the previous year. This came to a monthly average of 4,195 in 1979 and 1,693 in 1980. In the twelve years between 1969 and 1980 a total of 250,910 individual exit visas to Israel were granted. Of these, 250,187 Jews left.

The great number of exits in 1979 was widely interpreted as an appeal by Soviet authorities to world opinion, especially in the United States, as well as a result of internal pressures. Indeed, evidence suggests a connection, on the one hand, of political and economic relations between the United States and the USSR and Soviet policy toward the exit of Jews to Israel; on the other hand, there is a connection between the division of exit quotas among the various republics and cities and inner policy considerations of the authorities, regardless of the wishes of Jews in certain places to emigrate.

The reduction in the granting of exit visas began gradually. In January 1980, 3,266 individual visas were granted. By June this figure had shrunk to 1,489; in December it plummeted to 969. This would suggest the existence of a determined policy to severely curb the rate of emigration rather than a random or arbitrary practice. Among the more than 250,000 Jews who have succeeded in leaving during the past decade, many left relatives behind, including a wife or a husband or children. Thousands of newly divided families were thus created.

One estimate is that those who emigrated since 1968 left more than 500,000 relatives.

The decline in emigration reflects a change in the hopes of Jews to emigrate. This already has caused alarm and anxiety among Soviet Jews, accelerated by significant procedural changes and bureaucratic obstacles. For example, in letters sent to relatives in Israel, many Jews complain of nondelivery of affidavits sent to them by registered mail. This obstruction, caused by the Soviet Security Services, prevents the submission of an appeal for emigration. A prerequisite to submitting an application for emigration remains the possession of the affidavit from relatives in Israel. Three hundred and eighty thousand Jews received such affidavits in recent years, thus creating a special problem. The 380,000 people still in the USSR, in addition to the relatives of the 250,000 who left, are defined by the Soviet Security Services as an "unreliable element." As a result of these policies, not only has there been a substantial increase in the number of new refusals, but there has been little progress for veteran refuseniks who have been waiting for many years. For some time the number of refuseniks had been relatively stable, and about 25 to 30 percent of those who were known in the United States received exit visas each year. Their places, however, were soon taken by new refuseniks.

Reflecting the new procedures, the list of refuseniks known in the West jumped in 1980 by nearly 60 percent, reaching 4,741 persons (1,661 families), in addition to the thousands of families whose requests were rejected on the basis of insufficient family kinship. Most of the recently refused families do not know how to publicize their plight or are frightened to do so. They are not activists and generally are not psychologically prepared for the struggles of the older refuseniks.

The total number of Jews affected by the new restrictions has already reached several thousand. A conservative estimate is more than 10,000, including those who receive a refusal as well as those whose initial applications are not even accepted. As a result of the new restrictions, many Soviet Jews have decided to postpone submitting their applications despite other pressures that may be encouraging many people to leave, such as increased job and educational discrimination. The new restrictions also caused shifts in the exit groups of the various republics and cities. In certain republics, such as the Ukraine where regulations are widespread, the number of visas granted was 22.7 percent of the 1980 total. In the preceding four years (1976-79), it had been 45 percent, or 48 percent of the total. The number of visas granted in Byelorussia went up in 1980 to 15 percent as compared with 6.6 percent in 1979 and 3.9 percent in 1978.

Of some interest is the fact that several hundred Jews from among those who received exit visas to Israel in 1980 did not leave by the end of that year. It is assumed that the majority could not manage to complete all administrative procedures connected with their departure. Some of them might have renounced—or were forced to renounce—their right to emigrate, and some died while waiting to leave. We have no data concerning renunciation of the right to leave by those who actually received visas. It could be, of course, that some submitted applications but altered their desire to emigrate during their wait because of pressure on the part of the authorities, or because other members of their families never received visas. There is no confirmation, however, of recent Soviet claims that many Jews renounced their exit visas.

The years 1971–72 marked the beginning of growth in the number of exit visas to Israel given to Jews in the USSR. In 1971 this figure was 14,310; in 1972 it jumped to 31,478. Jews in the USSR sensed that for the first time there was a reasonable chance to receive an exit visa. As a consequence more and more began to request, and receive, affidavits from relatives in Israel. During the first year of accelerated permits 40,794 Jews requested and received affidavits from relatives in Israel. In 1973 this figure increased to 67,895. In 1975–76, as permits were cut back, a decline in the number requesting and receiving affidavits also followed. This would suggest that the changes in the number of Jews requesting affidavits may be directly related to the possibilities, at any given time, of securing the desired exit visa. Policy thus leads, in part, to self-regulating practices. This was in evidence in 1979, the peak year for exit visas, when 128,891 Jews who appealed to relatives in Israel to send affidavits received them. On the other hand, 1980's shift in government policy intimidated many Jews who foresaw rejections, and a natural deterrence was created. Only 32,335 first requests were received, the steepest decline since 1970.

According to the available data since 1968, 630,414 individual and first-time affidavits were sent. Of these, 191,000 Jews requested, and received, renewed affidavits. This was necessary in part because in many instances the first affidavit sent was not delivered to the addressee. In other cases the emigration authorities claimed that the affidavits had become outdated. Over 630,000 people requested and received affidavits for the first time by 1980. Nearly 35 percent of the total Jewish population in the USSR has taken the critical first step in the emigration process. Doubtless, nearly all those who received those affidavits but have not yet presented them to emigration authorities would not hesitate to do so were they to learn that they had a fair chance to get an exit visa. We should, therefore, consider the overwhelming majority of this group to be potential candidates for emigration.

The number of those who requested affidavits, expressed as a percentage of the total Jewish population in the USSR, varies significantly from republic to republic. Utilizing empirical and impressionistic data, we can surmise that these variations depend on a variety of factors:

(*a*) A quota for the specific republic. Since the number of those who request affidavits is influenced by the likelihood of a positive response from local authorities to the application, this also is self-regulating.
(*b*) The degree of discrimination experienced by an individual in respect to admittance to higher educational institutions or work promotion.

Table 2.1. Emigration from the USSR since 1967 [2]

Year	Visas (for Israel) issued in Moscow	Jews who left the USSR	Those to Israel	Those to other countries	First vyzovs sent (per individual)
1968	379	229	231	—	6,786
1969	2,902	2,979	3,033	—	27,301
1970	1,046	1,027	999	—	4,830
1971	14,310	13,022	12,819	58	40,794
1972	31,478	31,681	31,652	251	67,895
1973	34,922	34,733	33,477	1,456	58,216
1974	20,181	20,628	16,816	3,879	42,843
1975	13,139	13,221	8,531	4,928	34,145
1976	14,138	14,261	7,279	7,004	36,104
1977	17,159	16,736	8,348	8,483	43,062
1978	30,594	28,864	12,192	16,867	107,212
1979	50,343	51,320	17,614	34,056	138,891
1980	20,319	21,471	7,570	14,078	32,335
Total	250,910	250,187	160,561	91,060	630,414

(c) The variety and intensity of a local anti-Semitic campaign in the mass media.
(d) The degree of Jewish identity and the sense of being part of a Jewish people.
(e) The contents of letters from Israel and other Western countries describing the nature of the absorption process, including "success stories."

In areas where Jewish ties were strongest, the percentages of people requesting and receiving affidavits were highest: more than 50 percent in Lithuania, Latvia, Tadzhikistan, Uzbekistan, and Moldavia, and nearly 75 percent in Azerbaidzhan. (It may be of interest to note that the figure is over 100 percent in Georgia. This may demonstrate some of the difficulties in relying totally on official data. According to the 1970 census, 55,400 Jews were registered, although 66,144 Georgian Jews requested and received affidavits since 1968!) In those republics that were part of the traditional heartland of the Jewish population, but had a high degree of assimilation, the percentages reflected differing attitudes toward matters of "Jewishness." This worked out to nearly 33 percent in the Ukraine (246,571 persons), less than 25 percent in Byelorussia (31,220 persons), and slightly under 14 percent in Russia itself (111,821 persons), using the older 1970 data.

The percentage of people requesting and receiving affidavits significantly differed from republic to republic, and sometimes even from district to district in a given republic (namely, the west and east portions of the Ukraine). This could be attributed to the degree of assimilation and lack of Jewish motivation. It also might suggest fear inspired by local authorities, although this possibility needs to be assessed in the future. The degree of success in receiving the exit visas also differed from region to region. In Lithuania, Latvia, Estonia, and Georgia, more than 50 percent of those requesting and receiving affidavits were granted exit visas. Compare this with the RSFSR, Byelorussia, and the Ukraine, where about a third of those who received affidavits were given exit visas.

In general the percentage of dropouts (those Jews leaving the USSR who choose not to go to Israel) has continued to climb, from the beginning of 1980 when it hovered about 55 to 60 percent, until October 1980 when it ballooned to 78 percent. The 1980 average was more than 65 percent, compared with 66 percent the previous year. The dropout phenomenon is a function of many factors. While many persons often avoid explaining why they decided not to go to Israel, information gathered from Jews arriving in Vienna makes it clear that the decision often was made while they were still in the USSR. In Vienna many dropouts do state reasons that influenced their decision, including fear of the "strange and difficult climate," concern about war and Israel's future, and sometimes difficulties in the absorption process. These latter difficulties have indeed been cited as the decisive factor in the decision of many not to proceed to Israel. The phenomenon, however, reflects a more complex set of problems, of which the difficulties of absorption in Israel are only one. Is it safe to assume, for example, that Jews from Odessa did not encounter worse conditions than those of Chernovtsy? Nor were Jews from Kishinev treated better than Jews from Kiev. Still, the percentage of dropouts from Odessa and Kiev is much larger than from Vilnius, Riga, Chernovtsy, and Kishinev, most of whose Jews came to Israel.

Extensive improvements in Israel's absorption process, although necessary, could not solve the problem in its entirety. The phenomenon would appear to be a function of many factors, notably:

(a) For those under Soviet rule since 1917, over six decades of forced assimilation brought about by the lack of Jewish education, isolation from Jewish religious and nonreligious sources, and nearly total estrangement from any sentiments of ethnic or religious identity, in a society with more than one hundred other nations and nationalities.
(b) A sustained attack on Israel, Zionism, and Jewish history by all the media, creating negative images among many Jews and non-Jews.
(c) Fear of armed conflict between Israel and Arab states, and the sense of insecurity among new immigrants prevalent since the 1973 war.
(d) Moscow's campaign against unfiltered and objective news of Israel, as seen in the jamming of Israel's broadcasting facilities and the careful searches of Israeli visitors by Soviet airport customs.
(e) The insulation of Soviet Jews from friends and relatives in Israel through systematic interference with communications by phone or mail.
(f) Many mixed marriages, and the problems such families would encounter in Israel.
(g) Actual absorption difficulties, especially problems connected with absorbing academicians, or even some professionals, in addition to Israel's critical economic environment.

(*h*) Failure to understand or accept Israeli social and political patterns, which were often at variance with self-created images or expectations.
(*i*) An atmosphere of seeming economic or financial competition by Jewish community institutions in other countries, with substantive resources, and the moral authority this suggests.
(*j*) The creation of new Jewish population centers in countries other than Israel.

Some suggest that Soviet authorities may be exploiting the fact that many Jews have gone to the United States, Canada, and elsewhere in recent years, and so are unable to provide their closest relatives still in the USSR with Israeli invitations. The first-degree kinship refusals have been most evident in cities and towns in the Ukraine where the dropout rate has on occasion reached 95 percent. If so, this might endanger the continuation of any Jewish emigration, in addition to closing exit gates for the families who remain. As long as Jews who left the USSR with Israeli visas continued on to Israel, Jewish emigration was in accordance with accepted principles of repatriation and family reunification. This created no precedent for a claim of free emigration on the part of other national groups who had relatives in the United States and Canada. But the increased dropout phenomenon in the last few years slowly changed the nature of Jewish departure to a more normalized emigration, one which the Soviets view with increasing discomfort. Indeed, at the 1980–81 conference held in Madrid to review compliance with the Helsinki Final Act, Soviet delegates were quick to note that Jews hold affidavits from Israel but go to the United States, and suggested that the matter was being "investigated."

The deliberate decrease of Jewish departures from republics and cities conspicuous for their high percentage of dropouts, and the growth in exit quotas from regions and cities with a low percentage of dropouts, may indicate certain considerations of the Soviet authorities in regard to the dropout phenomenon. In any event, the dropout phenomenon, while not the only cause of the new emigration practices, has contributed to it substantially. At the very least it has become an exploitable issue for Soviet propagandists and, presumably, anti-Western hardliners who do not wish to encourage Jewish emigration under any conditions.

The worst aspects of current Soviet emigration practices are most evident in the ways in which refuseniks are treated. These Jews, whose applications for exit visas have been rejected, live in a world where their human condition worsens. The majority of refuseniks, following the submission of their applications, are fired from their jobs. Their children are driven out of high schools and tormented in primary schools when their parents are declared "traitors." Quite often male refuseniks who are driven out of the universities are summarily drafted into the Soviet army. In this manner, Soviet authorities simultaneously punish the refusenik family and create an additional pretense (security) for refusing exit visas for at least five additional years.

It is not possible to determine the exact number of refuseniks living in the Soviet Union today. Some of them have submitted applications, been rejected, and, out of fear of harming relatives or as a result of false promises made by the local authorities, decided to be temporarily reconciled with their fate and wait quietly. They may even have given up their right to receive exit visas. A substantial part of the refusenik group, however, is not reconciled with the verdict of Soviet authorities. They continue to fight for their right to get exit visas and are careful to continue legal efforts to circulate news of their situation, and that of their friends, among friends and relatives in Israel. It is this small group who have become best known in the West and who have become the symbol of all refuseniks. To some extent, they continue to be seen as the spearhead of all emigration activities, for they are the only visible and articulate voice for any Jewish issue in the Soviet Union. The number of refuseniks at the end of 1979 totaled 1,093 families (2,984 persons), as compared with 845 families at the end of 1978 (2,259 persons). The next year their ranks grew significantly and the number of known refuseniks reached 1,661 families or about 4,700 persons. This increase was much higher than any other in recent years. Among the refuseniks are about 80 persons (36 families) who have been struggling for more than ten years, in addition to 400 persons (130 families) who have been waiting from five to ten years to leave the Soviet Union.

Soviet authorities generally base refusals on security grounds. In most cases these considerations fail any objective standard in the West, especially for individuals fired from their jobs five to ten years earlier. If members of these families possessed information that might be considered as secret in the USSR, these data lose their importance and value over the years. The common assumption, therefore, is that these refusals remain a method for harassing those seeking to emigrate, especially those with higher education and professional skills. This method is a means of punishing those wishing to leave and who serve as a positive model for other Jews. Keeping them in limbo serves to intimidate sections of the Jewish population and deter them from presenting their own applications. These refuseniks live on meager savings and/or on assistance from relatives abroad. In most cases they are cut off from their professions and subjected to periodic harassment by the Soviet authorities, including sudden searches, phone disconnections, surveillance by the secret police, confiscation of mail, and occasional arrests. Many refuseniks have become frustrated and, in despair, have withdrawn into the security of their homes and families. This negative mood has been sensed by other Jewish emigration activists, especially younger ones attracted to the emigration movement within the last few years.

Even as emigration is suppressed, pressure builds up that compels more Jews to seek emigration. The admission of Jews to higher institutes of learning has declined dramatically, for example, and Jews may soon find themselves virtually shut out from prestigious academic institutions. Until 1968, in spite of a quota system, Jews were well represented at top universities and scientific institutes. One-third of the Jewish community was university-educated, compared with only 4 percent of the overall population. But since the late 1960s admission of Jews to higher institutes has declined dramatically. They are virtually excluded from the better schools by a system worked out for lowering the examination marks of applicants. The system is administered by specifically selected examiners who give Jewish students unusually difficult oral entrance examinations, notably in mathematics and physics. Documents of the Moscow Helsinki Monitoring Group explain how difficult it is to demonstrate this widespread discrimination since school records, if they exist, are kept secret. According to reliable sources in the USSR, in the academic years 1977–78 and 1978–79 not one Jew was admitted to the faculty of mathematics in Moscow University. In the year 1979–80 about 1 percent, or four Jews, were accepted out of the annual intake of 400 to 500 students. In the past this figure had been about 10 percent. Jews have little hope of achieving solid entry-level positions, much less any chance of getting near the top of their fields. This discrimination against merit is compelling Jews to seek to leave as future options become increasingly restrictive.

A parallel expression of anti-Semitism is the continuing, vitriolic propaganda campaign vilifying the Jewish people, the Jewish religion, and the State of Israel. The USSR is among the largest producers of anti-Semitic materials in the world. Its campaign of slander, conducted in the mass media and publications, is sensed by many Jews as a threat to their own security in the USSR. Discrimination may explain, in part, why so many Jews in recent years have chosen to leave. Their desire may be motivated by personal considerations, as they see fewer options for their children in the Soviet Union, and as a way to improve living standards. We do not know, of course, how many Soviet Jews still retain a sense of identity or consciousness. For decades Soviet authorities have suppressed the Jewish religion and culture. The USSR is the only country with a Jewish community in which there is not a single approved Jewish school or a means for passing on Jewish history and religion.

After more than six decades of Soviet rule there is no accurate way to measure the impact of purge trials, anti-Semitic propaganda, anti-Jewish discrimination, or repressive acts against Jewish activists. There is no method to measure the impact of a ban on Hebrew, a lack of Jewish historic materials, or of a nonfunctioning theological seminary in Moscow. Yet, one unusual opinion survey found a high degree of identity and interest in Jewish culture. The survey was organized by Soviet-Jewish activists in 1976 to test feelings about Jewishness among those who had not taken steps to emigrate. The study's main weakness was its sample, which could be neither random nor scientifically selected because of the Soviet government's opposition to polling outside of official auspices. The study is, however, instructive. While anyone who had applied for an exit visa was excluded, the analysis reported that most of the Jews who opposed emigration as a solution said they would like their children to learn Yiddish or Hebrew, and to be able themselves to buy books on Jewish history. The respondents were divided on the desirability of continuing to have nationality listed on internal passports, which now label citizens as Russian, Jewish, Ukrainian, and the like. But even the majority of those who would not list their children as Jewish said they would like to buy books on Jewish history.

Apparently, many of those who might register their children as non-Jews and who now oppose emigration to Israel want more opportunities for Jewish culture and education than are currently available. Soviet opposition to satisfying this objective is as adamant as it has been since the end of the Second World War, as evidenced by the recent Soviet attack on refusenik scientist Viktor Brailovsky.

For the last nine years a growing number of Jewish scientists who have been denied the right to leave, and some who have not, have maintained informal or unofficial scientific-educational seminars. The idea was born in 1972 when scores of persons who had requested permission to emigrate to Israel, and had been refused, were dismissed from their positions or demoted. The seminars were a means of demonstrating solidarity as much as an effort to maintain scientific literacy. Lacking adequate material or equipment, these scientists used their homes as substitute classrooms and theoretical laboratories.

The investigation into Brailovsky's association with the samizdat publication *Jews in the USSR*, claimed by officials to be anti-Soviet in nature, served as a quick pretext for his arrest. His imprisonment was to be a warning to others who might agitate for their right to emigrate, while at the same time halting a publication that had become a vital and popular link in the refusenik network.

Jews in the USSR was founded in Moscow in October 1972 to meet the growing demand by Soviet Jews for materials about Jewish history, culture, and identity. The early issues of the quarterly were prepared by Aleksandr Voronel, Viktor Yakhot, and a group of friends. Unlike other samizdat publications, it listed the names of its editors on the title page. The early editions were devoted to "the History, Culture and Problems of the Jews of the Soviet Union." While Voronel was editor, the journal dealt mainly with issues related to the national awakening of Jews in the Soviet Union and with the search for Jewish identity. A section entitled "Who Am I?" was a permanent feature. As the magazine matured and its typewritten pages grew from approximately eighty to 250, its scope broadened to include topics other than the status of Soviet Jews, such as world Jewish history and culture, and religion in Israel and other countries. Russian translations of works by Saul Bellow, Isaac Bashevis Singer, Rabbi Abraham Joshua Heschel, and articles from *Commentary* and other Jewish journals were published in *Jews in the USSR*. Poetry appeared, along with such diverse material as the life story of the "inventor" of modern Hebrew, and the "Jewish question" as viewed by two early twentieth-century Russian philosophers. Space also was given to works by non-Jewish writers and to interviews with selected members of the Human Rights Movement, notably Evgenii Barabanov and Andrei Sakharov. Because of the difficulties involved in the magazine's reproduction, the total number of copies per issue seldom exceeded thirty or forty. Printing and duplicating equipment was unavailable. Each edition had to be typed several times on old machines that made poor copies, by typists whose enthusiasm often surpassed their proficiency. Nevertheless, the magazine gradually became well known in the capital and later found its way to Kharkov, Leningrad, Kiev, Riga, Vilnius, Kishinev, Sverdlovsk, and Novosibirsk. Each copy was passed from hand to hand, one fragile onionskin issue being read by perhaps as many as one hundred people.

The policy of *Jews in the USSR* was stated in each issue of the publication: it would not pursue political aims, it would not contain "lies or offensive attacks," and it would be of high quality. These principles were reaffirmed by a succession of editors, each of whom left his individual stamp on the journal before entrusting it to the next one when his turn for permission to leave for Israel finally came. Viktor Brailovsky was the last in this chain.

Seemingly, Brailovsky's association with the magazine was but one of many concerns to Soviet security forces. Irritation with his activities as a spokesman for the refusenik community and his leadership in scientific circles had led to previous harassment and arrests. Viktor and his wife, Irina, both cyberneticists, were discharged from their jobs in 1972 when they applied for permission to leave for Israel. For some years the couple hosted a weekly Sunday seminar for the Jewish scientists. The International Seminar on Collective Phenomena, a yearly event attended by scientists from the West, also was convened by the Brailovskys. The authorities' growing irritation erupted when Brailovsky summoned Western reporters to his apartment early in November 1980 to inform them of hunger strikes being planned by frustrated refuseniks to coincide with the opening of the Madrid conference to review progress under the Helsinki Final Act. Many of the strikers were new to the emigration cause, a consideration not overlooked by the KGB.

Viktor Brailovsky's case is fateful for the Jewish activist and emigration movement, since he is also the first scientist-refusenik arrested by the Soviets who was deeply concerned with Jewish interests. In arresting Brailovsky, authorities attacked both scientific activists and those involved in self-education. Since Brailovsky's arrest, scientists who attempted to attend their Sunday seminar, as usual, have been periodically barred from his apartment by the police.

The situation had its desired impact: it silenced protestors. And if the message was not clear, within a few months other long-term refuseniks in Kiev, including Kim Fridman and Vladimir Kislik, also were arrested. As if tighter emigration restrictions were insufficient, the assault against Jewish emigration activists in the Ukrainian capital has been escalated.

The more than 250,000 Soviet Jews who emigrated between 1970 and 1981 suggested a positive change in regard to emigration. If the more recent cutback reflects a connection between the policy of Soviet authorities toward the emigration of Jews and the state of bilateral relations with the United States, Soviet Jews are now in a tragic situation: they are kept virtually as hostages. If their basic right to leave is conditioned upon a set of relations over which they have no control, their fate becomes even more desperate.

3. Brezhnev and Soviet Anti-Semitism

William Korey

Pronouncements against anti-Semitism in the USSR are scarcely characteristic of Soviet party leaders, especially not in the course of their major policy addresses. Indeed, such statements are rare and virtually unprecedented. It is this that makes a passage in the five-hour speech of Leonid Brezhnev to the Twenty-Sixth Communist Party Congress on February 23, 1981, unique.

At no previous party congresses had the principal policy address of the party leader ever referred to anti-Semitism, although Vladimir Lenin in various public statements did condemn it, as did Joseph Stalin on one occasion. The last time a high Soviet official had denounced anti-Semitism was sixteen years earlier, on July 18, 1965. On that date the late Premier Aleksei Kosygin, during a relatively brief period when some aspects of an enlightened human rights policy appeared on the Soviet horizon, sharply criticized manifestations of anti-Semitism in a speech at Riga that was carried in *Pravda* the next day. Later, on September 5, 1965, *Pravda* vigorously editorialized against anti-Semitism, citing Lenin's comment that it was a "malicious exaggeration of . . . national enmity."

Since then, such views have totally disappeared from authoritative sources and been replaced by the flat assertion—as Kosygin himself would declare— that "there has never been and there is no anti-Semitism in the Soviet Union."

The Brezhnev acknowledgement of the existence of anti-Semitism in the USSR and his sharp rejection of it came in the course of comments on the nationality question of the Soviet Union, which, oddly enough, had nothing to do with the Jewish issue. Brezhnev had taken note of the sizable movement into various Soviet republics of persons belonging to ethnic groups that were not indigenous to the specific republics. Observing that the indicated ethnic groups had "specific requirements in the spheres of language, culture and everyday life," he strongly suggested that these "requirements" were not being met, with the consequent emergence of bitter interethnic tensions. He asked that the party leadership on regional levels "penetrate deeply into such issues and propose ways of resolving them in good time."

The recommendation was immediately followed by the usual party soporific on the Soviet nationality question: "The national feelings and national dignity of each person are respected in our country." The next sentence—the key one— was notable for juxtaposing the expected general party message with a totally unexpected example. It read:

> The CPSU [Communist party of the Soviet Union] has fought and will always fight resolutely against such phenomena [interethnic tensions] which are alien

to the nature of socialism as chauvinism or nationalism, *against any nationalistic aberrations such as, let us say, anti-Semitism or Zionism* [emphasis added]. We are against tendencies aimed at artificial erosion of national characteristics. But to the same extent, we consider impermissible their artificial exaggeration. It is the sacred duty of the party to educate the working people in the spirit of Soviet patriotism and socialist internationalism, of a proud feeling of belonging to a single great Soviet motherland.[1]

The chosen illustrations of "nationalistic aberrations" would appear to be largely irrelevant as Soviet anti-Semitism is certainly not the primary expression of interethnic tensions in the USSR flowing from internal geographic mobility and migration. Indeed, the reference to anti-Semitism seems almost accidental. However, nothing is accidental in the party leader's policy speech, which is broadcast over radio, carried in the press, and, most importantly, carefully studied for guidance and implementation in all party organs.

Why, then, the stunning critical reference to anti-Semitism? Two separate, although complementary, hypotheses can be advanced. The first relates to external considerations, the other, far more critical, to internal factors. That there existed an urgent need to refurbish the Soviet image, by now badly tarnished through public disclosures of the Kremlin's virulent anti-Semitic propaganda campaign, must have been patently obvious to Kremlin policy makers. The Council of Europe in Strasbourg had officially documented the massive hate drive as had an Australian parliamentary inquiry. The Conference on Security and Cooperation of Europe, meeting in Madrid in November and December 1980, heard an elaboration of the charges of Soviet anti-Semitism, most notably by the Belgian delegate, René Panis. Indeed, the Belgian's accusation was one of the rare occasions during the Madrid proceedings that prompted an angry and emotional response from the Soviet delegation. That response had taken the form of a vehement denial of the existence of Soviet anti-Semitism, which evoked laughter from the participants.

The Kremlin leadership may very well have reasoned that the maintenance of detente and of the Helsinki Final Act necessitated the elimination, or at least the diminution of the more extremist manifestations of anti-Semitism. Significantly, Brezhnev vigorously emphasized the value of detente several times in his address, in particular observing that "the vital interests of the European peoples" demand following the "path . . . which was laid in Helsinki." The process of Madrid, he said, should continue "uninterrupted." Acknowledgement and public repudiation of Soviet anti-Semitism could conceivably help the process. Certainly, the Kremlin's image was badly in need of polishing.

Strikingly, a Soviet diplomatic initiative in Washington, D.C., in late February and early March of 1981, which focused upon the American-Jewish community, gave emphasis to the Brezhnev speech. Sergei Rogov, a prominent Soviet aide, in a rare effort approached B'nai B'rith and several other Jewish organizations in Washington to call specific attention to the public repudiation of anti-Semitism. Rogov emphasized a reference in the Brezhnev speech to ensuring "the security and sovereignty of all the states of this [Middle East] region, including Israel."

The initiative was obviously linked to Soviet anxiety about the Reagan administration's tough approach to the USSR. Since Soviet leaders not infrequently accept the assumptions of their own propaganda—that American Jews play a crucial, if not decisive, role in policy making—it is not surprising that an initiative to placate American Jewry was undertaken.

Still, image-building is far less important to Soviet officials than maintaining the power of the reigning Kremlin elite. How did Brezhnev and his close associates assess the burgeoning anti-Semitic vituperations in the mass media? Was Jew-baiting perceived as a serious challenge confronting Brezhnev's rule? The question is by no means as bizarre as it might seem. Exactly two years before the Brezhnev speech to the party congress, on February 23, 1979, a six-page typescript article replete with anti-Semitic invectives was placed in mailboxes throughout Moscow and distributed in Leningrad.[2] The striking aspect of the article was its open attack upon Brezhnev and seven of his associates on the politburo as "Kremlin Zionists." They were distinguished from the "faithful sons" of Russia on the politburo—top ideologist Mikhail Suslov, Leningrad party chief Gregory Romanov, party second secretary A. P. Kirilenko, and the late Prime Minister Kosygin.

The article reflected the rising chauvinist and xenophobic Russian nationalism that has deep roots in the party and its leadership. Signed by an anonymous "Russian Liberation Organization," the anti-Semitic essay offered the following physical characteristics as guidelines for recognizing Zionists: "hairy chest and arms," "shifty eyes," and "hook-like nose." The first guideline obviously pointed to Brezhnev. His name was seen as part of an elaborate secret code designed to help "hidden Zionists" recognize one another. He was openly denounced for "blatantly usurping" the presidency of the USSR by ousting Nikolai Podgorny.

The fact that the reproduction and widespread distribution of this hate literature could take place in the monolithic Soviet totalitarian society testifies to the serious and growing challenge of Russian extremism. After all, duplication machines are strictly controlled and allocated by the authorities in Soviet society. Moreover, there is no indication that the racist perpetrators of the article have ever been apprehended despite the powerful KGB police apparatus. That an intense internal struggle for power in the USSR has already developed is extensively documented by two perceptive émigré scholars, Vladimir Solovyev and Elena Klepikova, in the journal *Time and We*, published in Israel. According to these scholars, a "Russian Party" with roots deep in the Communist party apparatus as well as in the populace is seeking domination. The struggle continued to intensify as Brezhnev's aging infirmities deepened prior to his death. The authors further speculated that "the heir of Brezhnev is likely to become in essence Stalin's heir."[3]

In Eastern Europe anti-Semitism has been and remains a potent tool in political struggles, whether to seize power or to maintain power. The historic device is, indeed, manipulated even without the presence of Jews, in violation of sociological "laws" governing anti-Semitic causation. Recent startling episodes in Poland and Romania testify to the value and validity of the tradition, from which the USSR has ben no means been immune. Party power struggles in the 1920s were heavily permeated with anti-Semitism. Under Stalin and Secret Police Chief Lavrenti Beria, the racist weapon was continually wielded.

It was not only from anonymous, subterranean sources that Brezhnev might have perceived threats to his authority. Several months before the "Russian Liberation Organization" article appeared in Moscow, the Philosophy Institute of the prestigious Soviet Academy of Sciences produced an anti-Zionist booklet designed for a very limited and select audience—only 500 key party officials. The booklet, *Zionism in the Chain of Imperialism*, was written by one of the Soviet Union's most notorious anti-Semites, Yevgeny S. Yevseev.[4] Yevseev, who in numerous book and newspaper essays had resurrected the basic themes of the old fabrication, "The Protocols of the Elders of Zion," now charged that Zionism was "more dangerous than German, Italian and Spanish Fascism." In his view Zionism was "destroying the spiritual and moral health of the working class." The "enemy" was not merely abroad; its agents also could be found within the borders of the USSR. Yevseev criticized Soviet literature, movies, and television because "from time to time, people of Jewish origin appear as positive heroes or as supporting heroes." The challenge went deeper. Prominent Soviet literary officials, including Sergei Narovchatov, the chief editor of the major Soviet journal *Novy Mir*, and philosophy specialists like B. Kefrov and Mark B. Mitin, were declared to be "Zionist supporters" on grounds that they had written that Jews are an ancient people and that Zionism appeared historically as a reaction to anti-Semitism.

Far more significant than the booklet itself was the question of how it was produced. The printing was done not in a publishing house but by a facility housed in the Ministry of Internal Affairs, which supervises Soviet police work. Clearly, authority to produce the booklet had been granted at the very highest state levels.

Those accused of being "Zionist supporters" bitterly complained, and on March 11, 1979, the issue was formally aired in the Central Committee where Yevseev was reported to have been verbally chastised. Yet neither he nor the Philosophy Institute, which had sponsored the booklet, were punished; even chastisement was seen, in some quarters, as unwarranted. Two months later, scores of influential people received a mimeographed letter signed by a pseudonym—Vasily Ryazanov—which charged that "a powerful Zionist lobby" existed within the very Central Committee of the Soviet Communist party.[5] How the "lobby" functioned was detailed in the following manner: "They do not allow themselves to be attacked with the excuse that this would bring on accusations of anti-Semitism, negative reactions in world public opinion, and damage to the policy of detente." Whoever "Ryazanov" was, he did have well-placed protectors; use of a mimeograph machine made that evident.

High-level concern about a growing chauvinist thrust with distinctive anti-Semitic features became even more pronounced in 1980. This was disclosed in an extraordinary and unprecedented discussion between a Soviet-Jewish researcher and a key official in the secretariat of the party's Central Committee. The discussion was triggered by a two-year research project undertaken by Ruth Okuneva, a refusenik and former historian and researcher at the USSR Academy of Pedagogical Sciences. She assembled in three parallel columns statements concerning the character and culture of Jewry and proposals for solving the "Jewish Question." One column carried the assertions of the reactionary Russian "Black Hundreds" organization (during the tsarist epoch); the second carried the statements of Nazi Germany's ideologists; and the third carried extracts from recent and current Soviet anti-Zionist books.

The study, entitled "A Few Pages of Analogy," ran to eighty-seven pages. The documentation of anti-Semitic propaganda that echoed tsarist and Nazi hate was devastating. Okuneva sent the study to Brezhnev, as party general secretary, on April 12, 1980, with a covering letter noting that a half-dozen Soviet authors producing the massive anti-Zionist propaganda in articles and books were "violating the ideals of socialist internationalism that form the basis of the Communist party's national policy." Her summary of the findings was sharp: "Their works are full of savage hatred of Jews, not of Zionism, and they do not conceal it. They present the Jews as the enemies of the Soviet state, as counter-revolutionaries, spies, accomplices of Hitlerism."[6]

On June 23 a surprised Okuneva received a postcard from the Central Committee requesting her to call Anatoly Aleksandrovich Sazonov, a committee official. Sazonov met with her on July 4. His queries and comments were cordial. Noting that her documentation was "very thorough," he went on to say that "It will be of use to us." Sazonov's observations were revealing. According to Okuneva, he said: "Don't think, however, that you have invented the bicycle. We are also working on this matter; i.e., we are concerned about exaggerations in this literature."[7] Sazonov went on to say that he agreed with Okuneva's "evaluation" of specific Soviet authors, including Yevseev, Vladimir Begun, Valentin Pikul, Lev Korneyev, and Valery Yemelyanov—all literary hate-peddlers.

Sazonov's comments, while encouraging in their indication of the depth of concern in some official quarters, also suggested that the issue of the hate-mongers' propaganda was far from being resolved. Sazonov told Okuneva that "we are not always able to keep track of all their tricks; these authors often manage to evade our control." Clearly, powerful forces were yet in contention.

Still, it was apparent that Brezhnev's men in the party apparatus were profoundly concerned with the emergent anti-Semitism in the media and were determined to confront it head-on.

Party officials concerned with internal matters may have believed that the struggle against extremist anti-Semitism could produce an additional useful bonus. The party leadership had decided some time earlier to cut back the Jewish emigration rate and, since late 1979, had instituted harassment that reduced the exodus flow at first by approximately two-thirds, and later by three-quarters. Whatever the motivations for the cutback (which ranged from a fear of brain drain, to the perception of Jews as "hostages" to the state of American-Soviet detente relations), Soviet authorities still had to cope with the burgeoning internal Jewish pressure for exodus.

One way to ease emigration pressure was to reduce anti-Semitism. Marxist dissenter Roy Medvedev, whose contacts with Central Committee officials were never totally severed, had warned for some time that the single most important factor generating Zionist impulses among Jews was official anti-Semitism.[8] Significantly, on the eve of the Twenty-sixth Party Congress, 130 prominent Soviet Jewish activists sent a ten-page plea to the delegates, forcefully asserting that the anti-Semitic media campaign was one of two "principal causes" for the rapid rise in the number of applications for emigration. (The other was the lack of facilities for cultural self-expression.) The Jewish activists appealed for a "change in the party's attitude to Soviet Jewry," in particular the "virulent anti-Zionist campaign" that had reached "hysterical proportions" and "was coloring" the public's attitude toward Jewry.

Even before the Brezhnev denunciation of anti-Semitism, close students of Soviet propaganda noticed a quantitative reduction of anti-Semitism in the media. The number of hate articles in the press during 1980 was certainly less than during 1979. In that sense Sazonov's assertion to Okuneva that he and at least some of his party colleagues were "concerned" and "were working" on the matter is not without substance and significance.

Nonetheless, anti-Semitic propaganda has by no means ceased, and its qualitative character, echoing the tsarist "Protocols of the Elders of Zion," remains unchanged. The plea of the 130 Jewish activists to the Twenty-sixth Party Congress called attention to articles of crude bigotry in *Pionerskaia Pravda*, a tabloid organ of the powerful Komsomol for nine to fourteen year olds. An article in the tabloid's October 10, 1980, issue by the notorious hate-peddler Lev Korneyev is not unusual. The following excerpt is characteristic:

> In view of the fact that Zionism is the instrument of the big Jewish bourgeoisie, it is backed by its enormous resources that are being pumped out from the gold, diamond and uranium mines of South Africa, the workshops and industrial plants of Europe, American and Australia. Zionists are trying to infiltrate into all the spheres of public life, into ideology, science, commerce. Even "Levi's" jeans are part of their operation; the profits from selling the pants are used by the firm for helping Zionists. Most of the major monopolies producing arms are controlled by Jewish bankers. The business made on blood brings them enormous profits. Bombs and shells explode in Lebanon— the bankers Lazars and Leobs are counting their profits. Bandits in Afghani-

stan are poisoning school children by gasses—and stacks of dollars multiply in the safes of the Lehmans and the Guggenheims. It is understandable that for Zionism peace in the world is the main enemy.

Korneyev's other assertions carried similar thrusts. The Jewish concept of the chosen people was said to be a "racist invention" of the Zionists who "instill enmity and hatred towards all non-Jews." Practitioner of subversion and espionage, of racism and racial discrimination, of militarism and imperialism, Zionism was declared to be "the Fascism of today."

The Korneyev article highlighted the basic limitation of the Brezhnev denunciation of anti-Semitism. The coupling by the party general secretary of anti-Semitism with Zionism, to a significant degree, reduced and constrained the struggle against hate propaganda. Zionism, since 1967 and especially since 1971, had become the code word for Jewry, just as "cosmopolitanism" had been the code word during the Black Years of Stalin's anti-Semitism, 1948–53. It was precisely the media drive against Zionism that unleashed and gave sanction to the stereotypes, images, and formulations of vulgar anti-Semitism.

The inadequacy of the Brezhnev condemnation was glaringly revealed by an instructive article in the principal journal of Byelorussia, *Sovetskaia Byelorossia*, on March 6, 1981, only two weeks after the Brezhnev address to the party congress. Written by an especially infamous anti-Semitic propaganda specialist, Vladimir Begun of Minsk, the article was entitled "Danger: Zionism," but its theme, stripped of Aesopian formulations, is one of the most incendiary to have appeared in recent years.

The Begun article was formally designed as an answer to a letter that the newspaper is said to have received from a "war veteran." The letter had posed the following query: "At the beginning of the 1950s, the press carried articles about the Zionist organization 'Joint' and its activities on behalf of the enemies of peace. I am interested in learning whether this organization still exists." The specific reference to the 1950s and the pointed question about "Joint" are extraordinary. The early fifties is precisely the period when anti-Semitism in the USSR reached its most extreme form with the secret trial and execution of Jewish intellectuals and writers (July and August of 1952) and the unveiling of an alleged "Doctors' Plot" (January through March 1953), which generated an especially dangerous pogrom atmosphere in the Soviet Union. "Joint," or, more precisely, the American-Jewish Joint Distribution Committee, had been singled out in a massive propaganda campaign as the master instrument of World Zionism in a plot to murder all top Soviet leaders. The agents of "Joint" were said to be nine Soviet doctors, mainly Jewish.

Had the "Doctors' Plot" campaign reached its climax, the mass expulsion of Soviet Jews to Siberia and Central Asia would have followed together with executions of the principal "culprits." Only the death of Stalin on March 5, 1953, brought a halt to the unfolding catastrophe and saved Soviet Jewry. Shortly afterward, the "plot" was disclosed by Stalin's successors to have been a total fabrication. Nikita Khrushchev would later reveal in his "secret speech" to the Twentieth Party Congress how the plot was concocted by Stalin and how torture was used to extract fraudulent confessions.

The "Doctors' Plot" was so totally discredited and repudiated in official statements at the time that references to it—and to "Joint"—disappeared from the media. The positive resurrection of the affair is unprecedented and a stunning reminder that those seeking a violent resolution to the Jewish problem continue their efforts.

The appearance of the Begun article on the twenty-eighth anniversary of Stalin's death, almost to the exact date, must have triggered powerful—and dangerous—associations. Putting the query in the mouth of a "war veteran" was clearly designed to reinforce patriotic and chauvinistic memories, even as it dredged up the passions of Jew-hatred. The article itself regurgitated discredited myths about the "Elders of Zion," about how "powerful Jewish magnates—Kuhns, Loebs, and Lehmans"—manipulate Zionist-Jewish organizations, about how "Joint," acting as the instrument of the World Zionist Organization, engages in espionage in the socialist countries and subsidizes "the Zionist secret service."

A final indication that the campaign against Zionism, by its very nature in Soviet surroundings, mocks the condemnation of anti-Semitism even when articulated at the highest level of the party was the planned publiction of a new book by Trofim K. Kichko, *Judaism and Zionism—Adherents to Racism*. It was scheduled for publication during the second quarter of 1981 by Molod, a Soviet Ukrainian youth institution.[9]

Kichko has been called by Western observers the Soviet Union's "Julius Streicher," after the notorious Nazi hate propagandist and editor of the infamous *Der Sturmer*. The Soviet writer had acquired the reputation from his book *Judaism Without Embellishment*, published by the Ukrainian Academy of Sciences in October 1963. (As early as October 1, 1953, it was revealed by a Soviet source, *Literaturnaia Gazeta*, that Kichko had "compromised himself" during the Nazi occupation of Vinnitsa. The tantalizing disclosure was not elaborated upon further.)

Not until February 1964 did a copy of the Kichko work make its appearance in the West, stunning civilized society with disbelief. The Ukrainian work boldly repeated ancient canards: that the Torah teaches Jews to steal from goyim; that the Talmud "morally corrupts people" through instilling the "spirit" of "extortion"; that Judaism is "impregnated" with "greed," the love of money, and the spirit of egoism; and that synagogue leaders are distinguished by "speculation . . . thievery, deception and debauchery."

Kichko linked these features of the Jewish religion to Zionism, which he characterized as the instrument of colonial expansion in the Middle East. And, as in Nazi mythology, the Rockefellers were identified as an integral element in the Zionist conspiracy of conquest. Incorporated into *Judaism Without Embel-*

lishment were a number of crudely drawn cartoons portraying the Jew with hooked nose, uncouth facial and neck features, and wearing traditional religious garb. The scurrilous stereotypes produced at first incredulity, then shock.

By the third week of March 1964 Communist parties in the West were consumed with the issue. A storm of criticism, rare in the annals of international communism, welled up. *L'Humanité* reprinted a sharply angry commentary demanding Soviet disavowal of the book. The Italian party's *Paesa Sera* urged the withdrawal of the book, while *L'Unita* warned that the book's anti-Semitism threatened Soviet prestige. A chorus of similar attacks appeared in the organs of the Dutch, Swedish, Norwegian, Danish, British, American, Canadian, and Australian Communist parties. The explosion of indignation at what seemed a resurgence of Nazi-type anti-Semitism threatened a serious confrontation between the Soviet motherland and international communism.

It was the Soviet Communist party that retreated with an historic and unprecedented apology. The Ideological Commission of the party's Central Committee denounced the Kichko book as carrying "serious mistakes," including "erroneous statements" and illustrations that "may offend the feelings of believers and might be interpreted in a spirit of anti-Semitism" (*Pravda*, April 4, 1964). The work was soon withdrawn from bookshelves.

The new Kichko book is destined to repeat and extend the themes articulated in *Judaism Without Embellishment*. This is evidenced by its brief description in the bibliographical source work. The author is said to "reveal" the "criminal activities of various Zionist organizations and of Zionist-inspired Judaism" and to provide "a thorough critique of the age-old people-hatred of Judaism." Kichko's bigotry has by no means been modified over the past eighteen years. On the contrary, in the half-dozen articles and essays that he has written since his return to publishing in October 1967, he offers a continuous flow of vulgar hate material. Now, however, he has been provided by the authorities with a major book outlet. Twenty-five thousand copies of the work will be published, more than twice the number published of *Judaism Without Embellishment*. Unlike the first book, which was printed in Ukrainian, the new book is printed in Russian and thus will reach a much broader readership.

That the publishing privilege has again been extended to Kichko is an additional indication of the respectability still enjoyed by anti-Semitism in the Soviet media. Effective constraint of the propaganda of hate has yet to be realized, notwithstanding the danger such material poses for the party leadership and the damage it does to the state's image. The historic Brezhnev repudiation of anti-Semitism remains an act largely empty of meaning.

4. Soviet Jewry and Soviet-American Relations: A Historical Analysis

Robert O. Freedman

The issue of Soviet-Jewish emigration from the USSR has been an important element in Soviet-American relations since the early 1970s when the Jackson-Vanik amendment sought to tie American trade concessions to the Soviet Union to emigration of Soviet Jews. While the Soviet leadership has long asserted that there can be no "linkage" between Soviet-American relations on the one hand and what the Soviet leaders call "internal" matters of Soviet policy (such as Jewish emigration) on the other, it seems clear that such a linkage has operated in Soviet-American relations for the last decade. Soviet desires for American grain and technology, Soviet hopes for conclusion of the SALT I and SALT II agreements, and Soviet fears of a Sino-American alliance directed against the USSR have combined to motivate the Soviet leadership to allow the emigration of more than 250,000 Jews from the Soviet Union since 1970 (see Annex I).

Yet the issue of Soviet Jewry as a factor in Soviet-American relations does not begin only in the 1970s. There is evidence to indicate that Soviet Jewry played a role, albeit not a major one, in Stalin's planning during World War II, and it does not seem accidental that the worst period for Soviet Jewry, 1948–53, coincided with the worst years of the Cold War between the United States and the Soviet Union. In addition, there is considerable evidence that Nikita Khrushchev, who ruled the USSR from 1955 to 1964, also was sensitive to American and other foreign nations' expressions of interest in the fate of Soviet Jews. Thus, while the bulk of this analysis will be devoted to a study of Soviet Jewry as a factor in Soviet-American relations in the last decade, particularly during the period of the Carter administration, an examination also will be made of the impact of Soviet Jewry's role in Soviet-American relations in the Stalin and Khrushchev eras.

The Stalin Era

It is not possible to present a detailed examination of Stalin's attitude to Soviet Jews here. There is, however, one important element to note. A number of Stalin's top rivals in the Communist party were Jews (Trotsky, Kamenev, and Zinoviev), and he was involved in a power struggle with them until the late 1920s when he was able to assert his full control over the Soviet state and eventually eliminate them (and other Jews) from positions of power. To what degree memories of this power struggle influenced him later in life is impossible to determine.[1] However, he did dissolve the *Evsektsiia*, the Jewish section of the Communist party, in 1930, at least in part because of "Jewish nationalist tendencies."[2] As a result, there was no central Soviet-Jewish organization until the Jewish Anti-Fascist Committee was formed in 1942.

In the early stages of the German attack on the Soviet Union, Stalin was fairly desperate for Western assistance, and the Jewish Anti-Fascist Committee was one outgrowth of his quest for Western aid.[3] As Joshua Gilboa has stated in his study of Stalin's policy toward Soviet Jewry, "Soviet authorities attached great significance to the influence of world Jewry in shaping general public opinion in the West, whose support in the war against Germany was considered vital."[4] By organizing the Jewish Anti-Fascist Committee and sending its top leaders (Solomon Mikhoels, director of the Moscow Jewish State theater, and Yitzhak Feffer, a noted Soviet-Jewish poet) on a tour of Jewish communities in England, Canada, Mexico, and the United States, Stalin hoped to gain increased Western (and Jewish) economic aid, increased military assistance, and also the early opening of a second front against the Germans on the continent of Europe, thereby relieving some of the German pressure on the Red Army.

Interestingly enough, however, while Stalin's aim in establishing the Jewish Anti-Fascist Committee was to gain Western support, the committee soon developed a life of its own and served, albeit informally, as an organization for Soviet Jews during World War II. Indeed, there were a number of Soviet Jews who wished to greatly expand the domestic role of the committee. As the poet David Hofstein stated: "The Jewish Anti-Fascist Committee must become the center of Russian Jewry, and not merely an agency for raising funds in the United States."[5]

While Stalin permitted a rise in Soviet-Jewish consciousness through the establishment of the Jewish Anti-Fascist Committee, as well as through the production of a large number of Jewish wartime literary works, many of which were infused by specifically Jewish and anti-German themes, the end of World War II and the onset of the Cold War were to bring about a major change in his attitudes. While there is some evidence that one of Stalin's goals in giving diplomatic and military support to Israel in its war of independence against the Arabs was to influence the Jews of the United States and prevent the consolidation of the Anglo-American alliance,[6] by early 1949, with NATO established and the Cold War in full swing, Stalin cracked down hard on Soviet Jewry. By this time Stalin appeared clearly paranoid, and he was not willing to tolerate any manifestations of Jewish nationalism. The ties Soviet Jews had with their coreligionists abroad, which had been an asset for Stalin's strategy during World War II, now became a major liability for the Soviet Jews themselves when the United States and Britain became Russia's Cold War enemies. Stalin's destruction of Jewish culture during the 1948–53 period, and his murder of top Jewish poets and writers are, unfortunately, too well known to have to be described in detail.[7] Essentially, the leader of the Jewish Anti-Fascist Committee, Solomon

Mikhoels was murdered, the committee itself was dissolved, all Yiddish publishing houses were closed down, Jewish books were removed from Soviet libraries and bookstores, Jews were accused of being "cosmopolitans" and eliminated from many areas of Soviet life including the foreign service and foreign trade ministry, Jews were accused of "economic crimes" and made scapegoats for Soviet economic difficulties in the early 1950s, and in 1952 twenty-four leading Jewish writers were murdered as Stalin evidently sought to destroy the Jewish cultural leadership in the Soviet Union. An even more serious action against Soviet Jewry seemed in preparation in early 1953 with the announcement of the "Doctors' Plot" where "doctor murderers tied to the Joint Distribution Committee, that International Jewish Zionist Organization [working] . . . for the bosses of the U.S.A.,"[8] were accused of trying to murder Soviet military and civilian officials. Fortunately, after Stalin's sudden death, the "Doctors' Plot" was shown to have been a hoax and a possible major Soviet pogrom averted. Nonetheless, the cultural liquidation that he instituted against Russian Jewry was not reversed after Stalin's death, although, as the world situation changed and the Cold War faded, his successors would show themselves to be more sensitive to Western concerns for Soviet Jewry.

The Khrushchev Era

When Nikita Khrushchev consolidated his power in the Soviet Union in 1955 he was not burdened with Stalin's general paranoia, or his paranoia about the Jews. However, Khrushchev did suffer from what might be termed a "native" anti-Semitism, as his occasional anti-Semitic remarks indicated. In addition, unlike Stalin, who had eased Soviet antireligious efforts during World War II and its aftermath, Khrushchev revived the Soviet antireligious campaign and closed a large number of Soviet churches and synagogues.

Nonetheless, it was not too far into Khrushchev's period of rule that international considerations began to affect the Soviet leader's treatment of Soviet Jews. In the first place, China changed from an ally to an enemy, thereby precipitating a competition in the international Communist movement between China and the Soviet Union where Moscow, to a certain degree, had to court West European Communist parties. Second, Khrushchev's grandiose economic plans ran into difficulty and the USSR began to seek American grain. These factors were to lead to a small amelioration of the condition of Soviet Jewry. Thus, in 1961, for the first time since Stalin had obliterated Jewish cultural institutions in the USSR in the late 1940s, a national Yiddish periodical, *Sovietische Heimland*, was introduced. As Soviet minister of culture, Yekatarina Furtseva, reportedly stated several months earlier to the vice chairman of the Franco-Soviet Cultural Society, "If the USSR did anything at all for Yiddish culture, it would not be for domestic reasons, but to please our friends abroad."[9]

Another indication during the Khrushchev years of a certain amount of

Soviet sensitivity to Western pressure is the Soviet government's relaxation of a ban on the baking of matzoth in state bakeries in 1963 in response to protests from the West.[10] Yet another case of Soviet sensitivity can be seen from the consequences of the publication of Trofim Kichko's virulently anti-Semitic book, *Judaism Without Embellishment*, in 1963. Coming at a time when the Soviet Union was beset by a very poor harvest and a serious slowdown in economic growth, the book slandered Judaism as a religion that fostered "speculation" and other illegal economic activities, many of which allegedly took place in synagogues.[11] The publication of this book precipitated a wave of protest in the West, not only from Jewish groups, public officials, and clergy of all faiths, but also from the leaders of Western Communist parties whose allegiance the Soviet Union was then actively seeking because of the Chinese challenge to the USSR for leadership in the international Communist movement.[12] The end result of the protests was a decision by the Soviet leadership, which had been forced to seek grain from the United States because of its poor harvest in 1963, to mildly condemn Kichko's book because "it might be interpreted in the spirit of anti-Semitism."[13]

The Brezhnev Era

Part I: The Nixon-Ford Years

If the Khruschev regime had shown some sensitivity to Western concern over the plight of Soviet Jewry, the Brezhnev leadership was to display considerably more sensitivity, particularly over the emigration issue, although often in a rather disjointed manner. This may have been due to the fact that Soviet leaders never quite made up their minds as to how to handle Jewish emigration, whether permissively or through harsh crackdowns. Part of the problem may have stemmed from the fact that the drive of the Brezhnev regime for improved relations with the West, in which the emigration of Soviet Jews was to play a role—Prime Minister Kosygin's December 3, 1966 statement on the reunification of families, which was reprinted in *Izvestia*, appears to have been a gesture in this direction—was upset by two important international events in the 1967–68 period: the June 1967 Arab-Israeli War and the liberalization movement in Communist Czechoslovakia that was aborted by the Soviet invasion of August 1968. Paradoxically, while the Soviet propaganda media were to blame a so-called "alliance of Zionism and imperialism" for both the 1967 war and the liberalization movement in Czechoslovakia, the two developments were to activate a hitherto dormant Soviet Jewry that earlier had been characterized as "the Jews of Silence."[14]

Heartened by Israel's victory in the June 1967 war, an event that restored their Jewish national pride and proved that Israel was a viable state, and convinced that liberalization in the USSR was no longer possible after the invasion of Czechoslovakia, activists among Soviet Jews began to apply to emigrate to Israel. The Brezhnev regime, perhaps spurred by its two bloody border skirmishes with China in March 1969 (and possibly hoping that once bereft of leaders, the Jewish emigration movement would die down), permitted more than two thousand Soviet Jews to leave in 1969. This may have been a calculated effort to gain Western support, or at least neutrality, in case the Sino-Soviet border battles were to escalate into a more serious confrontation.

As more Soviet Jews applied to emigrate in 1970, however, the Soviet leadership changed its policy, holding a series of show trials that appeared aimed both at stemming the flow of valuable scientists and engineers which the regime could not afford to lose, and also at deterring other Soviet Jews from emigrating. By the spring of 1970 the Sino-Soviet border confrontation had diminished, and Soviet fears of a Sino-American alliance directed against the USSR had been reduced by the American invasion of Cambodia. These developments may have encouraged the Russians both to stage the show trials and to cut Soviet Jewish emigration in half during 1970. Nevertheless, the show trials were ultimately to prove counterproductive to the Soviet leaders, and emigration was soon to rise again.

The first show trial opened in Leningrad in December 1970. The defendants were a group of Soviet Jews who, having been refused exit visas to Israel, had allegedly conspired to hijack a plane (the hijacking never took place). The Jews were quickly found guilty and the two alleged leaders were given the death penalty.[15] The international outcry that greeted the death sentences and the trial itself forced the Soviet leaders to commute the sentences to long prison terms. It also had the effect of bringing the Soviet Jewish emigration question to the forefront of public attention in the United States and Western Europe, and this in turn resulted in an international conference on Soviet Jewry in Brussels in February 1971.

The Brussels conference, which could only further tarnish the Soviet image in the West (the USSR had not yet overcome the stigma of invading Czechoslovakia), was not the only problem facing the Soviet leadership in early 1971. Riots had broken out in Communist Poland in December 1970 as Polish workers had demonstrated in the streets in reaction to the Gomulka regime's decision to raise the prices of consumer goods. The disorders led to the fall of Gomulka and his replacement by Edward Gierek, and the Soviet Union was compelled to give Poland a large loan to help the country overcome the economic difficulties that had precipitated the crisis.[16]

It seems clear that the Soviet leaders, observing the riots in Poland, were concerned that a similar development might occur in the USSR where consumer goods were also of poor quality and in limited supply. Soviet leaders believed that popular unrest could be averted by Soviet importation of Western goods and technology, preferably on a long-term, low-interest, credit basis. It also seemed advisable to set some limits on the strategic arms race between the United States and the USSR so as to conserve scarce Soviet resources.

Given the fact that the Soviet economy was only one-half the size of the American economy, and that, unlike the United States, all of the Soviet Union's resources are committed every year, it appeared that a strategic arms agreement would be considerably more valuable to the USSR than to the United States. Reportedly, President Nixon tried to exploit this situation by indicating, in a series of messages to Brezhnev beginning in early 1971, that the United States might be willing to help assist the Soviet economy if the USSR would make concessions in a number of political areas, such as Vietnam and the strategic arms negotiations.[17] It was, therefore, perhaps not coincidental that in a major speech to the Twenty-fourth Party Congress in April 1971, Brezhnev pledged a significant increase in consumer goods production[18] and that one month later the USSR made a major concession to stimulate strategic arms negotiations.[19]

In the interim, however, the Soviet-Jewish activists had not been idle. Undeterred by the Leningrad hijack trial, a number of Soviet Jews staged a sit-in at the Soviet Parliament in March 1971—just before the opening of the Twenty-fourth Party Congress when a large number of foreign newsmen were in Moscow. As a result of their action, the activists obtained a conference with a general from the Soviet Ministry of the Interior (which handles emigration visas), and many were later permitted to leave the Soviet Union.[20] Interestingly, while many of the sit-in activists were allowed to leave, the Brezhnev leadership, perhaps still unsure as to the proper way to deal with the emigration problem, staged another set of show trials in May and June. Nonetheless, this form of intimidation came to an end in July, and a major reappraisal of Soviet foreign policy was made necessary when Henry Kissinger made a surprise visit to Peking—the first official visit of a representative of an American administration since the Communist takeover of China in 1949. Kissinger's visit may well have aroused the concern of the Soviet leadership that the long-feared Sino-American alliance was now a real possibility. This concern, coupled with the large demonstrations on behalf of Soviet Jewry that greeted Kosygin on his trip to the West in the early fall of 1971,[21] may have been the impetus that prompted Soviet leaders to allow a massive increase in the emigration of Soviet Jews in the last three months of 1971—from about two hundred per month in the first three quarters of 1971 to three thousand per month by December.

The Soviet-Jewish exodus continued through the first seven months of 1972 as Nixon visited both Peking and Moscow. During his visit to the Soviet capital, Nixon signed a strategic arms limitation agreement (SALT I) and made a commitment to increase Soviet-American trade.

Meanwhile, Soviet leaders encountered a number of severe problems. In addition to the specter of a Sino-American alliance, they were confronted with the worst harvest since 1963. Thus, they were forced to begin negotiations for a major grain purchase from the United States.[22] Further, in July 1972 the Russians were ejected from their air and naval bases in Egypt by Egyptian President Anwar Sadat, an action that weakened their strategic position in the eastern Mediterranean. While the flow of Soviet Jews to Israel was not the cause of

Sadat's decision to expel the Russians (Sadat had been unhappy with the lack of Soviet military support for his confrontation with Israel),[23] it is clear that the increasing exodus of Soviet Jews to Israel, many of whom were of military age and possessing technical skills useful to the Israeli economy, was very unpopular with the Arabs.[24]

Soon after the Soviet departure from Egypt, the Brezhnev regime imposed a prohibitively expensive head tax on educated Soviet Jews seeking to emigrate to Israel.[25] This move may have been aimed at soothing Arab feelings at a time when the Soviet position in the Middle East was deteriorating, and increasing the likelihood of securing Western funding for the expensive Western technology the USSR needed. It also may have been another attempt to deter Soviet-Jewish scientists and technicians from emigrating. Or, as Brezhnev himself reportedly stated, it may have been a "bureaucratic bungle."[26] Whatever the cause, the head tax precipitated a very strong American reaction, spearheaded by Senator Henry Jackson who sought to tie the exodus of Soviet Jews to the trade benefits (most-favored-nation treatment on Soviet exports, and United States credits) sought by Soviet leadership in an agreement that was to be signed by the Nixon administration in October 1972, but that needed congressional ratification to become law. The Soviet Union's change of its position on the head tax was to be the most important example yet of Soviet sensitivity to Western concern on the emigration issue.[27]

Before proceeding further, it is important to note a development occurring at this time in Soviet–West German relations. There are approximately 1.9 million Soviet Germans, primarily descendants of colonists who were invited to Russia by Catherine the Great and Alexander I. Like the Jews, they have suffered a considerable amount of discrimination in the Soviet Union, particularly since World War II. Beginning in 1971 Moscow began to allow sharply increased numbers of Soviet Germans to leave the USSR.

The exodus appears to have been caused by two primary factors. In the first place, there was a concerted drive by a number of Soviet Germans, beginning in 1970, to emigrate from the USSR. Second, there was a Kremlin effort to exploit West German Chancellor Willy Brandt's *Ostpolitik*, which included trade benefits for the USSR, and to gain passage for the Soviet–West German treaty in the German Bundestag in the face of opposition from a number of Germans who opposed improved relations with the USSR. The end result of these circumstances was that the number of Soviet Germans allowed to emigrate rose from 341 in 1970 to 1,140 in 1971. This number increased to 3,418 in 1972, 4,487 in 1973, and 6,517 in 1974. While the number of emigrants dropped somewhat in 1975, to 5,827, it rose sharply again in 1976 to 9,791 and remained above 7,000 throughout 1979. It is no coincidence that Soviet–West German trade also rose rapidly during this period, from 544 million rubles in 1970 to 4.246 billion rubles in 1979.[28]

While it is not possible to go into a full discussion of Soviet-German emigration in this chapter, there are a number of parallels between Soviet-Jewish emigration and Soviet-German emigration.[29] Moscow was sensitive not only to pressure from West Germany, but to pressure from the United States as well. As congressional support for what became known as the Jackson Amendment to the trade bill began to rise, the Soviet leaders made a series of concessions. They exempted émigrés over the age of 55 from paying the head tax and reduced the required payment for others by the number of years a prospective emigrant had worked for the state. In addition, a number of Jews were allowed to leave without paying the tax.[30] As the chief of the Soviet Ministry of the Interior's visa department told a group of Soviet-Jewish activists, "The waiver of the exit tax in certain cases was not a change in the authorities' approach to the emigration problem, but a gesture toward a certain foreign power with which the USSR is seeking to develop commercial and economic relations."[31]

Gestures alone, however, did not suffice to quell the rising tide of congressional support for the Jackson Amendment, particularly since the head tax had been adopted as a Soviet law in December 1972. During a trip to the United States the following February, the top Soviet expert on the United States, Georgi Arbatov, and Soviet Deputy Foreign Trade Minister V. S. Akhimov learned of congressional support for the Jackson Amendment. One month later U.S. Treasury Secretary George Shultz met with Soviet leaders in Moscow and conveyed the same message. Presumably by this time Brezhnev understood the situation, because four days after the Schultz visit the Soviet leadership permitted forty-four university-educated Soviet Jews to depart the Soviet Union without paying the head tax. This action was explained several days later by Viktor Louis, a Soviet "journalist" with close ties to the KGB, who stated in an article in the Israeli newspaper *Yediot Ahronot* that due to congressional pressure the head tax would "no longer be operative, although it would not be cancelled or changed."[32]

This concession, subject to reversal at any time, did not stop the momentum of the Jackson Amendment. Nor did efforts by the Nixon administration, which, on a number of occasions, demonstrated a greater interest in detente than in human rights. However, Brezhnev went on to make a number of highly optimistic statements about the development of Soviet-American trade at the April 1973 meeting of the Communist party's Central Committee, so it appeared that the Soviet leadership was willing to make concessions on the emigration of Soviet Jewry to obtain the benefits of American trade and technology.[33]

Unfortunately for the Russians, Soviet-American detente received a number of blows in the latter part of 1973. In September of that year the noted Soviet physicist and dissident Andrei Sakharov spoke out against detente unless it was accompanied by democratization in the Soviet Union. One month later came the Yom Kippur War in which the Soviet leadership acted to enhance its own position in the Middle East and undermine the United States position. It did so by organizing an air and sea lift of weaponry to Syria and Egypt, by urging all the other Arab states to aid the Syrians and Egyptians in their conflict with Israel, and by opposing American initiatives for a cease-fire until the Arabs began to lose.³⁴ These Soviet actions caused many Americans to begin to doubt the wisdom of detente and to question a number of the Nixon administration's policies toward the USSR, including its offers of massive credits. This concern was transformed in 1974 into what became known as the Stevenson Amendment to the trade bill.

The Stevenson Amendment limited American credits to the USSR to a total of $300 million and also prohibited credits for the production of Soviet gas and oil.³⁵ This was a major blow to the Soviet leadership, which had hoped for multibillion dollar credits from the United States, including up to $40 billion in credits to develop Soviet oil and natural gas reserves in Siberia.³⁶ While the Stevenson Amendment stipulated that the credit ceiling could be lifted by the president if he determined it to be in the "national interest," congressional approval was required for such an action, and Stevenson himself stated that this approval would be dependent on Soviet concessions, not only concerning Soviet-Jewish emigration, but also concerning the Middle East, arms control, and other areas of Soviet-American relations.³⁷ Having been shown by Soviet behavior in the Yom Kippur War that the Soviet leaders would not hesitate to violate either the spirit or the substance of detente if such action would benefit the Soviet Union's world position, Stevenson and the majority of other senators were determined to oppose the subsidization of the Soviet Union's economy without clear political concessions in return. It is important to note that while the Soviet leaders appeared willing to live with the Jackson Amendment, and even apparently worked out a formula for Jewish emigration, via Kissinger's mediation, which both they and Jackson seemed to agree to, these concessions were predicated on the USSR's receipt of sizable American economic credits. When faced by the rigid credit limitations of the Stevenson Amendment in January of 1975, the Soviet leaders repudiated the trade agreement they had reached with the Nixon administration in 1972.³⁸

The Soviet leadership did not terminate Jewish emigration after repudiating the trade agreement. However, the 1975 emigration total of 13,000 was only about one-third the record level of 1973. The Soviet leadership's willingness to continue emigration, albeit at a reduced rate (the 1973 war and its aftermath also may have made Israel appear less desirable in the eyes of Soviet Jews), may have been due to three factors. First, there was a new American president, Gerald Ford, who had committed himself personally on the issue of Soviet Jewry. Indeed, according to Senator Jacob Javits, who together with Senator Jackson and Senator Abraham Ribicoff had visited Ford soon after Nixon's resignation, the new president had given his assurances that he would personally hold the Soviet Union to account for more humane emigration policies.³⁹ Second, another strategic arms limitation agreement was being negotiated (a preliminary arrangement had been worked out by Ford and Brezhnev at their November 1974 summit meeting at Vladivostok) and the Soviet leadership continued to put high priority on getting the agreement formally accepted. Third, the Soviet leaders wanted to hold a European security conference to ratify the postwar division of Europe, and they were compelled to give at least lip service to the principle of emigration for purposes of family reunification in order to get the Western powers to sign what has become known as the Helsinki Agreement.[40] Soviet leaders also appeared not to have given up hope of getting credits from the United States, which in 1975 was beset by a severe recession. The Soviets may have felt that domestic economic pressure in the United States might encourage the Ford administration to grant credits to the Soviet Union in order to put unemployed American workers back to work. Indeed, despite the Soviet repudiation of the trade agreement, Soviet-American trade increased sharply in 1975 and 1976 (see Annex II). Given this overall situation, elimination of Jewish emigration would have been counterproductive to the larger Soviet interest.

Thus, Soviet-Jewish emigration continued at a reduced rate throughout the Ford administration, although it was to rise somewhat at the end of 1976 as a possible signal to Jimmy Carter who had been elected president in November.

Part II: The Carter Years

Although the United States was weakened both internally and in its world position in the 1970s by Vietnam and Watergate, developments that led to a sapping of the power of the American presidency, a greater assertiveness on the part of Congress, and a public feeling against committing United States' troops to battle overseas, Moscow had three central concerns in dealing with the United States at the time Carter assumed the presidency. First, the Soviet military worried about possible American technological advances that would enable the United States to leap ahead of the Soviet Union strategically, much as it had done in the early 1960s.[41] And while the percentage of the American gross national product devoted to defense had been dropping since Vietnam, Moscow had to be concerned about a possible reversal of this trend because the American economy, despite its problems, remained about twice the size of the USSR's, and the gaps in such fields as computer technology and automation appeared to be widening.[42] For this reason, it remained more in the interest of the USSR than of the United States to achieve a SALT II agreement as speedily as possible.

A second Soviet concern related to China. While Moscow could only have been encouraged by the fact that a rapid rapprochement between Peking (Beijing) and the United States did not occur in the aftermath of Nixon's 1972 visit to China (in part this was due to continued difficulties over the future of Taiwan; in part it was due to the influence of a group of Chinese leaders, later branded as "The Gang of Four"), there remained the possibility of a Sino-American entente directed against the USSR. While Moscow had sought to prevent this by, among other things, initiating a series of summit talks with American leaders (there were four U.S.-USSR summit meetings between 1972 and 1976 to only one between an American president and the top Chinese leadership) and maintaining the exclusive SALT talks, the Soviet political elite could not be sure that this pattern would continue, particularly in the post-Mao era that began two months before Carter's election.

Third, despite its military advances, the Soviet Union remained in need of American technology, and the USSR was approaching a partial dependency on American grain.

While SALT, China, and trade were important Soviet concerns at the time of Carter's inauguration, the Soviet leadership was cognizant of the fact that Soviet-American relations had deteriorated sharply since the Nixon years. Soviet-American relations had seemed to be on the upswing in 1975 when the Helsinki Final Act was signed (ironically, this was to lead to increased dissent in Eastern Europe and the USSR rather than to an increased acceptance of Soviet domination over East Europe) and when the symbolic Apollo-Soyuz joint space mission was executed. But Soviet intervention in Angola in 1976 chilled relations to the point where President Ford stated in March 1976 that the word detente was no longer in his political vocabulary. In addition, the SALT talks had stagnated, in part due to Angola and in part due to disagreements over the American cruise missile and the Soviet backfire bomber, with the result that Brezhnev had to postpone a visit to the United States.[43] At the same time the United States called off three Soviet-American cabinet-level meetings, and U.S. Secretary of State Henry Kissinger announced that he would no longer either urge Congress to lift the trade restrictions it had voted against the USSR or support multibillion dollar investments to develop Soviet oil and natural gas deposits.[44]

Another area of Soviet-American conflict lay in the Middle East. While the United States had suffered losses in Africa and Asia in the mid-1970s, it had met with considerably more success in the Middle East. Not only had the United States replaced the Soviet Union as the dominant foreign influence in Egypt, the Arab world's most populous state, but it also dominated the Middle East peacemaking process in the aftermath of the Yom Kippur War. Soviet influence in the region, which had reached a high point during the 1973 war, dropped sharply. This moved Moscow to call for a resumption of the Geneva Peace Conference where, as cochairman, it could hope to rebuild its waning influence in the region.[45]

As the Carter administration prepared to take office, Moscow was anxious to improve relations for a number of reasons, including the reinvigoration of the SALT process, the lifting of United States trade restrictions, the continued prevention of a Sino-American entente, and the reconvening of the Geneva Peace Conference.

Once the election campaign was over, the Soviet leadership set about sending signals to the incoming Carter administration that it was interested in improved relations and would look forward to Soviet-American cooperation in many areas. A major signal to the Carter administration came during the meeting of the American-Soviet Trade and Economic Council at the end of November

1976 when Brezhnev appealed for an end to the freeze on the strategic arms discussions and called for a new agreement based on the Vladivostok Accord. He also used the opportunity to call for an end to U.S. trade discrimination against the USSR, stating that American firms lost between $1.5 and $2 billion because of it.[46] Two weeks later *Pravda* published a major article by Georgi Arbatov evaluating the state of United States—Soviet relations. After criticizing the "enemies of detente," Arbatov praised President-elect Carter's "positive" statements about improving Soviet-American relations and seeking ways to limit arms. Arbatov then went on to call for the resumption of the Geneva Middle East Peace Conference as quickly as possible.[47]

Another signal came in the last two months of 1976, when there was a sharp increase in the number of Soviet Jews allowed to leave the Soviet Union.[48] The most important signal, however, came the day before Carter's inauguration; at that time Brezhnev noted in a speech in Tula that the SALT I agreement would expire in October 1977 and appealed for the "consolidation" of the Vladivostock Accord and for a resumption of the Geneva conference.[49]

Despite these overtures, Moscow probably had some reservations about Carter's performance in the election campaign and in the postelection period before he took office. On the one hand, Carter had called for a more aggressive effort to achieve a SALT agreement and for a $5 to $7 billion cut in defense spending, sentiments that must have been welcome in Moscow. In addition, he called for the gradual withdrawal of all United States ground forces from Korea, and this, too, must have been greeted warmly by Moscow as yet another example of the retreat of American power. But Carter also had emphasized human rights during the campaign and had followed up his words with a telegram of support to Soviet dissident Vladimir Slepak after the election.[50] In addition, during the latter stages of the presidential campaign, on September 29, 1976, Carter had publicly praised the Jackson Amendment, stating that he shared Jackson's "deep concern over the protection of human rights and freedom of emigration in the USSR and throughout the world." Carter went on to tell Jackson that "the legislation which you coauthored, which is now the law of the land and which is aimed at securing these rights, will be effectively implemented by a Carter-Mondale administration."[51]

Carter's emphasis on human rights, perhaps to the surprise of the Soviet leaders, accelerated after he became president and led to a major clash with Moscow within a month of his taking office. In seeking to understand the violent Soviet reaction to Carter's championing of human rights,[52] there are two major factors to take into account. First, as Adam Ulam has noted, members of the Soviet political elite tend to be "power hypochondriacs," seeing in the demands of the Soviet dissidents a threat to their power position, however remote.[53] Second, the Soviet reaction to the human rights campaign may be seen as part of a test of wills with the Carter administration. After all, the Soviets not only had signed the Helsinki Final Act, but had disseminated it publicly. By harassing and arresting those Soviet citizens seeking to monitor compliance with the "basket three" (human rights) provisions of Helsinki, the Soviets were, in effect, challenging the Western nations who had signed the agreement to see whether or not they gave anything more than mere lip service to the ideals contained in the document.

The Soviet attack on Carter for his human rights stand came soon after Carter's inauguration speech, which was positively received in Moscow as "restrained and modest."[54] The attack was precipitated by a formal declaration by the United States Department of State that by trying to intimidate Andrei Sakharov, the most prominent of the Soviet dissidents, the USSR was violating the principles of human rights.[55] While, initially, Moscow sought to distinguish between its criticism of the State Department and President Carter, this ploy ceased after Carter endorsed the State Department action.[56] Perhaps as a response, the Soviets then arrested another key dissident, Aleksandr Ginsburg, and expelled an Associated Press journalist, George Krimsky.[57]

These actions prompted several questions to Carter at a February 8 news conference as to whether he thought that the USSR was testing him by making the two moves, and whether he was concerned that his speaking out on human rights might jeopardize the American relationship with the USSR on other matters. Carter replied that he did not interpret the Soviet acttions as a test of his administration, and that he rejected the concept of linkage between human rights and other issues. His reply on the second issue is worth quoting in full:

> This brings up the question that is referred to as linkage. I think we come out better in dealing with the USSR if I am consistently and completely dedicated to the enhancement of human rights, not only as it deals with the Soviet Union but all other countries. *I think this can legitimately be severed from our inclinations to work with the Soviet Union, for instance in reducing dependence on atomic weapons* [emphasis added] and also seeking mutually balanced force reduction in Europe.[58]

While Carter felt that he could sever the human rights issue from the SALT talks, Moscow took a different position. Two days after the press conference Yuri Orlov, head of the unofficial Soviet Helsinki Monitoring Committee, was arrested. And, on February 12 a *Pravda* editorial blasted Carter's human rights campaign, citing Brezhnev to reinforce its view that such American actions impeded detente and amounted to interference in the internal affairs of socialist countries.

Carter did not appear deterred by the *Pravda* statement, for two weeks later he personally met with Vladimir Bukovsky, a leading Soviet dissident who had been allowed to emigrate from the USSR as part of a trade for Chilean Communist leader Louis Corvalan. This presidential action (which contrasted with President Ford's refusal to meet Aleksander Solzhenitsyn in 1975 "lest it harm detente")[59] was bitterly criticized in the Soviet press and precipitated a series of personal attacks on Carter. These included an article in *Pravda* on March 13 that deprecated the American president's assertion that it would be possible to separate detente and talks on reducing strategic arms from "attempts to interfere in our internal affairs under the false flag of 'defending human rights.'"

Brezhnev himself made the strongest attack in a speech on March 22 in which he attributed the continued stagnation in Soviet-American relations to the Carter administration's human rights campaign, stating, "We shall not tolerate interference in our internal affairs by anyone, under any pretext." While attacking the United States on human rights, Brezhnev did state that the USSR was still interesting in pursuing cooperation with the United States in the areas of limiting strategic arms and chemical and bacteriological warfare, developing trade (if the United States removed its discriminatory trade barriers), and forging a peace settlement in the Middle East. On the latter issue Brezhnev presented the most detailed and moderate Soviet peace plan to date, although one that was still unacceptable to both Israel and the United States because it did not include an insistence on the establishment of diplomatic, economic, and cultural relations between Israel and its Arab neighbors once a peace treaty was signed.[60]

When asked in a news conference about Brezhnev's remarks, Carter replied that he considered the speech to be "very constructive."[61] This statement might be termed either an overly optimistic view of the world or a case of naiveté. Whatever it might be called, this optimistic attitude vis-à-vis the USSR was evident in the Carter administration's view of the Soviet Union until, as Carter himself admitted, the invasion of Afghanistan served to shock the president into a new outlook.

In the light of Soviet threats about linking U.S. human rights policies to the SALT talks, the Carter administration might have waited a bit before pursuing the strategic arms talks with the USSR. Instead, less than a week after Brezhnev's speech, Secretary of State Vance went to Moscow with the Carter administration's multiple SALT plans. This action (which actually was a mistake in protocol since it was Gromyko's duty to come to Washington to meet the new American leadership) was interpreted by the Soviets as an overeagerness to achieve a SALT agreement, creating another problem that was to weaken the United States bargaining position on SALT over the next three years. In any case, by publicly announcing his SALT proposals before Vance left, Carter had doomed the plans.

Soviet leaders were used to the quiet methods of Kissinger and were undoubtedly surprised by Carter's public style. Given the influence of the Soviet military-industrial complex on Soviet policy, it was highly unlikely that Brezhnev would immediately agree to the major cuts that Carter had publicly proposed.[62] The Soviet Union not only rejected the Carter SALT program, it did so in a way that appeared aimed at publicly insulting—if not intimidating—Carter. Extensive articles in *Pravda* and *Izvestia* denounced the U.S. SALT position,[63] and Soviet Foreign Minister Andrei Gromyko called a rare press conference in which he attacked both the SALT proposals and the human rights policy of the Carter administration, stating that the latter poisoned the atmosphere and was an impediment to the resolution of other issues between the USSR and the United States, including strategic arms.[64] Gromyko attacked the efforts of the United States to include the backfire bomber in the SALT agreement and criticized sharp cuts that the United States sought in heavy MIRVed missiles, calling these proposals an attempt to seek "unilateral advantage."[65] He also called for a ban on the U.S. B-1 bomber and Trident submarine (two forthcoming weapons in the U.S. arsenal) and threatened to bring up the matter of forward-based U.S. nuclear delivery systems in future SALT discussions. He did, however, hold out hope for improved Soviet-American relations if the United States changed its policies: "We would like to express the hope that the leadership of the United States will adopt a more realistic position, that it will give greater consideration to the security interests of the Soviet Union and its allies and will not seek to obtain unilateral advantages."

Gromyko's use of the term "realistic" is a particularly interesting one, since that is the term used by the Soviet media to refer to Western statesmen who recognize that the "correlation of forces" is shifting against the West and who "adjust" their policies accordingly. This theme of the Carter administration's lack of "realism" was to be continued in the Soviet media. *Pravda* on June 19 went so far as to claim that "even the bourgeois press" of the United States had "noted with increasing frequency the lack of requisite realism" in the Carter administration's approach to international affairs.

At this point Carter began to adjust American policies to better meet Soviet sensibilities. Thus, for example, he publicly stated that he would not meet with the wife of recently imprisoned Soviet Jewish dissident Anatoly Shcharansky,[66] although he took pains to point out in his news conference of June 13 that Shcharansky never had any sort of relationship with the CIA as the USSR had charged.[67] Even more to the USSR's liking, however, must have been Carter's decision on June 30 to discontinue plans for production of the B-1 bomber. This was, to put it mildly, a unilateral gift to Moscow since Brezhnev in his speech to the Twenty-fifth Party Congress had spoken of mutual concessions on such weapons systems as the B-1.[68] It may well be that Moscow, having demanded that the U.S. show more "realism" in its policies, seemed satisfied with the result of its policy of intimidation—particularly since Gromyko in his April 1 press conference had called for a ban on the B-1 bomber.[69] However, as if to press the Soviet advantage, the B-1 decision was dismissed as essentially a propaganda trick (the Soviet media noted that research on the weapon would continue), and the Carter administration was intensely attacked for its plan to develop the neutron bomb and MX missile, thereby "moving toward a new upward spiral in the arms race."[70]

It was perhaps to correct what he saw as a continued Soviet misperception of American policy (at a news conference on July 12 Carter stated that he did not know how to explain the unfriendly rhetoric coming out of the USSR against him) that the president gave a major address at Charleston, South Carolina, on July 21, 1977, in which he dealt extensively with Soviet-American relations. In

4. Soviet Jewry and Soviet-American Relations   53

his speech Carter called for an increase in the areas of cooperation between the USSR and the United States "on a basis of equality and mutual respect."[71] The areas he mentioned included SALT, arms limitation in the Indian Ocean, and peace in the Middle East. In discussing the Middle East Carter remarked that "we have begun regular consultations with the Soviet leaders, as cochairmen of the prospective Geneva conference, to promote peace in the Middle East." The president also called for increased trade between the United States and the USSR, and referred warmly to Brezhnev (this was in sharp contrast to the Soviets' continued attacks on Carter), even quoting from one of the Soviet leader's speeches, which Carter called "sincere." He also stated, as he had done many times before, that U.S. advocacy of human rights was not an attack on Soviet vital interests. Finally, he outlined the overall strategy of the Carter administration toward the USSR, stating that he wanted to see the USSR "further engaged in the growing pattern of international activities designed to deal with human problems—not only because they can be of real help, but because we both should be seeking a greater stake in the creation of a constructive and peaceful world order."

This speech may have been seen in Moscow as yet another example of the eagerness of the Carter administration to have good relations with the USSR. Not only had Carter emphasized such terms as the USSR's "vital interests" and "mutual respect" (areas that Moscow had claimed Carter had violated with his human rights and SALT policies), he also offered cooperation in the areas most important to the USSR and appeared to grant the USSR equality in dealing with key world problems, including the Middle East. In making this speech Carter placed himself in the school of those analysts who see Soviet policy as essentially defensive in nature; he sought to meet Soviet sensibilities. Unfortunately, an offensive Soviet Union took advantage of these policies over the next two years.

The initial Soviet response to the Charleston speech was mixed.[72] Georgi Arbatov, writing in *Pravda* a week later, appeared to give the official Soviet response to it.[73] Although he attacked the Carter administration for worsening the political atmosphere and for not lifting the "artificial barriers it created in the way of developing mutually advantageous cooperation," Arbatov stated that "some of what Carter said in his Charleston speech can be seen as positive." He quickly qualified even this gesture, however, by attacking the Carter administration for its decision to deploy cruise missiles and create a neutron bomb. Interestingly enough, Arbatov also deemed it necessary to reject the "fabrication" that the USSR was more interested in U.S.-Soviet detente and economic ties than was the West (the frequent repetition of this theme in the Soviet press would appear to indicate Soviet sensitivity on this issue). Arbatov ended on a positive note, however, stating that it was still possible to develop improved relations, but warned that "unlike disputes, peace and good relations require willingness and realistic efforts on both sides."

The first area in which the Carter administration was to demonstrate its "realism" by making concessions to the USSR was the Middle East. As mentioned above, the United States had dominated Middle East diplomacy since 1973, but the Carter administration in 1977 was moving away from Kissinger's step-by-step diplomacy toward the convening of the Geneva conference, thereby moving to meet one of the central Soviet demands. In an effort to prepare the diplomatic path toward the reconvening of Geneva, Secretary of State Vance set out for a trip around the Middle East in early August 1977. Prior to departing, he stated that he had been in contact with the Soviet leaders about his trip and they had indicated a willingness to "use their influence" with some of the parties to "encourage flexibility."[74] This, unfortunately, was to be yet another overly optimistic evaluation of Soviet policies. The Soviet media openly attacked Vance's efforts during his trip,[75] and Palestinian leader Zuheir Mohsen later stated that he had been told by the Russians at the time "not to have any trust in American promises."[76]

Vance's trip proved a failure, and the Carter administation evidently decided that, by itself, it could not arrange the Geneva conference because of opposition from Syria and the Palestine Liberation Organization. It was decided that Soviet assistance was required, and at the end of September the administration negotiated a joint statement with the USSR on the Middle East. The statement, which was released on October 1, called for the convening of the Geneva conference by December 1977.[77] In making this move, which brought the USSR back into the heart of the Middle East peacemaking process for the first time since 1973,[78] the Carter administration clearly sought to create a climate of cooperation with the USSR. Subsequently, both superpowers agreed to continue abiding by the SALT I agreement (even though it formally expired on October 3),[79] moved ahead on the SALT II negotiations, and also went forward on negotiations to limit naval forces in the Indian Ocean.[80]

It was in this general thrust of policy that the Carter administration requested Congress to consider changing the Jackson-Vanik Amendment to the trade bill so as to eliminate the need for Soviet emigration assurances. Instead, the President was to be allowed to grant tariff benefits on an annual basis if he determined emigration levels to be "adequate."[81]

Perhaps as a result of this shift in American policy, or because of the Helsinki follow-up meeting in the fall in Belgrade, Soviet-Jewish emigration rose by almost 2,500 in 1977 to a total of 16,736. Much of this increase took place in the latter half of the year when Soviet-American relations began to improve.[82]

Improvement in Soviet-American relations was soon disrupted by events in the Middle East and by a further Soviet crackdown on dissidents, including Jewish dissidents. Anwar Sadat changed the face of Middle East diplomacy by his historic trip to Jerusalem in November 1977, an event that relegated Moscow to the sidelines in Middle East diplomacy. Moscow profited, albeit only temporarily, from the anti-Sadat alignment of Arab states that formed in response to the Egyptian leader's trip to Jerusalem and the subsequent Camp David agreements.[83]

Another issue that worsened Soviet-American relations was the massive Soviet intervention into the Horn of Africa. Beginning one week after Sadat's visit to Jerusalem, Moscow airlifted some 20,000 Cuban soldiers to Ethiopia. The Soviets also provided three generals to direct the Ethiopian army as it moved from the defensive onto the offensive against Somalia, with which it had been fighting a border war. With Soviet and Cuban aid, Somali troops had been driven out of Ethiopia by March 1978.[84]

The sharp influx of Soviet and Cuban forces into Ethiopia, the second such Soviet move in Africa since 1975, precipitated a major outcry in Washington. However, the American reaction was a very confused one, and this confusion in itself helped ensure the success of the Soviet venture. The Carter administration seemed at first confused over whether or not to arm Somalia, promising the Somalis arms and then retracting the promise.[85] The administration seemed divided over how to respond to the Soviet intervention.

On January 12 President Carter, again in a highly optimistic statement, asserted, "I hope we can induce the Soviets and Cubans not to send either soldiers or weapons into that area."[86] When Moscow ignored Carter's statement, a dispute broke out in the administration as to how best to respond to the Soviet move, with Zbigniew Brzezinski publicly calling for a linkage of the African situation to the SALT talks. Andrew Young and Cyrus Vance opposed such a policy. Carter himself seemed to come down on the side of the doves by stating at a press conference on March 2 that there was no administration policy of linkage between the Soviet involvement in the Horn and SALT.[87] One week later, however, at another news conference in which he announced that Somalia was withdrawing from Ethiopia, he stated his hope that once Ethiopian forces had re-established control over their own country "withdrawal of the Soviet and Cuban combat presence should begin."[88] This was to turn out to be yet another case of unwarranted optimism. The only concrete step the United States finally took in response to the Cuban-Soviet move into Ethiopia was to temporarily discontinue talks on arms limitation in the Indian Ocean.

Moscow, by contrast, was pursuing a consistent policy. By February 1978 the Soviets seemed to be utilizing Carter's hopes for a quick SALT accord as a cover for their activities in Africa and sought to put the Carter administration on the defensive for not doing enough to achieve SALT. On February 11, at the height of the Soviet build-up in Ethiopia, *Pravda* published a major editorial blaming the United States for the standstill in the talks. The editorial noted that while Carter had publicly stressed the importance of achieving a new SALT agreement "from the standpoint of ensuring security for the U.S. itself and from the standpoint of the positive development of Soviet-American relations," "practical deeds" had to follow up such statements. Three weeks after denouncing Brzezinski's attempts to link SALT to Soviet policy in the Horn of Africa, *Pravda* sought to demonstrate that many Americans, including President Carter, opposed such linkage as well, thus underlining the confusion in the American administration over the issue.[89]

In a response to the Soviet activities in Africa and propaganda on SALT, Carter gave a major national defense speech at Wake Forest University on March 17, 1978.[90] After discussing the rise in Soviet military power, he stated the United States was prepared "to cooperate with the Soviet Union toward common social, scientific and economic goals," but that if Moscow "failed to demonstrate restraint in missile programs and other force levels and in the projection of Soviet or proxy forces into other lands and continents, then popular support for such cooperation with the Soviets will certainly erode." Carter went on to say that even while the United States was searching for arms control agreements, it would continue to modernize its strategic system and revitalize its conventional forces.

Moscow reacted forcefully to Carter's speech, with *Pravda* claiming on March 19 that the president was shifting emphasis from efforts to achieve arms control to "a course of threats and the aggravation of tension." In a more extensive critique, Arbatov, writing in *Pravda* on March 28, attacked the United States for creating "dangerous new types of weapons, such as the neutron bomb," and for the efforts of some "leading" administration figures to link SALT with the "course of events in the Horn of Africa." Finally, Arbatov issued a thinly veiled warning that the time had come for

> a choice of a path for the years to come: either an agreement on the basis of which one can make progress in the area of arms limitation and reduction and the development of peaceful and mutually advantageous cooperation, or the rejection of an accord, which would mean the torpedoing of the Soviet-American dialogue on fundamental questions of the two powers' security and international security, and a significant worsening of the overall atmosphere in relations between the USSR and the U.S.[91]

From Moscow's viewpoint, these repeated warnings may well have had some effect, because on April 7 Carter announced that he was deferring production of the neutron bomb—a weapon long feared by the USSR. As with the case of the B-1 bomber decision, Moscow may have seen this action as a response to Soviet pressure, since it appeared to reverse the Wake Forest assertion that the United States was continuing to modernize its strategic forces, and because the USSR had mounted such a major propaganda campaign in the West against the weapon.

Interestingly enough, however, just as Moscow had publicly deprecated Carter's B-1 bomber decision, so too did it minimize the importance of the neutron bomb deferment. On April 9 *Pravda* complained that the decision did not affect work on the development of neutron warhead carriers. Brezhnev, in a speech to the Young Communist League Congress in late April, did make a gesture in response to Carter's action by stating that the USSR would not produce the neutron bomb if the United States did not.[92] The United States, however, was well ahead of the USSR in neutron bomb research and development at the time of Brezhnev's "concession," and the value of the Soviet move was therefore doubtful. Brezhnev also reported some progress in the SALT talks as a result of the Vance visit to Moscow in April 1978.

Soon after this exchange, in the spring of 1978, Zaire rebels, operating out of Angola, attacked the mineral-rich province of Zairan Katanga, an action that led to a further deterioration of U.S.-Soviet relations. The United States blamed the USSR for the attack, since Angola was allied to the Soviet bloc and the rebels had been trained by Cuba, which had a large military force in Angola.[93] In an effort to stop the invasion the United States organized a force of African soldiers who, together with Belgian and French troops, succeeded in defeating the invaders. This American move was denounced by the Soviets, who claimed that they had nothing to do with the invasion. Moscow also criticized the NATO decision to increase defense expenditures by 3 percent annually, a development that, while not precipitated by events in Zaire (the budget rise had been under discussion for some time), certainly was enhanced by them.

Despite events in Africa, Carter clung to his "no linkage" position and stated in a press conference on May 25 that the "SALT agreement is so important for our country, for the safety of the entire world, that we ought not to let any impediment come between us and the reaching of a successful agreement."[94] However, Carter qualified his statement by asserting:

> There is no doubt that if the Soviets continue to abuse human rights, to punish people who are monitoring the Soviets' compliance with the Helsinki Agreement [Yuri Orlov had just been sentenced to seven years in jail], which they signed of their own free will, and unless they show some constraints on their own involvement in Africa and on their sending Cuban troops to be involved in Africa, it will make it much more difficult to conclude a SALT agreement and to have it ratified once it is written.

The Soviets may have been puzzled by the contradictions in Carter's speech. Nonetheless, on the basis of Carter's previous concessions on human rights, the B-1, and the neutron bomb, they may have assumed that he would back down once again if the USSR pressed hard enough—particularly in threatening a collapse of the SALT talks, which Carter had publicly stated he wanted so much. Consequently, beginning in the late spring of 1978, Moscow stepped up its persecution of Soviet dissidents, including Jewish dissidents. As it mounted its campaign against the dissidents, Moscow had to be aware of a new development that was likely to affect Soviet-American relations, the move toward a closer relationship between the United States and China, and Moscow was to couple its crackdown on the Soviet dissidents with warnings to the United States not to get too closely involved with China lest SALT be harmed.

The post-Mao succession struggle in China finally ended in February 1978 with the coming to power of Hua Kuofeng and Teng Hsiao Ping. At the Fifth National Peoples Congress in February, Hua set forth a program calling for the rapid modernization of agriculture, industry, national defense, science, and technology, and the Chinese government announced a heightened interest in

Western credits and technology.[95] At the same time China rejected a Soviet request for improved relations, setting forth the condition that no improvement would be possible unless the Soviets made a major withdrawal from Chinese borders. A pro-Soviet coup d'etat in Afghanistan in April 1978 heightened Chinese suspicions of Moscow as did a Soviet raid across the Ussuri River in early May. Therefore, when National Security Advisor Zbigniew Brzezinski, by now a bête noire of the Russians (Moscow's clear favorite in the administration was Secretary of State Cyrus Vance, a "realist"), made a visit to China in late May, the stage was set for a rapid improvement of Sino-American relations. The first fruits of this development came on June 8 when the United States approved a sale to China of infrared scanning equipment that had been denied to the USSR.

Meanwhile, Carter issued yet another speech in an effort to clarify American policy toward the Soviet Union, this time at the United States Naval Academy in Annapolis on June 7.[96] Once again, as in the case of the Wake Forest speech, he seemed to give the USSR a choice between increased cooperation and confrontation, although there were some additional nuances. He indicated that while the United States wanted to increase collaboration with the USSR, it also wanted to do so with China. While citing the huge losses suffered by the USSR in World War II and his conviction that the people of the Soviet Union wanted peace, he also strongly criticized the USSR for exploiting areas of instability in the world. For the first time in his presidency, he came close to joining the school of thought that saw Soviet policy as essentially offensive, stating, "To the Soviet Union, detente seems to mean a continuing aggressive struggle for political advantage and increased influence." He again denounced the "abuse of basic human rights" in the USSR and Soviet attempts to "export a totalitarian and repressive form of government." Nonetheless, he reiterated his call for improved relations with Moscow and once again stated that the United States had "no desire to link the negotiations for a SALT agreement with other competitive relationships."

The first official answer to Carter came in a June 17 *Pravda* editorial that brought up the linkage question as far as SALT was concerned by warning the United States against playing the "China card":

> Washington's latest intrigues, or to be more exact, "petty intrigues" with China do not in the least serve to strengthen confidence. In and of itself, the desire to play the "China card" in the global game is nothing new for American politicians. But until now, it seemed that U.S. leaders were aware that they could not play that card without endangering the cause of peace and indeed, without danger to themselves and to the United States' own national interest.
>
> To all appearances, however, certain officials who occupy important positions in Washington are now so overwhelmed with anti-Soviet emotions that these dangers are being ignored. These officials are closing their eyes to the

fact that alignment with China on an anti-Soviet basis would close off the possibility of cooperation with the Soviet Union in reducing the threat of nuclear war and, of course, limiting arms.[97]

In a major speech in Minsk a week later, Brezhnev himself reiterated the Soviet warning against playing the China card.[98] He also drew attention to a major Soviet initiative at the Mutual Balanced Force Reductions talks in Vienna where Moscow offered to withdraw three divisions and one thousand tanks from Eastern Europe. While this may have been a ploy to divide the United States from its European allies, which had more to lose if detente weakened, it might also have been a recognition of the fact that the possible entente between the United States and China required a further reinforcement of the Chinese front, particularly at a time when Soviet manpower resources were becoming strained. Nonetheless, the China card issue in Soviet-American relations paled temporarily as the dispute over human rights increased in intensity during the summer.

The Soviet harassment of dissidents in the late spring and summer of 1978 differed from the anti-dissident campaign in the early months of the Carter administration. This time, not only were Soviet dissidents persecuted (by June, Orlov had been sentenced to prison, and Vladimir Slepak and Ida Nudel, leading Jewish refuseniks, had been arrested), but so too were Americans residing in the USSR. On June 12, less than a week after the Annapolis speech, Francis Crawford, deputy director of the International Harvester office in Moscow, was arrested for currency speculation. Two weeks later, two American newspaper correspondents, Hal Piper and Craig Whitney, were accused by a Moscow court of libeling Soviet television, a Soviet action inconsistent with the Helsinki Agreement. While these actions may have been a response to the American arrest of two low-level Soviet UN aides on charges of espionage, they also may have been intended as a test of America's willingness to continue its defense of human rights.

Despite these events, during the early stages of the revived anti-dissident drive Carter continued to sound optimistic about relations with the USSR. On June 26 he stated, "I have a deep belief that the underlying relationship between ourselves and the Soviets is stable and that Mr. Brezhnev, along with myself, wants peace and wants to have better friendship."[99] He added that the United States opposed linkage and that it "never tried to threaten the Soviet Union" and "never held out on the prospect of increased or decreased trade if they did or did not do a certain thing that we thought was best." At a later news conference Carter said he hoped that he and Brezhnev might meet personally to ratify the SALT agreement. In addition to such verbal gestures with which President Carter sought once again to assure the USSR of America's good intentions, U.S. Ambassador to Moscow Malcolm Toon refrained from emphasizing the human rights issue in a July 4 address on Moscow television.

Perhaps encouraged by this apparent softness of the American position on human rights, on July 7 Moscow announced the treason trial of Jewish dissident Anatoly Shcharansky, a man whom Prsident Carter had publicly stated was not involved with the CIA. (In addition, two Jews were sentenced to death for so-called economic crimes in a trial where forty-four of the fifty-two defendants were Jews.)[100] In trying Shcharansky for treason (in effect calling Carter a liar), Moscow went too far even for Carter, and he decided to do more than protest verbally.[101]

Carter canceled a sale of sophisticated oil drilling equipment, thus depriving the USSR of the American equipment it needed the most (the USSR was far behind the United States in both computer technology and sophisticated oil drilling equipment). Carter also canceled a visit to Moscow by his science advisor, Frank Press (who had just visited Peking), as well as American participation in the scheduled sixth session of the joint Soviet-American Commission on Scientific and Technological Cooperation,[102] events in which Moscow stood to gain the most. The effect of these gestures was weakened when Carter sent Secretary of State Vance to Geneva in mid-July for another SALT meeting at the very height of the furor over the harassment of the Soviet dissidents and American reporters. Moscow took note of this and reiterated Vance's statement that the SALT talks, because of their enormous importance for the maintenance of peace, should not be "linked to other questions."[103] Another weakness of Carter's policy was his decision to allow once again the sale of oil field equipment to Moscow after Crawford was given a suspended sentence and the two American reporters were assessed small fines. While the Americans had gotten out of trouble, Soviet dissident Ginsburg and the refuseniks Shcharansky, Slepak, Nudel, and others remained in jail. American willingness to send the oil equipment despite the continued imprisonment of these persons may well have signaled to the Russians that Carter would use American trade pressure on behalf of Americans, but not on behalf of Soviet dissidents, and that his international human rights policies would continue to be limited to verbiage. Indeed, in a press conference on August 17, Carter had said: "We obviously don't have any inclination to declare a trade embargo against the USSR to stop all trade. It is to the advantage of our country to trade with the Soviet Union. I think embargoes that have been enforced in the past by previous administrations, for instance, unannounced and unilateral [embargoes] of shipments of feed grains and food grains and soybeans overseas have been very detrimental to our country. I do not intend to do that."[104]

The USSR had successfully mounted a major anti-dissident campaign in the face of American protests. Nonetheless, while Moscow may have felt that once again it had successfully pressured the American president into retreating in his human rights efforts with Carter's reversal of his position taken in the May 25 news conference that Soviet human rights violations would "make it much more difficult to conclude a SALT agreement," the Soviet leaders were to prove less successful in preventing Washington from playing the China card, a development that threatened Soviet security in Asia.

Indeed, from the Soviet perspective, the situation in Asia seemed to be rapidly deteriorating. Not only had the United States and China entered into a more friendly relationship, but Japan and China also were moving closer together. On August 12 Japan and China signed a Friendship and Cooperation Treaty in Peking, which *Pravda* labeled anti-Soviet because it contained an "antihegemony" article that was viewed as directed against the USSR.[105] The USSR sought to counter the Chinese rapprochement with Japan by trying to improve its own relations with the island nation, but these efforts proved unsuccessful when Japan refused to sign a cooperation treaty with Moscow unless the USSR agreed to return the four small islands just north of Japan seized at the end of World War II, something the USSR was unwilling to do. Adding further to the pressure on Moscow at this time was Carter's unexpected decision on October 18 to go ahead with production of the neutron bomb, although he qualified this move somewhat by stipulating that the components would be stockpiled instead of inserted into warheads.[106]

Possibly because Washington had played its China card, or possibly because of concern over the neutron bomb, Moscow became more forthcoming in the SALT talks and only a week after the neutron bomb decision *Pravda* reported that progress had been made in the talks.[107] At the same time there was another sharp increase in the number of Jews being allowed to leave the Soviet Union (the émigrés included Benyamin Levich, a prominent Jewish refusenik scientist who had been denied permission to leave for seven years, and Boris and Natalia Katz).[108] Thus, while only 1,899 Jews had been allowed to leave in July 1978, that figure rose to 3,286 in October and 4,197 in December—more than double the July exodus that had been the monthly average for the first half of the year.

While seeking to push ahead on SALT, Moscow also was moving to enhance its position in Asia. Soon after Japan refused the offer of a treaty with the USSR, Moscow moved to sign one with Vietnam, whose relations with China had become increasingly strained. The apparent goal of the treaty, coupled with large shipments of Soviet weapons to Hanoi in the fall of 1978, was to confront China with a powerful enemy on another border, thereby compelling her to deploy her military forces accordingly.[109]

Soon after the signing of the Soviet-Vietnamese treaty, Vietnam invaded China's ally, Cambodia, apparently on the assumption that its treaty with Moscow would deter the Chinese from any counterinvasion. China, in turn, played its "Washington card," indicating its willingness to normalize relations with the United States by making concessions on the Taiwan issue. The United States responded affirmatively, and on December 15 there was a joint announcement that formal Sino-American diplomatic relations would be established on January 1, 1979. U.S.-Taiwanese relations would be terminated the same day, although the United States would continue to maintain "commercial, cultural, trade and other [military] relations with Taiwan."[110]

As might be expected, Moscow did not look favorably on the acceleration of the Sino-American rapprochement, although Carter, in his typically optimistic fashion, reported that he had received a "very positive" message from Brezhnev on the development. Moscow Radio, however, and *Pravda* were quick to present a different interpretation of Brezhnev's message, noting that Brezhnev had stated that the Soviet Union would follow very closely the development of Sino-American relations and would "draw the appropriate conclusions for Soviet policy."[111]

A central Soviet concern was expressed in a Moscow Radio broadcast by Soviet commentator Valentin Zorin which indicated that Moscow was quite worried that the Chinese would now find it easier to acquire Western arms and modern military technology.[112] Other Soviet media expressed the concern that a military bloc of China, Japan, and the United States might be forming.[113] These fears were undoubtedly exacerbated during Teng Hsaio Ping's January visit to the United States in which he appealed to the United States to join China in an anti-Soviet front. While the United States officially disassociated itself from Teng's anti-Soviet remarks, a joint communique issued at the close of his trip calling for opposition to efforts to establish "hegemony" indicated to Moscow that the United States supported China's anti-Soviet stand.[114]

Subsequent events were to lessen Moscow's concern both about the Asian strategic situation and about the Sino-American alignment, albeit only temporarily. Less than two weeks after the end of Teng's visit to Washington, China invaded Vietnam with the apparent goal of getting the Vietnamese to pull out of Cambodia, thereby allowing China's ally, the Pol Pot regime, to regain power in that country. After several weeks of fighting, China was compelled to withdraw its forces from North Vietnam, although it stated that it had been successful in "punishing Vietnam." Vietnamese forces remained in Cambodia.

There was clear embarrassment in Washington over the Chinese move, and Moscow may well have thought that the Chinese invasion would slow the Sino-American rapprochement.[115] As far as Sino-Soviet relations were concerned, while Moscow issued several warnings to China during the invasion, the period of fighting was so short that the USSR did not have to follow through on its warnings. In addition, while China moved after the war to denounce its 1950 treaty with the USSR, it also called for new talks with Moscow, this time without the preconditions demanded in 1978. Moscow could only be heartened by this Chinese retreat and by the subsequent Chinese government announcement that its 1978 modernization goals had been too ambitious and that they would have to be revised downward.[116]

In sum, while China remained a major threat to the Kremlin, and while U.S. Vice President Walter Mondale's visit to China in the summer of 1979 signaled the continuation of cordial Sino-American relations, the immediacy of the danger precipitated by the Sino-Japanese treaty and the Sino-American rapprochement seemed to have been, at least temporarily, averted.

Nonetheless, for the first time since the 1971-72 period, the three main factors that had caused the Soviet leadership to permit large numbers of Soviet Jews to emigrate in the early 1970s were again present: Soviet fear of a Sino-American

4. Soviet Jewry and Soviet-American Relations   63

alliance, the Soviet desire for a SALT treaty, and an American administration willing to grant the USSR trade benefits. By early spring of 1979 when the SALT talks were in their final stage, the U.S. Commerce Department permitted the computer sale that had been canceled in 1978, and there was a growing (albeit not yet majority) sentiment in Congress to raise the $300 million limitation on grants to the USSR as well as to lift the Jackson-Vanik Amendment.[117] In such a situation Jewish emigration from the USSR again increased (reaching a record 51,320 in 1979), and Brezhnev made a number of other gestures to the United States on the issue of Soviet Jewry by pardoning five Soviet Jews involved in the alleged hijacking of the Soviet airliner in 1970 (Boris Penson, Anatoly Altman, Arieh Knokh, Wolf Zalmanson, and Hillel Butman), who then were allowed to emigrate to Israel. Brezhnev also traded Soviet-Jewish activists Eduard Kuznetsov and Mark Dymshitz, both of whom had been sentenced to death in 1970 for their roles in the alleged hijack attempt, along with Russian dissident Aleksandr Ginsburg, Ukrainian nationalist Valentin Moroz, and Ukrainian Baptist Georgi Vins (all of whom were well-known Soviet dissidents) for the two Soviet spies caught in the United States on April 27. These actions coincided with the Moscow visit of a U.S. congressional delegation that included Charles Vanik, coauthor of the Jackson-Vanik Amendment.[118] It should be noted, however, that while the emigration of Soviet Jews reached record heights and a few well-known dissidents were released, there was no general easing of the crackdown on Soviet-Jewish and non-Jewish dissidents, including long-term refuseniks. The Soviet leadership clearly separated the emigration issue from that of the dissidents. In addition, there was a rising tide of anti-Semitic propaganda being published in the USSR and an increase in other forms of anti-Semitism as well.[119]

Despite the harassment of Soviet dissidents, the overall atmosphere for Soviet-American relations had been greatly improved from its low point in April 1977, and it was not long before the negotiations on SALT II were completed and a date was set for a summit between Carter and Brezhnev to sign the agreement.

The summit took place in Vienna (reportedly out of deference to Brezhnev's health), although it was Brezhnev's turn to go to the United States. Of particular interest was Carter's speech during the summit's first day. Again expressing an optimistic view, he stated the hope that "our new SALT treaty could provide the basic framework we seek to reduce tension and conflict throughout the world."[120] Indeed, in an apparent effort to entice the USSR to take a more cooperative position in the Third World, the United States made several concessions to Moscow during the summit. Carter agreed to the resumption of the Indian Ocean naval limitation talks, which had been interrupted after the Soviet and Cuban intervention in Ethiopia, despite the fact that the Cubans remained in Ethiopia in large numbers. In addition, the United States publicly committed itself to strengthening trade ties with Moscow and "recognized the necessity" of working for the "elimination of obstacles to mutually beneficial trade and financial relations."[121]

The Vienna summit ended with a few more American than Soviet concessions, but with the expressed hope by President Carter that Soviet-American relations would improve and that the USSR would show restraint in the Third World. Such, however, was not to be the case.

One of the areas of increasing contention between the USSR and the United States was Afghanistan. Noor Mohammed Taraki, who had seized power in a military coup in April 1978 and who had signed a Treaty of Friendship and Cooperation with the USSR in December 1978, was in deep trouble. Although Soviet military aid and advisors had poured into the country after the coup, and Taraki had begun to institute major land and social reform programs in the rural areas of Afghanistan, he had incurred the wrath of the Islamic religious and tribal leaders who resisted his government's efforts to extend its control to their areas. It was not long before virtually the entire country was in a state of rebellion.

Moscow blamed the turmoil on outside forces, including Egypt, the United States, and Pakistan. As the summer of 1979 progressed, Moscow followed up warnings against "outside intervention" in Afghanistan by increasing still further its military involvement in that country,[122] thereby disregarding a series of American statements opposing the heightened Soviet military commitment. In a speech on August 2 Brzezinski, citing "prudent" American restraint during the Iranian crisis, said, "We expect others similarly to abstain from intervention and from efforts to impose alien doctrines on deeply religious and nationally conscious peoples."[123] Brzezinski's warning, however, was taken no more seriously by the Soviets than was Carter's plea in January 1978 that Soviet and Cuban troops not get more heavily involved in Ethiopia. Indeed, several days after Brzezinski's statement, Soviet forces helped put down an attempted coup in Kabul;[124] the build-up of Soviet military advisors and military equipment also increased, although the rebels continued to score victories against the highly unpopular Taraki regime and against Taraki's successor, Hafiz Amin, who overthew Taraki in Mid-September 1979.

If Moscow disregarded American warnings about Afghanistan, it acted similarly during the imbroglio over the so-called Soviet brigade in Cuba. When Carter proclaimed that the United States found the "status quo of the Soviet brigade in Cuba unacceptable"—despite the fact that the Soviet troops there did not violate the Khrushchev-Kennedy understanding of 1962—the American president soon had to back down when the USSR stood firm, thus, in effect, accepting the status quo that he previously said he found "unacceptable." The end result was that the Soviet brigade in Cuba stayed in place (although Carter promised it would be watched closely and that a new U.S. Carribean Joint Task Force would be created). Meanwhile, Carter pressed ahead to get the SALT agreement ratified—despite a series of personal attacks directed against him in the Soviet press over the brigade issue.[125] Indeed, Moscow may well have seen this as yet another example of Carter's weakness and vacillation, and *Pravda* on October 3 noted that in his speech announcing the end of the

4. Soviet Jewry and Soviet-American Relations   65

crisis Carter "was forced to admit . . . that the presence of Soviet military personnel at military training centers in Cuba is certainly no reason to return to the cold war." The *Pravda* article also cited Carter's pleas to the Senate to ratify SALT II.

Almost as damaging to the credibility of the Carter administration during the summer of 1979 was the acknowledgment by American UN Ambassador Andrew Young that he had met "accidentally" with the PLO representative to the UN. Young later resigned, admitting that the meeting had been planned, and finally claimed that the State Department had known all along about the planned nature of the meeting, which violated both U.S. policy and a clear commitment to Israel. In watching the handling of the affair by the Carter administration, Moscow may well have concluded that the administration not only was a vacillating one but that the president could not control his chief assistants.[126]

If the Soviet brigade and Andrew Young affairs might have raised questions in Moscow about Carter's competence, there was no such questioning of the competence of the American farmer. By early October, because of another poor harvest in the USSR, Soviet orders for American grain spiraled to 25 million tons. The USSR continued to hope for the lifting of trade restrictions, and Carter's decision to appoint former IBM Chairman Thomas Watson (an advocate of increased trade with the USSR) rather than a professional diplomat to be ambassador to Moscow may have signaled to the Soviets that the U.S. president also was genuinely interested in an increase in trade. Nonetheless, Congress now seemed unwilling to grant Moscow most-favored-nation status, a development that must have galled the USSR, since China seemed well on its way to achieving this standing.

While Moscow was unhappy over the lack of congressional action on trade, it was even more unhappy with congressional opposition to the SALT II treaty.[127] Indeed, after the treaty was signed, Soviet leaders warned the Senate against any changes, and visits to Moscow by Senate majority leader Robert Byrd and Senators Joseph Biden and Richard Lugar did little to change the official Soviet attitude.

Nor could Moscow have been too pleased with President Carter's actions in the area of strategic weaponry. Gone were the days of unilateral concessions such as those on the B-1 bomber and neutron bomb. Instead, Carter decided, in an action that was clearly within the letter of the SALT II agreement—although the Soviets made charges to the contrary—to push ahead with the mobile MX ICBM that was seen as a hedge against Soviet first-strike capability on the increasingly vulnerable U.S. land-based ICBM force. In addition, Carter announced his agreement to a 5 percent increase in overall defense spending (hitherto he had supported only a 3 percent increase). The USSR attacked both of these actions as payoffs to Senate hawks whose approval was needed for SALT passage.[128] Even more upsetting to Moscow were Carter's efforts to get NATO to agree to deploy in Western Europe U.S. medium-range, nuclear-tipped ballistic missiles (Pershing IIs) and ground-launched cruise missiles that had the capability of hitting the USSR.

While Moscow later claimed that the NATO decision and the Senate's stalling on SALT and trade had caused the sharp deterioration of Soviet-American relations in 1980, the major reason was the Soviet invasion of Afghanistan at the end of 1979. In response to that Soviet action President Carter announced the withdrawal of the SALT II treaty from Senate consideration, imposed a partial grain embargo and a high technology export ban, and canceled approval for the participation of U.S. athletes in the Moscow Olympics. At the same time the U.S. Academy of Sciences announced a suspension of scientific exchanges with the USSR. In addition, the United States stepped up its search for Middle East bases for its newly created rapid deployment force and sought to arrange an anti-Soviet alliance of Muslim states in the Middle East.

For its part the USSR called the United States an "unreliable partner" and took the opportunity to exile the Soviet Union's leading dissident Andrei Sakharov from Moscow to the city of Gorky. As Soviet-American relations deteriorated, so too did conditions for Soviet Jews. Emigration dropped sharply (to a total of 21,471 in 1980 with only 789 leaving in November and 889 in December), and there was an increase in the harassment of refuseniks.[129] Relations between Washington and Moscow plummeted almost to the level of the Cold War. November brought the election of Ronald Reagan, a confirmed anti-Soviet political figure far to the right of Jimmy Carter. The initial acts and statements by the president-elect and his hard-line Secretary of State Alexander Haig were strongly anti-Soviet and reminded many observers of John Foster Dulles's comments and actions during the Cold War of the early 1950s.

The advent of the new administration provides a useful point of departure for drawing some conclusions about the role of Soviet Jewry in the Soviet-American relationship in the period since World War II.

Conclusions

Despite their protestations to the contrary, it is clear that Soviet leaders have been sensitive to Western interest and pressure on the issue of Soviet Jewry. Stalin sought to use Soviet Jews as tools to gain Western support during World War II and established the Jewish Anti-Fascist Committee for this purpose, but he turned on the Jews sharply during the Cold War. Khrushchev, in the face of Western pressure, made some minor concessions to Soviet Jewry, including the publication of a national Yiddish magazine and the withdrawal from publication of a virulently anti-Semitic book. Under Brezhnev the USSR showed its greatest sensitivity on the issue of Soviet Jewry: large numbers of Soviet Jews were allowed to emigrate, and Soviet leaders backed down from enforcing a head tax on prospective emigrants—despite the fact that the tax had been published as a Soviet law.

To be sure, these concessions were not made for humanitarian reasons. There were two concrete objectives that the Soviet leadership wanted: trade benefits from the United States and the conclusion of a SALT agreement. Soviet leaders also were very concerned about the possibility of a Sino-American alliance. When it looked as if Moscow might achieve its goals, and when Sino-American relations were becoming very close, as in the 1971–73 and 1978–79 periods, Soviet-Jewish emigration skyrocketed. When one or more of these goals seemed out of reach, as in the 1975–77 and 1980–81 periods, Jewish emigration dropped sharply. In many ways the emigration level serves as a barometer of Soviet-American relations.

If Western pressure—or the Soviet desire for Western benefits—has been instrumental in achieving the emigration of more than 250,000 Soviet Jews, this pressure has been far less potent in improving the status of Judaism in the USSR. In part, this may be due to Soviet sensitivity on matters deemed "internal," but it should be remembered that Moscow also called the emigration and head-tax issues "internal."

Another factor that might be operative is a lack of concerted human rights interest on the part of the executive branch of the United States government on behalf of Soviet Jews seeking to practice their religion in the USSR. During the Kissinger era, the United States tended to downplay human rights, and it was primarily congressional pressure that forced the lifting of the head tax. In the case of Jimmy Carter, while the former president started out strongly on human rights, his efforts soon lagged as he appeared not only to vacillate on the issue (as he was to do on so many others), but also to allow himself to be browbeaten by the Soviet Union as he appeared to be on the B-1 bomber and, initially, on the neutron bomb. It remains to be seen, therefore, what would be the effect of a firm president who remained consistent in support of human rights in the Soviet Union and linked U.S. trade and SALT benefits to such a policy and to Soviet adventures in the Third World.

5. The Welcome Home: Absorption of Soviet Jews in Israel

Theodore Friedgut

As a state based on mass immigration since its inception, Israel has developed a sophisticated network of administrative institutions designed to ease the new immigrant's adaption to life there. Divided between the Jewish Agency of the World Zionist Organization and the government's Ministry of Immigrant Absorption, with other agencies and the Ministry of Labor and the prime minister's office handling some particular portions of the process, this machinery often has been called an instrument of Darwinian "survival of the fittest," discouraging the weak in spirit by bureaucratic despotism over the public it was meant to serve. Nevertheless, this machinery existed and was ready to serve, for better or for worse, when the mass immigration from the USSR began in the early 1970s.

Part of Israel's national mythology is the image of survivors of the Holocaust being borne to shore from the beached ships of the illegal immigration fleet on the shoulders of sturdy volunteers from the Yishuv, the prestatehood Jewish community. This myth is contradicted by the bitter witticism that "Israelis love immigration, but can't stand immigrants." Not unlike other countries that have experienced great waves of immigration, Israel has been torn by friction between newcomers and the established population, however newly arrived it may be. Within Israel with its barely crystalized social structure and national identity, and with a rapidly changing economic environment, these social frictions are easily exacerbated.

Each wave of immigration has its own specific characteristics, demanding flexibility of attitude and response from both the administrative organs charged with facilitating absorption and from the public—neither of which can be expected to display such sensitivity of response. Israel had some experience responding to the diverse needs of various groups in its first years of mass settlement. At the start of the 1950s Kurdish, Yemenite, Polish, Romanian, and Moroccan Jews all demanded recognition in the procedures of settlement and socialization. Nonetheless, Soviet-Jewish immigrants of European, Georgian, Bukharan, and Dagestani origin, all with vastly different outlooks and even different languages,[1] initially caused some confusion and difficulty among those Israeli institutions charged with absorption.

Another unique characteristic of the Soviet-Jewish immigration was its "high culture." Reflecting the high level of education and the socioeconomic standing of Soviet Jews, this wave of immigrants brought with it a large proportion of university graduates with professional backgrounds.[2] While the trickle of North American and West Europeans immigrants had a similar professional profile, they posed a totally different absorption problem, for they came gradually rather than in a wave, and generally could plan and prepare for their immigration during preliminary visits, rather than being thrown raw into Israel's pressure cooker society. It goes without saying that immigrants of this nature are very different clients in their needs and demands than were the immigrants from North Africa and the Islamic countries of Asia who composed the previous mass immigration.

Another cause of strain between Soviet-Jewish immigrants and Israeli society was a discrepancy in the perceived status and motivation of the immigrants. In Israel there exist the concepts of an "immigration of salvation" and an "immigration from countries of hardship." The general Israeli view of the USSR and the emotion aroused in the Israeli public by discussion of Soviet anti-Jewish propaganda created an image of Soviet-Jewish immigrants as helpless and impoverished "Jews of Silence," rescued from a lion's den of imminent holocaust. The "rescuers" expected some expression of gratitude for their hospitality. The immigrants, however, saw themselves as having single-handedly conquered the bureaucracy of the mighty Soviet state, breaching the Iron Curtain by moral force, and marching as a militant reinforcement to a small, far-off, and beleaguered Jewish homeland. Certainly it was not for them to express appreciation to Israel. This perception gap caused considerable social malaise among Soviet immigrants in the first years of the mass immigration.

The Dynamics of the Soviet Immigration

As early as 1957 Nikita Khrushchev had spoken of the possibility of letting all those who wished leave the USSR. A substantial number of Jews had come to Israel by way of Poland in 1956 and 1957. Soviet-Jewish emigration to Israel in substantial numbers began in 1965 when 1,444 Jews came from the USSR to Israel.[3] This may be taken as the beginning of the present wave of immigration, which by the end of 1980 brought some 160,000 Soviet Jews to Israel.

The actual beginnings of the Jewish emigration from the USSR preceded the public enunciation of an open emigration policy by nearly a year. At the end of 1966 Premier Alexei Kosygin, speaking of Soviet Jews at a press conference in Paris, said that "as regards family reunions, if there are, in fact, some families which would like to meet, or to leave the Soviet Union, the way is open before them, and this constitutes no problem." Publication of this statement in the Soviet press informed the Soviet public that this was official policy.[4] Since 1966 family reunification has been the only justification on which any Jewish emigration has been allowed, though there exists no foundation for this in Soviet law, neither as a right nor as a limitation.[5]

Soviet circumspection as to the exodus of Soviet Jews was paralleled by a similar Israeli discretion. The only mention of the growing number of Soviet Jews arriving in Israel was in a scattering of newspaper articles referring to young people of a high educational and cultural level now arriving in Israeli schools and youth institutions as part of a family reunion arrangement. This discretion was abandoned after the June 1967 war when the Soviet Union stopped the emigration, and Soviet Jews decided on public protest as a tactic.

Jewish emigration from the USSR has moved in cycles of considerable magnitude since then. Emigration increased slowly from 1968 to 1971, and then jumped from 12,819 to 1971 to 31,652 in 1972. Between 1973 and 1974 the number of Soviet Jews arriving in Israel dropped from 33,477 to 16,816. In 1977, 1978, and 1979 the numbers were 8,348, 12,192, and 17,200. A sudden drop to about 6,000 occurred in 1980.

These extreme fluctuations in Soviet-Jewish emigration caused serious difficulties in the absorption process. Like any administrative process, absorption must be planned and funded ahead of time. However happy Israeli leaders may have been to receive Soviet Jews, the unpredictable nature of the emigration was a headache to administrators.

Among the problems were absorption centers to be prepared for professionals during the initial period of orientation in the country; the building of permanent housing, a long and drawn-out process in Israel; and the rental of temporary housing from private owners in periods when permanent housing was in short supply. Other needs included recruitment and training of absorption staff, language teachers, and social workers; planning and implementation of training courses; and provisions for acceptance of young people into universities and schools. All of these needs must be seen in the perspective of the particular characteristics of this wave of immigration and the relatively limited size of Israel as an absorbing society. Funds were provided from abroad in generous measure, whether as part of United States aid to Israel or as part of world Jewry's support of Israel, and thus were not a limiting factor in providing absorption capacity. But the judicious and effective application of these funds was badly hampered by the constant fluctuations in the number of immigrants.

The sharp quantitative changes had an impact on the immigrants themselves and on the Israeli society in which they were to be absorbed. The first trickle of immigrants was made up mostly of Jews with strong national and religious motivations for their emigration to Israel. But as the numbers arriving in Israel swelled each year, the character of the immigration changed. It was possible to detect a snowball effect in which Jews who had not previously thought seriously of leaving saw the comparative ease with which their neighbors, colleagues, or relatives were emigrating and decided to join the exodus. This placed pressures on Jews remaining in the Soviet Union. Employment opportunities narrowed as bosses at all levels considering promotions or hiring for their staffs bypassed Jews for fear they would later want to leave. Many Jews who considered themselves loyal Soviet citizens found themselves looked at askance for not joining their compatriots—and solved the problem by turning about and joining them. These immigrants naturally had less commitment to Israel and less patience with its overburdened and under-trained absorption bureaucracy than did the pioneers of the first wave of immigration. Serious tensions were thus unavoidable.

Similar tensions grew up in Israel. The mass immigration from the Soviet Union was hailed in Israel as a near-miracle. The sudden appearance of public protest by Jews in the Soviet Union, with open press conferences, mass petitions, and public demonstrations, was indeed newsworthy. The apparent success of this campaign, in the form of the growing number of immigrants from the USSR, was greeted effusively by Israeli authorities and media who saw in Soviet-Jewish immigration the living confirmation of the Zionist ideal.

The degree to which this campaign was given prominence in the Israeli media, and the publicity generated around steps taken by the authorities to aid the immigrants, created a backlash in sectors of the Israeli public. In particular, lower socioeconomic groups of Asian and African origin saw in what they called "the Soviet Jewry festival" an expression of continuing discrimination against oriental Jews.[6] Although, in fact, Soviet-Jewish immigrants were given no rights that did not already exist, they were the first mass immigration to make use of the absorption centers and of the immigrant's right to purchase furniture and such consumer durables as automobiles without paying the taxes that make up two-thirds of the price of such commodities in Israel. In fact, such resentments had existed against North American and other immigrants, but these, arriving in small numbers and without fanfare, had never offered a target of any significant size, nor had they been the subject of general and prolonged public attention as were the immigrants from the USSR in the years from 1970 through 1973.

Public antagonism toward Soviet-Jewish immigrants was fed by reports of strikes and demands by new immigrants for specific jobs or living places. These strikes had two roots, one within the absorption administration, and another within the immigrant community. The absorption administration was, as has been mentioned, working under the strain of sudden changes in the number of immigrants. The attempt to handle this influx meant trying to match immigrants' skills to job openings and finding suitable housing, both difficult tasks. Sending immigrants to the small development towns where more housing was available often fit the government's plans, but not the skills or desires of the immigrant. The immigrant, from his side, already was conditioned by his experience in the Soviet Union to skepticism regarding bureaucrats and was reluctant to accept the official information and explanations offered him. Immigrants would arrive armed with letters from friends or relatives, saying "Don't go to Beersheva. Accept only Holon," and would put their trust in these. The result was antagonism that quickly became a public issue.[7]

All of this should be viewed within the context of the trauma experienced by Jewish émigrés. The emigration process is one of uncertainty and psychological strain. There are no certainties in an emigrant's life. He is totally at the mercy of the vagaries of Soviet raison d'etat. He may leave the USSR quietly and easily. Or he may be harassed, delayed, even physically attacked or subjected to trial and imprisonment. He may work until his last days in the USSR, or be dismissed immediately. Until he has left the borders of the USSR, the potential emigrant is like a soldier walking in a minefield blindfolded.

Once in Israel the new immigrant is subject to other strains. However well he may have prepared himself for his new life, he finds himself insecure and disoriented. Everything is different. The scale of the country, the climate, the scenery, the language, the cultural environment are totally unfamiliar. In his first hours or days in the country, while still dazed with the strain of leaving the USSR and fatigued with travel, he is required to make decisions with regard to such major issues as housing. As noted above, he may be subject to conflicting pulls from the authorities and from well-meaning friends and relatives. The strains of adjustment can last for months. The transition from a tense life in the USSR, dedicated to the exodus movement, to the routine daily life of a new immigrant in Israel is prolonged. Indeed, one of the benefits of the absorption centers and of the various preparation and training courses offered to the immigrants is the provision of a supportive framework of life and society during this period.

The Soviet Jews who scored the first successes of the exodus movement in the late 1960s and early 1970s did so by challenging the Soviet bureaucracy. Hunger strikes, public demonstrations, and open letters of demand for rights were all part of the campaign that caught the public eye and heart. It was only natural that similar tactics would be used by individuals and groups who felt that the absorption authorities of the Jewish Agency and the Ministry of Absorption were not sufficiently responsive to immigrants' needs. Strikes by immigrant dentists over retraining and licensing practices, strikes in individual absorption centers, protests to the press by families or individuals, and public protests by Georgian communities regarding settlement, cultural, and employment arrangements were common during the early mass immigration and continue sporadically, even today.

Within the general and individual problems of absorption, Georgian Jews presented a special case. Unlike the Soviet Jews from the European parts of the USSR, they were extremely family- and community-centered and fiercely resisted attempts to scatter them through different parts of Israel. Until the unique features of this community were understood, the application of standard absorption procedures was deemed to "harm, offend or demoralize" the Georgian immigrants.[8] Many Georgian Jews had lived in small communities in the USSR in which many aspects of traditional behavior, such as social inferiority of women and filial deference to parents, were a norm shared by the Jews and surrounding gentiles. The Georgians found the permissiveness and egalitarianism of Israel disorienting and disappointing, as had many of the North African immigrants a generation earlier.

While it is difficult to say whether the Israeli authorities and public made the best or worst of the immigrant situation, it is certain there were many factors that made the mass immigration of Soviet Jews a difficult and unique challenge for Israel's existing absorption practices.

As we noted at the outset, Israel had an infrastructure with facilities for caring for a varied immigrant population.[9] There were seventy-four urban and rural intensive Hebrew language courses, with the capacity to reach ten thousand students, existing in 1964.[10] Pension procedures for immigrants beyond working age were already in existence, though the new immigration brought need for adjustment,[11] and an extensive network for social and medical care of the aged had been set up.[12] Courses were available to retrain foreign-trained lawyers, doctors, and engineers by giving them language skills and preparing them to pass examinations of governmental regulatory commissions or professional associations. What was different about the absorption of Soviet Jews was again the mass nature of the immigration, the difficulty of planning in advance, and, of course, the particular differences in content, definition, and skills of Soviet-trained professions.

To help adjust Israel's absorption practices to the specific needs of immigrants from the USSR, a series of studies was commissioned.[13] These gave Israeli institutions an understanding of the training that professionals received in the USSR and the problems they faced in adjusting to Israeli standards. In addition, a special office was set up for evaluating the studies and degrees of immigrants from the USSR.

In many professions the absorption efforts were successful. Of a sample group of engineers studied, 90 percent were found to be employed within two years, mostly in the field for which they had been trained. Of the remaining 10 percent, it was found in most cases that termination of employment had been voluntary and tied to a search for better conditions or retraining.[14] Though some fields of engineering have presented fewer problems than others, more than five thousand engineers and architects from the USSR are employed in the economy of Israel, and one in every three engineers in the Israel Aircraft Industries is from the USSR.[15]

Some professions, such as nursing, were much in demand and posed little difficulty as far as adjustment of standards. Half of the immigrant nurses from the USSR were certified after one month of training and 80 percent by the end of six months. However, almost 50 percent of those surveyed were not considered eligible for R.N. status without extra training, though they had expected such status.[16]

Teachers' retraining and certification courses sometimes lasted as long as two years. This might be the case particularly in subjects such as history, where the selectivity and ideological bias given in the Soviet Union make applicability in Israel difficult, or in the case of specialists in Russian literature, which is incorporated in general literature courses in Israel. The percentages of teachers certified after such courses ranged from 80 percent of mathematics teachers to 25 percent of music teachers.[17]

For teachers, language training in Hebrew was clearly a major part of any preparation for work in Israel. For doctors this was less so, with the result that immigrant physicians from the Soviet Union burdened with a heavy quota of patients in the clinics were said to read less professional literature than their Israeli or English-speaking colleagues, affecting their eventual professional status. This, plus the fact that 62 percent of Soviet immigrant doctors were women, almost all of whom were married, might be thought to have created a difficult situation for such persons, yet an absorption survey found 90 percent saying that their work in Israel was compatible with their previous experience. Sixty percent found that their medical work in Israel met their expectations, despite the fact that half of those who had been ranked as specialists in the USSR did not receive similar status upon arrival in Israel.[18]

Between the professions (where some adjustment of existing skills could fit the immigrant into Israel) and working-class skills, which were easily translated into the Israeli context, lay a large area of lower- and middle-level administrative work. Here, government intervention both in training and employment was massive. Large numbers of immigrants were given training as bookkeepers, archivists, and similar skilled office occupations, and then hired by the civil service and public corporations. This solved the problems of many immigrants in their late forties and early fifties whose previous experience was inapplicable in Israel. Having acquired language facility and on-the-job experience, they could compete on the higher paying private job market if they so desired, but in any case enjoyed the economic and social satisfaction of stable employment.

Students in higher education were both a particularly important group and a privileged one. They were important since the acquisition of higher education enjoyed a high priority in the value system of Soviet Jews, and the inability to acquire higher education in the USSR was often a primary factor motivating families to leave. Success of children in higher education in Israel was therefore an important point in the overall absorption of Soviet-Jewish immigrants. The Student Authority of the Ministry of Absorption had been set up to facilitate the immigration of university-age youth. Under the programs of the Student Authority, students received grants covering tuition, living expenses, and part of their monthly rent, freeing themselves and their parents from most of the economic burdens associated with university training. A combination of language difficulties and sociopsychological adjustment problems led to the institution of a full-year preacademic course. In this course students concentrated on acquiring Hebrew and English language skills (both of which were necessary since in many of the social and natural sciences the bulk of reading in Israeli universities is in English, while lectures and classroom discussions are generally in Hebrew). They also took part in introductory courses in their fields of study, plus introductions to Jewish history and to Israeli society and politics, all in the Russian language. Throughout their years of study, new immigrants from the Soviet Union suffered from inadequate knowledge of English and difficulties in reading large assignments in Hebrew. Nevertheless, the introductory year, which gave basic skills and helped the immigrant student get over the initial year adjustment problems, improved both morale and academic performance.[19]

In the cultural field, projects unique to the Soviet emigration were undertaken. Each immigrant group in Israel has its own native language newspaper, but the mass immigration from the USSR brought with it many of the Jewish journalists and writers who made up 8.5 percent of their profession in the USSR.[20] These persons, whose professional achievements were dependent both on a knowledge of language and an insight into the local environment, could not successfully compete for work in the Israeli media. To help them adjust, a whole publishing and translating industry was created in Israel, supplying both employment for the immigrants and cultural satisfaction for the entire Russian-speaking immigrant community. As emigration from the USSR grew, the possibility of turning such projects into self-sustaining sources of revenue increased. Both popular weeklies and serious intellectual journals have made their mark, and a new Russian-language edition of the *Jewish Encyclopedia* has been published.[21] These programs, however, as well as similar programs in music, are basically dependent on government subsidies and thus extremely vulnerable to budgetary crises.

Soviet-Jewish Absorption in Israel: A Balance Sheet

Much as the Absorption Ministry and the Jewish Agency have come under criticism for bureaucratic inefficiency, their programs to facilitate absorption and the effectiveness of the absorption of various sectors of the Soviet immigrant community have been impressive. Both in the adaptation of existing facilities to the particular characteristics of new Soviet immigrants, and in the establishment of new programs, the absorption authorities belie the stereotype of passive and unyielding bureaucrats. Yet a good part of the success of the absorption process is undoubtedly inherent in the creation of a culturally and socially self-sustaining community of Soviet-Jewish immigrants. The first such newcomers were characterized as being "without connections, without relatives, alone and friendless."[22] At some point, however, probably around the end of 1973, by which time 80,000 Soviet Jews had arrived in Israel, a "critical mass" was attained and many of the factors that had caused absorption difficulties eased or disappeared.

First of all, immediately after the October 1973 war, immigration dropped sharply. Where 33,477 Jews had arrived from the USSR in 1973, only 16,816 came the following year. This eased the strain on the absorption apparatus, which was geared to the previous higher scale of immigration. Moreover, the psychological crisis that followed the war made Israelis feel more solitary and appreciative of those who were coming to share in the burdens and sorrows of the time.

The presence in Israel of a large settled community of Soviet-Jewish immigrants was influential both in changing the public's antagonism toward them and in easing problems of absorption. One of the research findings regarding hostility to immigrants and immigration was that such feelings are strongest among those who have least contact with newcomers.[23] By the end of 1973 the 80,000 Soviet Jews had ceased to be only television or newspaper stories and had become reality. They were to be found in every place of work as engineers, technicians, football players, wrestlers, chess champions, civil servants, and school teachers. Above all, they were appearing in large numbers in Israel's army and in reserve service, the most important socializing institution in Israeli society. Here was a case in which familiarity did not breed contempt. Reduced to life size, and sharing equally in all the burdens and strains of life in Israel, Soviet Jews finally found their place in the mosaic of immigrant communities that is Israel.

The "critical mass" referred to previously became one of the important instruments of absorption for newcomers. While the first immigrants were like pioneers in a wilderness, those arriving later had relatives, former neighbors, friends, or colleagues already in Israel to whom they could turn for reliable advice and information. The absorbed played a crucial role in easing absorption for the newcomers by shortening the learning process, informing the newcomers of their rights, and guiding them in the field of employment. Leonard Schroeter considered the matter of "knowledge of rights" central to the difficulties of newcomers.[24] Absorption surveys showed information from friends and relatives to be an important source of guidance in employment.[25] Since assistance in finding employment has been found to be one of the important factors in creating a sense of identification with Israel, this absorptive activity of the established immigrants takes on added importance.[26]

Culturally, too, large community size made absorption easier and improved the quality of life in what is to this day the weakest side of Soviet Jews' absorption in Israel. The presence of a large audience made possible the maintenance of frameworks of cultural creation and consumption that could compensate in some measure for the community's being largely cut off by language barriers from films, theater, radio, and newspapers.[27] Visits by poets and performers using the Russian language generated large audiences that made such performances viable commercial propositions. A market for translated books existed, and journals and other publications whose original raison d'etre had been to provide employment for immigrant writers became the focus of widespread intellectual activity, sparking the formation of circles of intellectuals that rushed to do battle with each other in heated polemics, in the best tradition of the Russian intelligentsia. The Society of Immigrants from the USSR became a center for political and social lobbying, and volunteer associations of religious immigrants worked to propagate traditional Jewish rituals and values in the community. Institutions thus existed that provided an outlet for almost any type of activity. The climax to this activity was the declaration of three separate groups of Soviet immigrants regarding their intent to contest the elections to the Israeli Parliament in June 1981.

Table 5.1. Comparison of areas of life in Israel with life in the USSR[29] (in percentages)

Area	Better	Same	Worse
Social life	29	33	38
Social status	32	40	28
Living standards	51	27	22

Economically, the Soviet-Jewish immigrants have done well for themselves. A survey of four hundred Jewish immigrant families from urban centers of the European part of the USSR showed that three and a half years after arrival male workers were earning 8 percent more than the Israeli average and female workers 25 percent above the Israeli average. Among university graduates, male immigrants were earning 3 percent less than average, but women were earning 25 percent above the national average. The family income for new immigrants from the USSR was a full third above the average of all Jewish families in Israel, and 20 percent above the average for Israeli families of European or North American origin.[28] The picture drawn in this research project is one of a highly skilled population gainfully employed and working intensely (the investigators found that women in particular were working longer hours than the average Israeli) to establish themselves. Despite these economic achievements and an overwhelming sense of improvement in material life (88 percent reported that their general satisfaction with housing, consumer goods, and diet was better or much better than in the USSR), half the group polled felt that their social status had declined, and 86 percent declared that their cultural life was inferior to what they had experienced in the Soviet Union (see table 5.1).

An earlier study based on fifteen hundred new immigrants had reported similar, though less polarized, tendencies. At that time the sample investigated had given the following patterns of change comparing their life in the USSR with their life in Israel. While a direct comparison cannot be made because of differences in the populations investigated and in the framing of the questions, the two research projects point to the field of social and cultural adjustment as more problematical and less tractable than the material problems. In this sense, however, there is nothing unique in the experience of Soviet-Jewish immigrants. Most first-generation immigrants in any country cluster together socially and culturally, existing on the margin of the established society of their new homeland, the degree of their comfort or discomfort determined by the makeup of the absorbing society.

The ultimate measure of absorption, though, is the re-emigration rate of any immigrant community, and in this respect the immigrants from the USSR show unusual stability by both Israeli and international standards. Countries of immigration such as Australia and the United States have had overall re-emigration rates of up to one-quarter of all immigrants. In Israel the overall re-emigration rate after three years is about 15 percent. For immigrants from the USSR it is only 5 percent over the whole period of the Soviet-Jewish immigration. More strikingly, as the dropout problem has developed, and the immigrants arriving in Israel represent a select group motivated positively by the idea of life in Israel, the re-emigration rate has dropped to about one-half of 1 percent.[30]

Our conclusion therefore must be that however painful—and sometimes needlessly painful—the absorption process may have been, it nevertheless has been largely successful. A responsive and flexible administrative structure and a self-sustaining, active immigrant community have played their parts in this success, but the basic and essential ingredient would appear to be the motivation and dedication of the immigrants themselves.

6. A New Soviet Jewry Plan

Fabian Kolker

Editor's Note

The issue of dropouts, or noshrim, *has become a highly sensitive one for the world Jewish community. Initially, virtually all of the Soviet Jews who left the USSR emigrated to Israel; in the aftermath of the 1973 war, however, increasing numbers of Soviet Jews opted to go to the United States and other Western countries instead of Israel. The various reasons for this development have been given in previous chapters; the new element is that the Jewish Agency, long unhappy with the dropout phenomenon, in 1981 succeeded, after a great deal of debate, in convincing the Hebrew Immigrant Aid Society (HIAS) to refrain, for a three-month trial period, from aiding emigrating Soviet Jews who chose not to go to Israel, unless they had a first-degree relative in the West. The Jewish Agency claimed that the recent (1980–81) drop in Jewish emigration was caused by the fact that the Soviet authorities, angered that the emigrating Soviet Jews were going to the United States instead of Israel, decided to cut the number of Jews allowed to leave. Other Jews, both in Israel and the United States, have asserted that the reduction in the number of Jews allowed to leave has been caused by the deterioration of Soviet-American relations. Indeed, these observers recall that while Israeli officials back in 1977 were warning of a drop-off in emigration because of the dropout phenomenon, in reality emigration reached a new record in 1979 despite the fact that the vast majority of these emigrating Jews did not choose to go to Israel. Not unexpectedly, therefore, Soviet-Jewish emigration continued to drop in 1982 despite the new HIAS policy. In May 1982 HIAS returned to its previous policy of aiding all Soviet Jews who, upon arriving in Vienna, chose to go to countries other than Israel. In any case, the debate about* noshrim *has become an increasingly bitter one. In the article below, Fabian Kolker, a long-time American activist on behalf of Soviet Jewry, suggests a compromise solution.*

—Robert O. Freedman

Emigration of Jews from the Soviet Union began in sizable numbers in 1971 when some 13,122 Jews emigrated, 98 percent of whom went to Israel. In the four years preceding 1971 a total of less than five thousand Jews were permitted to leave, virtually all of them going to Israel.[1] Emigration in 1972 increased to approximately 32,000 and in 1973 to approximately 35,000, but fell to 20,000 in 1974. In these three years, approximately 85 to 100 percent of the emigrants went to Israel. The dramatic increase in those going to the United States began in 1975 and 1976, when some 37 percent in 1975 and 50 percent in 1976 of the Soviet Jews who arrived in Vienna did not continue on to Israel. The term "dropout" began to be used in this period.

Since then, the dropout issue has become an increasingly severe political problem in the Jewish world, one that has precipitated heated debates for which no solution has yet been found.

The "Kolker Plan" is being offered as a solution to this vexing problem. It is a plan that has been developed after five years of research. This research has included discussions with colleagues, with Jews who emigrated from the Soviet Union, with Jewish leaders, and with "grass-roots" Jews in America, Israel, and the Soviet Union. It has furthermore involved a great deal of personal agonizing and soul-searching. My personal involvement in the Soviet Jewry cause began just prior to 1960. It has spanned two decades and three continents. It has included six trips to the Soviet Union and eleven trips to Israel.

My grandparents were émigrés from tsarist Russia, albeit almost a century ago. I consider Russian Jews as my family and their welfare as my responsibility. Many American Jews, of course, have these same feelings toward our Russian "brothers and sisters." We want the very best for them and their children. At the start of the 1960s I was one of the world founders of the Soviet Jewry Movement. During the two decades since that time I have discussed the Soviet Jewry issue with several American presidents, starting with President John F. Kennedy; with several Israeli prime ministers and cabinet ministers; and with Soviet Premier Alexei Kosygin, in Moscow, on my fourth visit to the USSR.

At the beginning of the 1960s some of us in the American-Jewish community had thought of trying to bring about the re-establishment of Jewish culture and religion inside the Soviet Union. This concept was seriously discussed by the Jewish world in the mid-1960s, but after a brief period of attempts and failures, such plans were abandoned. It quickly became clear how thoroughly Joseph Stalin had completed his goal of destroying all Jewish institutions in the USSR, especially during the 1948–53 period (the "Black Years"). Only a few cultural and religious crumbs were thrown to the Jews of the Soviet Union following Stalin's sudden death in 1953. Among such crumbs were what I term the Soviet "matzo crumbs"—the right to bake a few matzoth in the USSR at Passover time, the sending of one or two rabbis to Hungary to train for the rabbinate and return to the USSR, and the right to publish and read the *Sovietische Heimland* and the *Birobidzhaner Shtern*, both of which are primarily a presentation of the Kremlin line in the Yiddish language.

Our fellow Jews inside the Soviet Union began, in the mid-1960s, to give us signals that their only hope for survival as Jews was to emigrate.[2] Fortunately, in the 1960s there existed the State of Israel where emigration could be directed following Premier Kosygin's famous December 1966 statement.[3] A headline in the newspaper *Izvestia* announced this new policy to the Russian people. Under the banner of family reunification and, implicitly, repatriation to the Jewish National Homeland in Israel, Premier Kosygin stated this new emigration policy on behalf of the rulers in the Kremlin. This change in Kremlin policy was, of course, influenced by the newly emerging detente with the West, particularly improved bilateral relations with the United States and the increase in Soviet-American trade.

Less than a year later, an event occurred in the Middle East that sparked many Jews in the Soviet Union to think of emigration. This was the rapid victory of the State of Israel in the June 1967 Six Day War. It was the catalyst that both inspired and impelled Soviet Jews to think in terms of their Jewish identity and of emigration to Israel.[4]

History records that the emigration movement gathered increasing strength following this victory of the Jewish state in 1967. But it became a dynamic and significant movement only following the Leningrad Trials of 1970 and 1971.[5] Unable by means of these trials to break the spirit of the small group of defendants who had been determined to fly to Israel, nor able to destroy the will of thousands of Jews inside the USSR to emigrate and live freely as Jews, Moscow grudgingly began to give ground. The government began to grant oficial permission to Jews to emigrate from the Soviet Union, something that had not been done to a significant degree since before the Communist revolution of 1917.

Following the Leningrad Trials more than a decade ago, some 250,000 Jewish men, women, and children have been permitted by Soviet authorities to emigrate. Further, the possibility now exists that many hundreds of thousands of additional emigrants will follow. It is an amazing accomplishment, one of truly historic proportions.

Let us now examine the factors that made possible the emigration of so many Soviet Jews.

One of the important factors, of course, has been the supportive actions taken by Western Jews. Equally important has been the leadership and financial support provided by people in the West. This leadership was provided by non-Jews as well as Jews. The non-Jews were primarily government leaders such as Senator Henry Jackson and Congressman Charles Vanik, and religious leaders such as Sister Ann Gilen.[6] Financial support was provided by Jews of generosity living on both sides of the Atlantic Ocean. Even more important were the actions—often brave and heroic—of the Soviet Jews themselves, who struggled inside the Soviet Union and who demanded the right to leave the USSR.

But it was obvious that the indispensable factor, the pivot around which this entire movement operated, the sine qua non, was the State of Israel. The Soviet Jewry Movement could not even have gotten started without the founding of the State of Israel, and without the thirty-five year struggle of the Israelis to make it the strong, viable country that provided invitations for the Soviet Jews who wished to emigrate.

In the cities of the Soviet Union, when more than ten years ago the possibility of emigration was opened, Soviet-Jewish families (and individuals) considered and made decisions that were to profoundly affect their lives. The decision was made first by a few, then by hundreds, by thousands, and later by tens of thousands. That decision was to uproot themselves from the USSR, to exile themselves from the land of their birth, where for most Soviet Jews their families had lived for many generations. Their decision to leave "Mother Russia" was, of course, a decision taken with mixed emotions and for many reasons. A primary part of this decision was always the totalitarian, authoritarian, and repressive Soviet regime under which they had been living. The regime was daily causing many problems for its Jewish citizens, often regarding those of the Jewish nationality as an unreliable element in the population. The Jewish minority was and is regarded as not worthy of the same limited rights, the same job opportunities, the same educational opportunities, the same religious and cultural privileges as Soviet citizens of the majority groups.[7]

The State of Israel, on the other hand, provided a home for Soviet Jews. At that time (thirteen years ago), and now, the State of Israel was true to its original concept as a homeland for homeless Jews, for Jewish exiles. At the request of Soviet Jews desiring emigration, the State of Israel came to their rescue. Soviet Jews began asking for invitations from relatives in Israel, and the Israeli people and the State of Israel responded. To date, over 600,000 invitations have been requested by Soviet Jews and mailed to the Soviet Union, corresponding to about one-third of the entire Jewish population of the USSR.

The seeking and sending of invitations from Israel for the purpose of family reunification is the basic emigration procedure required by the Soviet authorities. The invitation from Israel is, therefore, the basic document for the Soviet-Jewish exodus.

It is the State of Israel that is the central factor in the emigration process, and the plan presented below has as its goal the strengthening of the State of Israel through increased Soviet-Jewish emigration—while at the same time respecting the wishes of the Soviet Jews themselves.

The Kolker Plan

Exemption for Primary Relatives (Mother, Father, Sister, Brother, Child). There is an exemption to the new rules, stated below, for all Soviet emigrants who now have primary relatives in the United States (or other Western countries) and who choose to join their primary relatives. This exemption will be carried out in the city of Vienna.

Such emigrants, after arriving in Vienna, may choose to go to Israel along with the rest of the emigrants who do not have primary relatives in the United States (or other Western countries). However, they may choose the following procedure:

They can promptly advise the Jewish Agency in Vienna that they wish to join their primary relatives. Their papers will then be transferred in order to receive the necessary documents to be transported from Vienna to the Transit Center in Rome. After the proper waiting period in Rome and receipt of an American visa (or a visa from another country), they will be flown from Rome to the United States (or other Western country) to join their primary relatives.

Procedure Governing the Rules. For all Soviet Jews who make future requests for invitations from Israel, the following rules shall apply:

There will be mailed to the apartment of the Soviet Jew who has requested the *vyzov* (the invitation from Israel) an additional printed document called the "Rules." These two documents will be mailed together in the same envelope. They will be sent from Israel by registered mail, return receipt. The applicant in the USSR will therefore be fully aware of the rules prior to submitting his application to OVIR, the Soviet government office handling emigration, and prior to beginning his or her emigration process in the Soviet Union.

The Rules

Rule I. Soon after arrival in the transit city of Vienna, all Soviet Jews carrying documents with the destination of Israel shall fly to Ben Gurion Airport in Israel.

Rule II. On arriving in Israel, the Soviet emigrant may choose one of the following two categories, each of which is permitted under present Israeli law:[8]

(*a*) The status of Oleh
This entitles the immigrant to Israeli citizenship automatically in accordance with the Law of Return.

(*b*) The status of Temporary Resident A-1
This will entitle the immigrant to Temporary Resident status in Israel for a period of twelve months (minus one day), at which time the Temporary Resident will make known his choice.

Rule III. Freedom of choice. The Temporary Resident A-1 may choose at the end of twelve months (minus one day)[9] either of the following:

(*a*) to acquire the status of Oleh, which entitles the immigrant to Israeli citizenship,

(*b*) or to leave Israel to become a citizen of the United States (or other Western country).

Rule IV. Rules applying to those Soviet emigrants who choose to go to the United States. (If another country is chosen, the laws of that country will apply.)

(*a*) The applicant for an entrance visa to the United States will obtain the necessary documents from the U.S. Consulate in Tel Aviv.

(*b*) The applicant will fill out necessary forms required by U.S. law under the American Refugee Act of March 17, 1980.

(*c*) The applicant will be permitted to enter the United States and will be given the same resettlement benefits under American law as received previously by Soviet Jews on entering the United States from Italy, except that they will be flown directly from Tel Aviv to New York.

(d) The following suggestions are made to the Jewish organizations involved in this category:

(1) that HIAS and the American Joint Distribution Committee, through their offices in Israel, assist Soviet Jews in their transit from Israel to the United States in the same manner that they now render such assistance from Rome to the United States.

(2) that the Jewish Federations and Jewish community service agencies in U.S. cities assist Soviet Jews in their immigration and absorption into the United States from Israel in the same manner that they now assist Soviet Jews from Italy.

Rule V. The funds allocated to each Soviet Jew during his twelve-month (minus one day) stay in Israel shall be furnished by world Jewry in a manner similar to the way it is done in Italy by world Jewry. It shall not be a contribution by the State of Israel or the people of Israel. To prevent the possibility of objection by Soviet authorities to certain parts of the new "Rules" to be received by Soviet Jews with their *vyzov*, the following measures should be taken:

1. It is proposed that prospective Soviet-Jewish applicants for emigration will receive in another manner the knowledge of primary-relative exemption. No reference can be made in the actually printed "Rules" to "Exemption for Primary Relations" (this exemption, the essential elements of a living experience in Israel, and freedom of choice of final destination are basic to this plan).

2. Rules III, IV, and V above are obviously for the internal use of the Soviet Jewry Movement and cannot be sent to the USSR in their current form. In printing the "Rules" (to be mailed from Israel), no use of the words "the United States (or other Western country)" shall be in the document. Instead, it is suggested that the printed "Rules" will refer to the choice of the status of (*a*) Oleh, or (*b*) the status of "free agent to decide his future for himself."

3. The final language decided upon and printed in the "Rules" must, of course, be consistent with Soviet law and Soviet emigration practice.

Justification for the Kolker Plan

I feel that this plan will be far more successful in convincing Soviet Jews to become Israeli citizens than was the previous Jewish Agency program called the "Naples Plan." This was a plan evolved by the Jewish Agency that consisted of counseling Soviet Jews and briefing them about the benefits of living in Israel and giving them, in effect, a "crash course" on Judaism during their stay in Naples or Rome or another Italian transit point. This Italian plan began in November 1980. Its ultimate purpose was to influence people to make Israel their destination instead of the West. My own conclusion regarding this attempt to effect a change of mind after the Soviet Jew was already in Italy and on his way to the United States, or another Western country, is that the Naples Plan was a waste of Jewish energy and Jewish funds. From my own three visits to Vienna over the past few years (as well as to Rome), I can testify to the utter futility of such efforts. The reason is that the decision to emigrate to either Israel or the West is made back in the Soviet Union, in discussions with family and friends, before the emigration step is taken. It is not made when one sets foot off the train or plane on arrival in Vienna after exodus from the Soviet Union.

It is my feeling that if the Kolker Plan is adopted and implemented, that is, if Soviet Jews go directly to Israel for a twelve-month (minus one day) period, and all parties involved cooperate to the fullest, most Soviet Jews experiencing life in Israel will like it and decide to remain. Indeed, they are the first beneficiaries of this plan.

As stated above, I have frequently visited Israel and have held interviews with many Soviet-Jewish immigrants. In the spring of 1981 I made my fifth such visit for this purpose. Almost all of those interviewed at that time told me their lives were being fulfilled in Israel and that they were able to find employment and job opportunities in the fields for which they were trained in the Soviet Union. They advised me that they felt their choice to come to Israel to live was the correct one. They spoke of the good quality of life in Israel and the general spirit of camaraderie that characterized the people. "It's like being with family," they said to me over and over again. They told me that, in general, their own economic situation in Israel was better than in the USSR and that their children seemed to be adjusting well. They spoke to me of being proud of discovering their newly found Jewish heritage. They felt that they and their families were "making it" in Israel.

Over the past ten years 160,000 Soviet Jews have arrived in Israel. My study of their situation convinces me that their absorption into Israel has, in general, been successful. This has been accomplished not only with the help of the government of Israel and the Jewish Agency, but with the personal help of Sabras, older Israeli settlers, and primarily with the help of the Soviet immigrants already in Israel. Experience has shown that in Israel each new group of Russian immigrants receives a helping hand from the previous group of arrivals.[10]

In addition, the American Jewish community has been very generous in support of the resettlement of Russian-Jews in Israel. In 1980, for example, the United Jewish Appeal, with funds raised largely in the United States, sent the sum of $130 million to assist Soviet-Jewish absorption in Israel. These funds helped in housing, food allowances, language training, job and professional training, job placement, and social and medical services in Israel.

Through legislation initiated annually by the House of Representatives Subcommittee on Foreign Operations, chaired for many years by Maryland Congressman Clarence Long, the U.S. Congress has continuously granted $25 million annually to the State of Israel for the absorption of Soviet Jews in Israel.

Unlike other countries in the world, Israel is able to offer almost immediate job opportunities and employment in many fields. I refer to the fields of medicine, nursing, pharmacy, teaching, scientific research of many types, industrial research and development, and computer technology—the list is long. However, not enough publicity has been given to opportunities in Israel. The fact is that Soviet Jews hold key positions today in the Israeli economy and Israeli society.

One striking example of a yet largely unpublicized Israeli organization providing job opportunities for new Soviet immigrants is a group called METAR. Five years ago a new émigré to Israel, Soviet scientist Yisroel Averbuch, organized METAR and is now its director. METAR employs hundreds of people who work largely on their own, most of them newly arrived Russian engineers and inventors, in accordance with Averbuch's policy. Over the past few years these Russian engineers, living in various Israeli cities and operating under the aegis of METAR, have received profitable contracts—such as producing products and furnishing services for the Weizman Institute, the Technion, and the Israeli Aircraft Industry. Many of the contracts are for export items, and thus they are making an important contribution to the Israeli economy. Averbuch advises that there are job opportunities for many additional hundreds of Soviet engineers who would come to Israel.

During one recent trip to Israel, I visited several Israeli development towns and cities where large numbers of Russians now reside. In the city of Beersheba, for example, Ben Gurion University has provided tenured chairs for Russian scientists such as Herman Branover, a specialist in solar energy. Other Russian scientists and academicians have likewise settled in Beersheba and have received positions at the university. Tel Aviv University and the Hebrew University of Jerusalem also have given tenured chairs to Soviet scientists.

Israel has become a land of opportunity for Jews who leave the USSR. I have met dozens in the fields of medicine, law, the sciences, the arts, and the humanities who are carrying on their chosen professions and vocations in Israel. This includes people such as Professor Benyamin Levich, Professor Mark Azbel, Dr. Alexander Voronel, Dr. Alexander Luntz, Dr. Benjamin Fain, Victor Polsky, Avrum Shifrin, and many, many others.[11]

There live in Israel today almost all of the fifty or more Russian prisoners of conscience who were jailed in the USSR for their beliefs and who have struggled and succeeded in their fight to emigrate. These prisoners of conscience and other refuseniks have, by their sacrifice, pushed open the gates of the USSR for other Jews who wish to leave, and they now live a satisfied life in Israel.

The litmus test of successful absorption of Russian Jews in Israel is, of course, whether or not they decide, after living in Israel, to emigrate from Israel to the West. Contrary to what has been experienced with native-born Israelis and with non-Russian Jewish émigrés, the statistics of Soviet Jewish re-emigration from Israel to the West shows a startling difference: over the entire decade of the 1970s, less than 5 percent have re-emigrated to the West.

Over the same period the re-emigration rate of immigrants to Israel from the United States and Canada has been approximately 50 percent per year. This is clear testimony to the quality of absorption of Soviet Jews in Israel, once they have had the opportunity to experience Israel and correct any wrong impressions they might have obtained about Israel back in the Soviet Union. My observations over two decades about Soviet Jews and Israeli Jews is that these two groups are, in general, more compatible with each other than are Soviet Jews and American Jews. The re-emigration test of successful Israeli absorption speaks for itself. These figures attest to the general acceptance of Israel by the 160,000 Jews who have come to Israel from the USSR over the past ten years and more.

A second beneficiary of the plan would be the State of Israel. Soviet Jews are generally well educated, hard working, skilled professionally, and have a cultured life-style. My research convinces me that they have added a great deal to the sum total of Israeli life, culture, and progress over the past decade.

In addition to their professional contributions, the Soviet Jews also will contribute to Israel demographically. It is, of course, no secret that within the borders of Israel today there is an ever-expanding Arab population. Given the sharp difference between the birth rate of Israel's Arab families and the birth rate of its Jewish families, the demographic reality is that in the next twenty-five to fifty years Jews in Israel may no longer be the majority population. The danger of the State of Israel losing its Jewish character in the coming decades is therefore very real.

The hope of David Ben Gurion, Golda Meir, and other prime ministers of Israel that the American Jewish community, now numbering six million, would leave America in large numbers and emigrate to Israel is still unrealized. In my view it will never be realized to any sizable extent. The fact is that only a few thousand Americans per year emigrate from the United States to Israel, and, as previously stated, 50 percent return to America.

It is primarily from only one country in the world, I believe, that the future population growth in Israel can come. Emigration from that one country alone can help counterbalance the increasing Arab population that now lives in the State of Israel. That country is, of course, the Soviet Union. It is the country from which most of the founders of the State of Israel and most of the early pioneers and builders of the State of Israel came.

Russian immigrants to Israel now form a sizable group. The Kolker Plan, if adopted and implemented, will hopefully add many more Russian olim to Israel in the coming decades.

I feel that both the Soviet Jews themselves and the State of Israel and its people would benefit greatly if the Kolker Plan is adopted, since most of the Soviet Jews would want to remain in Israel. However, it should again be emphasized that the Soviet Jews retain freedom of choice under this plan, and should they wish to re-emigrate to the United States they would have that option. Indeed, after a year of life in Israel, any re-emigrating Soviet Jews can be expected to be enriched Judaically and Hebraically. The main purpose of the entire emigration movement—that the Soviet Jews, by leaving the USSR, will be given the opportunity to live as Jews—will be fulfilled regardless of the final destination of the Soviet-Jewish émigrés.

7. Soviet-Jewish Immigrants to the United States: Profile, Problems, Prospects

Zvi Gitelman

Between 1971 and 1980 over 300,000 people emigrated from the USSR, the first time since 1944-45 that so many people left the country, and the first time since the 1920s that large numbers have left legally. Of these 300,000 legal emigrants, about 50,000 were ethnic Germans, 8,000 Armenians, and 248,000 Jews. Approximately 12 percent of the Soviet-Jewish population has left the country in the past decade, a development unforeseen by Western (and probably Soviet) observers.

We do not know precisely why the Soviet authorities have permitted this emigration, fluctuating and controlled as it is. The most likely explanation is that it has resulted from a fortunate coincidence of external and internal pressure (from the dissident and Zionist movements) coming at a time when the USSR wanted to improve relations with the United States and needed congressional support (and, hence, the support of public opinion) to do so. The Soviet leadership perhaps believed that if it let a few troublemakers go, it could kill two birds with one stone: Western opinion would be placated and the Zionist movement within the USSR would die off. Of course, the Soviets underestimated the extent of Jewish (and German) alienation and, therefore, of the potential emigration. Moreover, they did not take into account the phenomenon of chain migration whereby emigration grows geometrically.

Emigration became a political football between East and West. Both in the case of Germans and of Jews, emigration has risen and fallen more or less in line with the ups and downs of the Soviet-Western political relationship. That is why 1979 was a peak year for Jewish emigration—51,000 Jews left—and why 1980—after the invasion of Afghanistan and after the SALT II agreement was blocked in the U.S. Congress—was a low year, with a 60 percent drop in emigration over the previous year, increased harassment of would-be émigrés, and tightening up of emigration requirements and eligibility.

After a decade of emigration, we can try to answer the following questions: (1) Who are the Soviet Jews who have emigrated, and how do the Israeli and American immigrants compare with each other? (2) What are some of the problems that Soviet immigrants in the United States encounter? (3) In what ways has Soviet-Jewish immigration affected the American-Jewish community? (4) What are the possibilities for a continued Soviet-Jewish emigration to the United States?

Table 7.1. Geographic origin of Soviet-Jewish immigration from 1974–June 30, 1979[1]

	Israel	United States
Georgia	9.8% (ca. 35% before 1974)	0.9%
Central Asia	12.1	2.8
Russia	7.6	18.3
Ukraine	20.9	64.4
Moldavia	20.2	3.9
Baltic	5.9	3.3
Byelorussia	2.9	4.3

Note: In 1980, 25 percent of the American immigrants came from the Russian Soviet Federated Socialist Republic and 35 percent from the Ukraine.

From 1971 through 1980 some 156,000 Soviet Jews emigrated to Israel, 79,806 went to the United States with the assistance of the Hebrew Immigrant Aid Society, and about 16,200 emigrated to other countries.[2] Within this period the changing trend is very clear. In 1971, of 13,000 Jews who left the USSR, only 290 came to the United States. But in 1974 a turning point was reached and 19 percent of those who left the Soviet Union did not go on to Israel. In 1976 this figure rose to 49 percent, and ever since then more than half of the Soviet-Jewish emigrants have been coming to the United States (about two-thirds in more recent years). I would say this trend is likely to continue for several reasons: (*a*) The chain migration—each arrival in America increases the likelihood that others will come. (*b*) The cultural and geographic characteristics of the émigrés. They are European, not Central Asian or Georgian, and are highly educated and highly acculturated into Russian culture, though not assimilated into Russian society because they are stigmatized as Jews. (*c*) The relatively successful absorption in the United States makes it more likely that others will follow. (*d*) The element of fashionability and peer pressure about emigration—the United States is now in fashion as a destination. (*e*) Israel's objective difficulties (housing, security, inflation), which are reported back to the USSR by immigrants and which are magnified by Soviet propaganda.

The Israeli and American immigrations are quite different from each other, with the non-Ashkenazic, more traditional, and more Jewishly conscious émigrés going largely to Israel. Let us look at the two immigrations in terms of their geographic origin.

Israeli immigrants came largely from areas that were absorbed into the USSR in 1939–44 (West Ukraine, Moldavia, the Baltic) or those areas that were not very Russified (Georgia and Central Asia). Only about 30 percent came from the European heartland, whereas about 87 percent of the American immigrants came from that heartland. Another way of looking at these figures shows that about 72 to 73 percent of all émigrés from Russia and the Ukraine go to the United States, whereas only 6 percent of the Georgians and 13 percent of those from Central Asia choose the United States over Israel.

7. Soviet-Jewish Immigrants to the U.S.

There is hardly any difference in the sexual composition of the Israeli and American immigrations. Women constitute 53 percent of the Israeli immigrants and 52 percent of American immigrants. There are more females in the older cohorts.

Surprisingly, given the high proportion of Asian Jews among the Israeli immigrants, the family size of the two immigrations is not very different. The American immigrant family has an average of 2.7 people (typically, the Soviet-Jewish family is a one-child family) and the Israeli, only 2.5, though among the immigrants from Asian republics and Georgia the unit size is 3.1. It should be noted that in 1970 the average size of an urban Soviet family was 3.5 persons, and that the units emigrating to Israel between 1971 and 1975 averaged 3.1 persons among Ashkenazim, 3.7 among Georgians, and 4.4. among Central Asians.[3] So, unless there is something wrong with the statistics, small family units have been arriving in the more recent period.

The Soviet-Jewish population is an aged one, with very low birth and high mortality rates. In 1970 in the RSFSR 26.5 percent of all Jews were 60 years old or older, and only 15 percent were under 20 years of age.[4] Emigrants are much younger. This is to be expected in light of the fact that young people are more mobile and are usually overrepresented in migrations. In the United States between 25 and 29 percent of the Soviet-Jewish immigrants (1974–80) were under 20; only 8 to 19 percent were over 60, though the trend was clearly to a higher proportion of older people (in 1980, 19 percent were over 61).[5] It may be that the younger Jews are the first to emigrate, with older relatives coming later. The median age of Soviet emigrants going to Israel is 33, while it is 35 years of age for those going elsewhere. Note, however, that the median age of heartlanders (those from the RSFSR and Byelorussia and the Eastern Ukraine) going to Israel is 40 and of Asians only 24. This seems to indicate thàt a young group of heartlanders is coming to the United States, and older heartlanders are gravitating more toward Israel.[6] This trend also is hinted at by the smaller family size of heartlander Israeli immigrants as compared with the American heartlanders.

In 1974–79 between 57 percent and 63 percent of the American immigrants were in the labor force. In 1980 this figure fell to 53 percent. There is a higher proportion of professionals and skilled workers among the American immigrants, but only because of the Asian-Georgian component of immigration. In the 1974–79 period, when that component dropped proportionately, the occupational profiles of Israelis and Americans became very similar; in fact, if one compares immigrants alone, there are more professionals among the Israeli immigrants. Of those in the labor force during 1974–79, 26 percent of the Soviet-Jewish immigrants to the United States had been professionals in the USSR; 15 percent had been engineers; 9 percent technicians; 15 percent had been in white-collar jobs; and 16.5 percent in blue-collar. Another 14 percent had been in the service sector, 3 percent in transportation, and 1 percent had been unskilled. Among the Israeli immigrants the proportions were very similar, except that there were more blue-collar and unskilled workers and fewer white-collar and service sector employees. Among the American immigrants there were many more women than men in the professions and in white-collar and service occupations, while men dominated the engineering and blue-collar categories.

Almost 12,000 Soviet-Jewish professionals arrived in the United States from 1974 through 1980. One-third of them were in the humanities, one-quarter in medicine, and nearly a fifth in the arts and entertainment. Together with the engineers and technicians, they made up half the working immigrants. Rarely has America seen such highly skilled immigrants. The potential of this Soviet immigration for self-fulfillment—as a benefit for the United States as a whole and for American Jewry in particular—is enormous. Is this potential being reached?

The truth is that we do not know. Somewhat surprisingly, the American-Jewish community has made no systematic national study of the Soviet immigrant resettlement, though a few community studies exist, notably of Baltimore by Jerome Gilison,[7] of Minneapolis–St. Paul by Steven Feinstein,[8] and of Cincinnati by Ellen Paul and Dan Jacobs.[9] Some information on resettlement in Detroit has been collected by the present author.[10] The Soviet-Jewish Resettlement Program of the Council of Jewish Federations has sponsored a resettlement study directed by Professor Rita Simon of the University of Illinois. The study encompasses seven hundred Soviet-Jewish immigrants living all over the United States. Consequently, this analysis relies largely on the studies cited, on my own travels and contacts, and on an oral history project in which I have been involved.

The latter study consists of 473 ex-Soviet citizens who emigrated to the United States in 1977–81 and is part of a larger study, "Bureaucratic Encounters in the USSR," conducted also in Israel and the Federal Republic of Germany.[11] Of the American immigrants surveyed, 331 had been registered as Jews on their Soviet internal passports. Interviews were conducted mainly in New York, Cleveland, Detroit, Chicago, Ann Arbor, and three other cities. The sample was divided almost evenly among men and women. Slightly more than 40 percent came from the RSFSR, 29 percent from the Ukraine, 15 percent from Moldavia, and 13 percent from the Baltic. Nearly half of those interviewed had received higher education, and only 10 percent had not gone beyond elementary school.

Major Issues

Housing

The major housing problem in Israel does not seem to be paralleled in the United States.

Employment

Employment seemed to be the major problem in the United States, especially in the sluggish economy of the 1970s and 1980s. My general impression is of some unemployment and of considerably downward occupational mobility, especially for former engineers and physicians. Nearly 60 percent of our sample, which included students and housewives, were employed, but an equal proportion of the employed claimed not to be employed in their specialty or profession. A few case histories will illustrate these points.

M. F., a thirty-three-year-old electrician from Uzhgorod, got his first job in a junkyard, earning $5.20 an hour: "After Russia . . . without language, without anything, that's big money, and I got a lot of overtime." Eventually he found a job as an electrician with a construction firm and was excused from the $80 union fee for electricians.

V. F., a television producer in Moscow, obtained a job in a textile factory in Des Moines, worked for twenty-five days, and then took a teaching position at a midwestern college.

I. K. was an editor and proofreader who, when she came here, worked in a bakery in Cleveland for three months. Then she started a course in computer programming and is very happy in her new vocation.

L. L., an engineer, had eighteen job interviews in Chicago before getting a job as a draftsman for $4 an hour. After three years he became a project engineer, and he now owns his own home and two cars.

L. M. was a mathematics teacher in Kiev. He now has two part-time factory jobs and attends English classes at night. He is over fifty and does not have much hope of ever being a teacher again, but he hopes to enter the computer field.

B. H., in his seventies, is a musician. In 1974, when he first came, he got $10 for playing the violin at a Bar Mitzvah, but later the local Jewish community center gave him $200 for a concert. He then got jobs as a conductor of several suburban orchestras and has conducted Handel's *Messiah* for two churches in his area. "So, you know, for my age . . . it's unbelievable that I received such possibilities to work in the United States." (He earned $7,000 in 1978.)

Z. K. was a doctor, specializing in sports medicine. She got a temporary job as a nurse in a Jewish hospital but lost it after nine months when the original jobholder returned. She has been unemployed for four months. Her husband, an engineer in a shipbuilding yard in the USSR, is working as a draftsman.

Resettlement and Satisfaction

The immigrants we surveyed are about evenly divided in their evaluation of the resettlement agencies and workers with whom they have come in contact, with slightly more than half tending toward a mildly negative evaluation. However, while they see most Americans as considerably more helpful and fair-minded than Soviet people, over a third of the Jewish respondents, and more than half of the non-Jews, feel that resettlement workers discriminate among immigrants and "play favorites." This was most often charged regarding assistance in securing housing, jobs, and loans. New Yorkers and Chicagoans were especially apt to complain of unequal treatment, as were non-Jews. Nevertheless, over 40 percent identified resettlement agencies as the main factor in helping them re-establish themselves; 35 percent identified family and friends. Clearly, there is an unofficial support network for the immigrants that has developed over the years, but the work of the resettlement agencies is still central.

Nearly 70 percent of our sample reported that they were satisfied or very satisfied with their life in the United States and thought other immigrants were equally satisfied. (There are no differences on this score between Jews and non-Jews.) The more educated people were less satisfied in America. On the other hand, they were more sure than the others that they would emigrate again if they had the choice. This is probably because they were more alienated from the Soviet system.

But even among the satisfied, employment and language acquisition and facility were identified as troublesome problems. Nearly 58 percent thought their standard of living had gone up since their arrival in the United States, and only 13 percent saw it as having declined (29 percent said it was the same as in the USSR). Therefore, it is not surprising that only 15 people said that if they "could do it over" they would not emigrate from the USSR. But almost one hundred people said they would choose a country of immigration other than the United States, and the numbers are divided among Western Europe (25, mostly non-Jews), Israel (22), Canada (21), and other destinations (29). If they missed anything at all of Soviet life it was friends and family, with non-Jews emphasizing the former, and Jews the latter. They also evaluated positively relations among people in the USSR and the cultural life in that country (I found the same evaluation in my surveys of Soviet immigrants in Israel in 1972–75 and in Detroit in 1976).[12]

A more objective, though partial, picture of resettlement is provided by some data on the employment of the immigrants. With about 60 percent employed, most of them not in their specialties, and with their recent entry into the American labor force, it is not surprising to find that over 40 percent of our sample earned less than $500 per month, and that an equal proportion earned between $500 and $1,100. Unemployment is more problematic in Detroit and Chicago than elsewhere, and Detroit and Cleveland have the highest proportion of people employed in fields other than their own. Undoubtedly the economic problems of the older industrial cities of the Midwest directly affect the immigrants.

American Culture and the Identity of the Immigrants

In Israel language seems to be a relatively minor problem except for the elderly. On the one hand, many Israelis speak more than one language, and, on the other, there is a long-established network of intensive Hebrew language courses. In the United States language acquisition seems to be a more serious problem, especially among the elderly who find it very difficult to learn English, which reinforces their social isolation. A Russian subculture is developing in the United States, as evidenced by the revival of the newspaper *Novoe Russkoe Slovo* and some Russian journals, as well as by the appearance of the weeklies *Novy Amerikanets* and *Novaia gazeta*, and of many original works of Russian literature published mainly by Ardis in Ann Arbor, Michigan. Over half of our sample followed the Russian-American press regularly and considered it to be a more important source of information for themselves than the local press or even television.

The immigrants displayed a marked ambivalence toward American culture. Its freedom and creativity were viewed as attractive; but its vulgarity and pandering to low tastes repelled them. For most of them American culture will forever remain alien. A perceptive immigrant has made the point most vividly:

> I don't have their memories, associations, past. I was not like them. I didn't collect baseball cards, didn't start driving at the age of 15, didn't throw newspapers on their manicured lawns, wasn't absorbed in comic books, didn't take psychological tests. I was different . . . . My personality and that of the Americans were formed differently . . . . As a friend of mine said, "language itself is not the important thing. Even if all of America began to speak Russian, we would still feel ourselves in a foreign country."[13]

The cultural gap between immigrants and established Americans is widened by distorted images of the United States that emerge in the Soviet Union, a country whose official portrayal of American life is sometimes overcompensated for by fantasies born of wish fulfillment and the impossibility of verification. One immigrant comments:

> Already in the USSR, just as soon as we decided to emigrate we . . . imagined America to ourselves . . . one big Las Vegas, millionaires all around, everyone in jeans, Cadillacs and Rolls Royces, and everyone bursting with joy when we arrive—in general, an eternal holiday, eternal music. The real American disappointed us. First of all it turned out (who could have imagined it!) that they speak English here. Secondly, no one burst with joy when we arrived. Thirdly, it turned out that the eternal holiday is temporarily postponed, that is, you have to search for work long and hard, and find it in order to stay alive. And even with the purchase of the second car and the home, the eternal music

does not begin. And our own disappointment in America we do not mention, we carefully hide even from ourselves; we take it out on the Americans.[14]

The same person realizes that immigrant children adapt more quickly to American ways and that they, not their parents, will be the first Americans culturally. It very well may be that the same skipping of a generation may occur in regard to Jewish, as well as general, culture.

Jewish Culture and Identity of the Immigrants

The immigrants have made no special impact on American-Jewish culture nor does there seem to be a consensus on how to transmit Jewish culture to them. The whole question of their Jewish identification and its substantive content remains an open one.

Israeli spokesmen and the media have often warned that Soviet emigrants to the United States would cease to identify with the Jewish community as soon as their dependence on it ended. The self-serving nature of this contention is obvious, but most observers would acknowledge it to be a reasonable supposition. It is therefore with some surprise that we observe a considerable amount of positive Jewish identification among our sample, as well as among those in the other studies cited. True, in these cases many of those interviewed were still dependent to some degree on Jewish communal organizations, but this dependence may not severely distort the subjective self-identification or activities of the respondents.

The majority of the respondents in our recent study still feel "Russian" in America most of the time. This is especially true among non-Jews, 79 percent of whom say that they "always" feel Russian. The Jews are identified informally, even by American Jews, as "Russians." The friends of 84 percent of the Jews in the sample (95 percent in New York) are other "Russian Jews," and few claim to have made American friends. The cultural preferences of the Russian-Jewish immigrants strongly reflect their country of origin. Over two-thirds would like their children to learn Russian, and among New Yorkers, where the intelligentsia is overrepresented, the proportion reaches 80 percent. However, when asked how they would like to be identified, three-quarters of the Jewish respondents answered as "American Jews" or "Jews" and only 20 percent simply as "Americans." Thus, they do not indicate a desire to assimilate into an undifferentiated American society.

When it came to Jewish activities, only 8 percent of the Jews identified themselves as religious, but, despite years of Soviet indoctrination, only one person claimed to be antireligious. Interestingly, exactly half of the rest said they were traditional, meaning that they observed some customs and holidays. The other half called themselves nonreligious. So the overwhelming majority clustered around the intermediate categories of traditional and nonreligious. Only 15 percent attended synagogue regularly, and the same proportion never attended at all. But over 40 percent attended two or three times a year. The regular worshipers are mostly elderly and have relatively little education.

Of the 149 Jews who had school-age children, fifty-nine (49 percent) were in Jewish schools, a far higher proportion than for the American-Jewish population as a whole, though this is due to their Jewish communities' encouragement and incentives. Only thirteen children attended afternoon or Sunday schools, and a bare majority of the children received no Jewish education whatever.[15] It remains an open question as to how long the day-school students remain in those schools and what the long-range consequences of this education will be. After all, two-thirds of the sample said they never participated in any Jewish organizational activity. About 12 percent of the Jews had spouses who were not officially registered as Jews in the USSR.[16] But, again, the younger generation may well have a very different "Jewish profile" from their parents.

Soviet Immigrants and the American Jewish Community

What impact has this most recent and largest emigration since the aftermath of the Holocaust had on American Jewry? First, it has mobilized many professionals and volunteers in efforts at resettlement. Considerable resources have been allocated by national and local organizations to immigrant resettlement. Second, it has changed the image of Soviet Jews from idealized heroes to real people, people with problems and shortcomings like everyone else. Third, the dropout issue has created tensions with the Israeli government and the Jewish Agency but has forced the American-Jewish organizational leadership to take an independent stand, which I see as a generally positive, healthy development. (See the discussion of this issue in the Epilogue.) Fourth, there may be some temporary demographic strengthening of American Jewry, which is badly in need of it, but in view of the small Soviet-Jewish immigrant families and their high potential for assimilation, one should not look to them for long-term help in reversing the decline of American Jewry. Fifth, Soviet immigrants already have made great contributions to the arts, especially in music, and will undoubtedly continue to do so. Finally, Soviet-Jewish immigration has forced some American Jews to confront their own Jewishness and re-examine whether they have taken full advantage of the cultural freedoms they have.

The official Jewish community has welcomed Soviet immigrants, but there is an undercurrent of hostility and resentment one senses among at least a part of the American-Jewish population. Some people believe the immigrants should go to Israel, though they themselves do not exercise that option. Others are disappointed that the immigrants are "not Jewish" enough, not observant. Both professionals and lay people sometimes express the feeling that the immigrants are not grateful enough for "all that is being done for them" and that they make unreasonable demands, based on arrogance or unrealistic expectations. These resentments arise in most countries vis-à-vis most immigrants, but they may be exacerbated here by the cultural gap between Soviet and American people. Yet the Hebrew saying has it, "What reason will not do, time will." The attitudes cited here are likely to fade with time.

The Future of Emigration

The Soviet system creates potential émigrés. The more that Jews emigrate, the more that educational and vocational opportunities for Jews are closed. The number of Jewish students in higher education has fallen 40 percent in less than a decade.[16] But the more that higher education is closed, the more that people decide to leave. Chain migration will be a second spur to emigration. The more Soviet émigrés there are, the more family and friends are likely to follow them.

There is reason to believe that emigration will increase if the Soviet leaders decide to try to improve relations with the existing American administration. Even if not, the potential for resuming a high level of emigration is there, and in the right political conditions, and with enough pressure from the West, that potential can be realized. Resettlement should therefore remain an item on the agenda of the American-Jewish community for the foreseeable future.

8. Aspects of Integrating Soviet-Jewish Immigrants in America: Attitudes of American Jewry Toward the Recent Immigration

Stephen C. Feinstein

The emigration of Soviet Jews to the United States is no longer regarded as a short-term episode. Nonetheless, there continue to be serious problems in many communities over the question of cultivating the Jewish bond, or as it has been called, the "Judaizing" of the immigrants. In fact, this particular issue has begun to grow as a fundamental question in many American-Jewish communities where the influx of newcomers may make them between 3 percent and possibly up to 5 percent of the total Jewish population. The basic question, of course, is whether Soviet newcomers, who had had minimal contact with the Jewish religious and social experience as understood in an American context, will have the interest and determination to remain Jews once they are in America. Certainly this is not a new issue; immigrants who came to the United States more than a hundred years ago grappled with the same question. Was America to be defined as the "golden land" or the "unkosher land"? Did not America, in retrospect, present the possibility of equality through assimilation? But did not America also offer the possibility for Jews to forget or reject their traditions, religion, and nation? These difficult issues, valid a century ago, are still very much alive in identifying some of the contemporary difficulties between Soviet newcomers and American Jews.

The beginning of the Soviet-Jewish immigration in 1973 caused a certain amount of enthusiasm on the part of American Jews who viewed very positively the prospect of newcomers adding strength and vitality to their community. Americans soon found out, however, that Soviet Jews were not really Jews in the same sense as American Jews perceived themselves. While strong in national identity and possessing a sense of Jewishness arising out of Soviet anti-Semitism and varying levels of oppression, Soviet-Jewish newcomers were rarely concerned with manifestations of Jewishness as a primary goal in their new American homeland. The honeymoon between American and Soviet Jews was over by 1980. Many American Jews, including community leaders who presumably possessed a greater depth of understanding about the Soviet Jewry issue, began asking hard questions relating to the lack of bonding between newcomers and American Jewish life and institutions. While scholarly studies have made it clear that Soviet Jews are culturally Russian,[1] the implications of this finding have yet to seep down into the American-Jewish community, and perceptions persist that a problem exists because of the failure of newcomers to become open participants in the cultural and religious structures made available to them in the United States.

With this problem in mind, the United Jewish Fund and Council (UJFC) of St. Paul, Minnesota, in August 1980 authorized the beginning of a twofold project designed (1) to provide information that might better define both the Soviet newcomers' attitudes and knowledge and (2) to find out what the native Jewish community felt about the immigration. The project envisioned two surveys. The first was to gather information with the ultimate aim of getting newcomers more involved in community life. This was done by establishing a questionnaire that would provide the basis for assessing newcomers' attitudes toward America generally and toward the Jewish community in particular to determine modalities of involvement that would be appropriate to community interests. The second survey was to question members of the American-Jewish community to determine what they knew and felt about the recent immigration. This was a project quite appropriate to small and moderate-sized Jewish communities characterized by close and well-defined community relationships. It was, however, an approach not viable in larger communities because of the complexity and heterogeneity of Jewish life and values found in such places. Certainly, it was understood at the outset of the study that American Jews and Jewish values are difficult to define, which in turn might produce all sorts of difficulties in evaluating information. However, the character of the St. Paul community, with a small population of 7,500 Jews having a very high rate of synagogue affiliation and high involvement with the fate of Israel, was viewed as acceptable for this type of study.

The community survey was designed to obtain information in three specific categories: Jewish community knowledge about Soviet immigration; community contact with the Soviet-Jewish immigrants; and community attitudes toward integration and resettlement of immigrants. Respondent information also was requested for age, marital status, sex, income, place of birth (St. Paul, "other city in Minnesota," "another state," or "another country"), synagogue affiliation, and Jewish organizational affiliation. This basic respondent information was used for cross-referencing and cross-tabulating the various answers.

There are two varieties of the community survey. The first, designed as a trial run, was composed of twenty questions and was administered by telephone to every twentieth person on the UJFC membership list. One hundred and twenty-two people replied to questions from this survey. The second variant of the survey was reduced to nineteen questions and was mailed out to two thousand people on the UJFC list. Five hundred and sixty-five responses were received, or a bit more than 28 percent.

The results of this survey provided information that may prove useful to various Jewish organizations in educating the Jewish public about the mechanics of the Soviet Jewry movement and resettlement process. One thing that became clear as the results were tabulated, for example, was the fact that while the

Soviet Jewry movement was more than ten years old, and although there had been a more or less continuous barrage of information toward the community on Soviet-Jewish issues, the local community indeed may have been taking the movement for granted during the last several years. Thus, most of the respondents did not know how many Soviet-Jewish newcomers had been resettled in their own community. The number that guessed the closest to the actual figure of three hundred newcomers represented only 22.8 percent of the sample. In terms of exposure to background information on the Soviet Jewry movement, 57 percent of those polled indicated that they had listened to a speaker on the Soviet Jewry issue. Despite a high percentage in this category, it was judged lower than anticipated relative to other factors in the community that should have been an impetus for greater contact. It was thought that the high synagogue affiliation of St. Paul Jews would have provided greater exposure to the Soviet Jewry issue, as this has been a major agenda item in most synagogues. But that did not appear to be the case.

Another question that might fall into the background category was whether or not Soviet-Jewish immigrants should go to Israel rather than to the United States. Given the intensity of this debate among major Jewish communal leaders and institutions during the past several years, results were expected indicating a preference for newcomers to settle in Israel. This was not the case in the survey. Only 15 percent of the respondents "strongly agreed" that Soviet Jews should go to Israel, and only 14 percent "agreed," making a total of 29 percent in the agreement category. However, 40 percent of those polled "disagreed," and 10 percent "strongly disagreed," making a total of 50 percent in the "disagreement" category. The remaining 19 percent of respondents were undecided. These responses were especially interesting as there had been much public talk and editorial opinion in local Jewish newspapers about the problems for Israel created by Soviet immigrants who opt for America, about the financial burden that Soviet immigrants were imposing on local resettlement services, and about the material and identity problems they faced in the United States. These issues, however, did not seem to be significant in the answer pattern for this question.

In terms of assessing why Soviet Jews have left the Soviet Union, St. Paul Jews seemed to have a realistic grip on the rationale of Soviet emigration. Fifty percent of the respondents indicated "political alienation" as a factor for emigrating, 43 percent indicated "education discrimination," 40 percent "desire for economic improvement," and 25 percent "concern for the future of their children." Surprisingly, only 15 percent indicated that anti-Semitism was a major reason for Jews leaving the Soviet Union, although all of the other answers do have some relationship to this response.

In evaluating the responses relating to familiarity with the resettlement process, 74 percent of the community members indicated awareness of the Jewish Family Service and Jewish Vocational Service efforts. Sixty-one percent of those polled were familiar with the activities of the St. Paul Jewish Community Center to attract immigrants (newcomers are given a one-year free membership plus invitations to come to special socialization programs), and 71 percent were aware of the host family program sponsored by the Jewish Family Service.

The host family program was adopted several years ago in St. Paul as a means of facilitating the immigrant's adaptation to American life. A host family is assigned to each immigrant family and, from the date of arrival, teaches the newcomers about the basics of American and Minnesota life and is a friend and potential confidant during the initial process of resettlement. However, though almost three-fourths of those polled were familiar with the host family program, only 8.5 percent had participated in it. This finding suggests one of the ongoing difficulties in the Soviet immigrant absorption process. In almost all cases the host family program has proved to be of substantial value in aiding the absorption of Soviet newcomers. However, in the case of St. Paul (and in neighboring Minneapolis) there has been a shortage of volunteer families to serve in this capacity.

The frequency of meetings between Soviet newcomers and St. Paul Jews was another factor judged to be significant in understanding and ultimately accepting Jewish immigrants in the community. The results of questions in this area suggested the problem of minimal contacts between newcomers and local Jewish residents. For example, 35 percent of those polled indicated they "hardly ever" came in contact with a Soviet newcomer and 14 percent "never," giving a total of 49 percent in these combined categories. Only 7 percent of the St. Paul sample saw newcomers on a "daily" basis, 27 percent on a "weekly" basis, and 14.5 percent on a "monthly" basis. Sixty-four percent of the native Jewish population had met and talked with a Soviet immigrant sometime during the past seven years. But a much smaller percentage actually had become involved with newcomers. Only 34 percent indicated that they had helped a newcomer with a problem, almost 19 percent had invited a Soviet immigrant to their home for a meal, 11 percent had taken a newcomer to synagogue, and 28 percent had become friends with an immigrant.

A debatable issue at stake here, of course, is whether or not one should expect more from a host community. In the St. Paul study there were only three hundred Soviet immigrants in a Jewish community of 7,500. Not every newcomer could be expected to make sufficient American friends to cover an entire community for survey purposes.

The questions and responses dealing with attitudes toward Soviet immigration, however, seemed to indicate that difficulties were perceived by local American Jews. For example, 66 percent of those who responded felt that immigrants had difficulty interacting with the local Jewish community; only 12 percent felt the opposite. On the other hand, close to 39 percent felt that newcomers were eager to become involved with Jewish life when they arrived in America, with 34 percent in disagreement, and 24 percent undecided on the issue. This seemed to indicate some discrepancy between the expectation level and reality. Respondents seemed to feel that immigrants were not taking much initiative in becoming involved in Jewish organizations (18 percent "agreed" that immigrants had become involved with Jewish organizations). In fact, there was a reasonable perception that Jewish newcomers might eventually be lost to the community as Jews. The statement, "There is a danger that recent Soviet-Jewish immigrants may be lost as Jews to the community," produced these responses:

Strongly agree	74	13%
Agree	211	37
Disagree	108	19
Strongly disagree	14	3
Undecided	148	26

Thus, 50 percent of the respondents agreed with the statement generally, while 22 percent disagreed, and 26 percent were undecided. This statistic alone appears to point to a common perception among the native Jewish population that there is insufficient fabric in immigrant life to guarantee the maintenance of Jewish culture. However, it should be pointed out that the immigrants themselves, in discussions and in some of the preliminary statistical data revealed in a concurrent survey of the newcomers, thought this response was erroneous. It also should be recognized that there is an implicit danger in this question, as it fails to establish clear criteria for defining "Jewishness." Nor does it measure religiosity or Jewish national identity among the respondents, although other questions in the survey did evoke answers regarding synagogue affiliation, participation in Jewish communal agencies' boards, and whether or not the respondents were contributors to the annual campaign. But the significant number of answers falling into the "agree" category on this question does seem to indicate some definite anxieties on the part of American Jews concerning Jewishness among Soviet newcomers.

Despite difficulties on those questions that dealt with personal contacts and emigration to Israel, the St. Paul sample seemed generally to accept the Soviet newcomers as well as the financial outlays necessitated for the support of the community social service network. Sixty-nine percent of the respondents felt that resettlement should be financed with Jewish charitable funds, and 83 percent believed that newcomers should have free access to Jewish schools and the community center until they became financially independent. Alternately, 94 percent expected that immigrants would become full members of the Jewish community as indicated by their contributing money to the United Jewish Fund and Council in the future. The sample responded in the following ways to the statement, "Soviet-Jewish immigrants should be solicited for charitable contributions to the United Jewish Fund and Council when they become financially independent":

Strongly agree	286	51%
Agree	252	45
Disagree	7	1
Strongly disagree	0	0
Undecided	21	4

A series of cross-tabulations were made to gain an additional profile of the St. Paul Jewish community in regard to age, sex, income, place of birth, and differences in attitudes attributable to religious (synagogue) affiliation. Some interesting and perhaps useful facts materialized from these data.

One item of interest was the range of American Jews who had contact with Soviet newcomers. The survey revealed that the group with the greatest contact on a daily basis were those over the age of sixty (10.16 percent of that age group), representing 46 percent of those having contact on a daily basis. The greatest amount of contact on a weekly basis occurred in the 46 to 59 age group. Thirty-one percent of that group indicated weekly contact. The group with the highest contact on a monthly basis was the 19 to 29 age group, with 17 percent of that group indicating contact. Each of these three percentage figures was higher than the average in the basic questionnaire, where only 7 percent of the total sample had daily contact, 27 percent weekly contact, and 14.5 percent monthly contact. The only category where there was consistency among age groups was the response of "hardly ever" to seeing an immigrant. There all categories from 19 to 60 years indicated a response in the range of 33 percent to 37 percent of the respective age group.

The survey also sought information on which groups actually had talked to immigrants and which of them had helped an immigrant with a problem. Both questions suggest a relationship of higher intensity than simple contact. The responses to the question of "met and talked with a Soviet-Jewish immigrant" indicated that the 35 to 45 age group had the highest contact and the over-60 age group the lowest, although the latter group still had a respectable figure of 50.8 percent contact. The 30 to 45 age group again prevailed when it came to helping an immigrant with a problem, although indicators of contact dropped from the 70 percent range for both the 30 to 45 and 46 to 59 age groups in talking with immigrants to the 39–43 percentage level of helping them.

The actual percentage of the St. Paul sample that became friends with Soviet newcomers was surprisingly high (28 percent), given the small number of newcomers relative to the community size. There was little differentiation from this percentage by age groups.

In regard to income, respondents with the highest rates of contact with immigrants (15 percent) had incomes of less than $15,000 per year; the lowest rate of contact (2.27 percent) occurred in families earning between $36,000 and $39,000 per year. Families with incomes of less than $15,000 also had the highest rate of weekly contact (32 percent), while families with incomes over $50,000 had the lowest weekly contact rate (19.5 percent). Still, the majority of respondents in most income groups stated that they "hardly ever" had contact with the immigrants. The only exception was the group under $15,000 income where 5.47 percent responded that they "hardly ever" came in contact with immigrants. There was some initial belief that those in the category under $15,000 income with high contact with newcomers might be Orthodox Jews. However, statistics indicated that this group was largely made up of Conservative Jews.

That the highest percentage of those having "daily contact" also would fit into the less than $15,000 earnings category takes on greater meaning when related back to the fact that the group with the greatest contact on a "daily" basis was that over 60 years of age. Since these people have retirement income that might fall into the below $15,000 category, it would seem that we are identifying the same group in both instances. This also reflects the fact that in the St. Paul community there has been a more visible interaction between retirees and newcomers. Those American Jews in the lower income brackets, presumably a large section of whom are retirees, indicated that they had become friends with Soviet-Jewish immigrants.

Those members of the St. Paul sample with incomes under $15,000 per year had the highest incidence of friendship with immigrants (34 percent), while those with the highest income had the lowest number of friendships (20.33 percent). Nevertheless, the majority of respondents in each category had not established friendships with newcomers.

The income group with the highest incidence of helping an immigrant with a problem was the $36,000–$49,000 group (43.18 percent). This figure was unexpected in one sense, as it presumably indicates high interaction between newcomers and an American group involved highly in its own work or professions, as indicated by income. However, this statistic also may be perceived as being logical, as that income group, possibly representing a managerial class, might be more likely to help newcomers. In this context, problems of newcomers should probably be read as job-related problems.

The most interesting information obtained in the survey related to place of birth of the respondents and their participation in the absorption process of newcomers. Native St. Paulites had less exposure to the issues and were the least receptive to the newcomers' presence than were non-natives. For example, 61 percent of those born in another country, 61.9 percent of those born in another state, and 59.26 percent of those born in another part of Minnesota had listened to speakers on Soviet Jewry, compared with 53.3 percent for St. Paul natives.

A remarkably high 50.6 percnt of those respondents who were born in another country had become friends with Soviet newcomers. This statistic reflects the shared immigrant experience and often a common use of Yiddish or Russian by these groups. Native St. Paulites placed last in this category, with only 21 percent having become friends with Soviet newcomers. Seventy-one percent of those born in another country had at least met new immigrants, while only 58 percent of native St. Paulites had done so. Native St. Paulites also placed last in the area of helping newcomers. Respondents born outside the United States saw newcomers on a more frequent basis in the daily, weekly, and monthly categories and had a very low incidence of "hardly ever" coming into contact with newcomers. Native St. Paulites also were least hospitable toward newcomers insofar as they were lowest (13.6 percent) in the percentage of having had a newcomer to dinner. In contrast, those from another country finished first, with 33.7 percent indicating they invited immigrants over to dinner.

Finally, although those born on foreign shores had established a high level of communication with Soviet newcomers, a majority felt the Soviet-Jewish immigrants would be better off in Israel. Fifty-three percent of those born in another country agreed that Soviet newcomers should go to Israel, while only 25 percent of native St. Paulites fell into the same category. While this statistic might indicate that the native St. Paulites would welcome newcomers because of their presumed preference to have these people in America rather than Israel, their quantitative and qualitative support on a volunteer basis for immigrants in the community indicated otherwise. Ironically, the group that gave the most support to newcomers felt that they would be better off in Israel.

Using sex as a basis for dividing the respondents, the statistics yielded information that may be summarized quickly. Women had greater contact with Soviet immigrants than men on a daily basis (9.7 percent of women to 5.4 percent of men) as well as a weekly basis (29.5 percent to 24.6 percent), although men indicated a higher level of contact on a monthly basis (16.9 percent vs. 11.3 percent). One might conclude, of course, that contact beyond a weekly frequency has little effect on the absorption process for the immigrant. More men than women, however, helped newcomers with a problem (37.7 percent vs. 29 percent). More women than men felt that newcomers were not being successfully integrated into local Jewish organizations (23 percent vs. 12 percent). More men than women (31 percent vs. 26 percent) felt that immigrants from the USSR should go to Israel rather than the United States, but both sexes felt that immigrants were in danger of being lost as Jews in the American experience (49 percent women, 50 percent men). Sex, therefore, appeared to be a minor factor in assessing community attitudes toward newcomers.

Another way of evaluating the community response toward the new immigration was by synagogue affiliation. This was a difficult task, mainly because there are only four large congregations in St. Paul, with the fifth synagogue being a small, informal congregation. Furthermore, the survey, by random method, evoked more responses from members of the Conservative congregations than from the Orthodox or Reform. Nevertheless, some generalizations from the data might be useful as a basis for future research.

The highest level of exposure (64 percent) of synagogue members to a speaker on Soviet Jewry occurred in a Reform congregation. This was followed by a Conservative synagogue (58.9 percent) and an Orthodox congregation (57.8 percent). All five congregations indicated more than 50 percent on this question, but none scored over 65 percent. Those who belonged to no congregation (15 percent of the sample) indicated a lower exposure to speakers on the Soviet Jewry issue (42 percent) and to other questions that dealt with Soviet immigration absorption problems. Members of the Orthodox congregation most commonly reported that they had helped an immigrant with a problem (57.8

percent). Only 32 percent of the Reform congregation, which had the highest exposure to speakers on Soviet Jewry, indicated that they had helped with immigrant problems. The Conservative congregation was in the middle on this question (with 36 percent). Only 23 percent of those without congregational affiliation reported helping an immigrant with a problem. Members of the Orthodox congregation appeared more idealistic about the intentions of the newcomers, possibly because of their higher level of involvement with them. Sixty-two percent of the Orthodox congregants believed that newcomers were eager to become involved in Jewish life in America, compared wth only 32 percent of the Reform congregation and 27 percent of the Conservative congregation. A majority of all congregants felt that Soviet immigrants might be lost as Jews in America, while only 37 percent of those without congregational affiliation shared this opinion.

Similarly, members of Jewish organizations were stronger in their perceptions about the eagerness of immigrants to become involved in Jewish life. Thirty-four percent of those who belonged to organizations felt this eagerness among immigrants vs. 42 percent of nonorganizational members. Members of organizations also had a higher frequency of contact with newcomers than did nonmembers. The former saw newcomers twice as often on a daily basis and 50 percent more often on a weekly basis than did nonmembers. Only 10.5 percent of those who belonged to organizations never saw an immigrant, compared with 20.6 percent of those who did not belong. When going beyond frequency of contact to friendship levels, however, there was no significant difference between the responses of members of organizations and nonmembers. Almost 29 percent of the members indicated they had made friendships with Soviet immigrants compared with 26 percent of nonmembers. When probed on the issue of whether or not immigrants should go to Israel (rather than the United States), more members of organizations (34 percent) responded positively than did nonmembers (17 percent).

Members of organizations also expressed greater anxieties about the future "Jewishness" of Soviet immigrants. When asked if Soviet newcomers might be "lost as Jews to the community," 53 percent of organization members responded positively (15.6 percent strongly), while only 43 percent of nonmembers agreed with the statement (7.6 percent strongly). This response reflects perhaps the larger problem in the Jewish community today regarding the definition of Jewishness. Obviously, those who belong to organizations assume that their membership is in some way an important manifestation of Jewishness. On the other hand, nonmembers may have a more casual approach to their Judaism, in which membership in organizations or synagogues is not a requirement of being a Jew. Having a casual attitude themselves, they perhaps expect newcomers to survive culturally in the same way during the absorption process.

The information in this report represents only half of the materials to be collected for the St. Paul Soviet immigrant project. The statistics from the interviews with the newcomers themselves provide the second part of the greater project, which taken together with the information from the community survey should provide ample material for rethinking or improving the absorption process in the St. Paul community.

There are many general statements that can be made as a result of examining the preliminary information in the community survey, which may form the basis of an active community policy. One item that came out very clearly was the substantial need for increased community exposure to the Soviet Jewry issue itself as well as to the realities of the absorption process. This appears to be a task that can be carried out by the Minnesota Action Committee on Soviet Jewry, as well as by the Jewish Family Service and Jewish Vocational Service.

While the community seemed to be aware of the presence of Soviet-Jewish newcomers, the immigration seemed to have taken on the characteristics of business as usual, thus leading many community members to assume that all problems were being handled successfully by the responsible professional agencies or synagogues. This, in reality, was not the case. Indeed, experience in the Twin Cities area as well as in other cities seems to indicate that the most successful absorption results not from agency outreach, but from personal contacts and guidance. One very crucial aspect of this finding is to make the local St. Paul community aware of how closed its native-born population is to outsiders. That native St. Paulites placed last in the questions dealing with hospitality and friendships is significant in predicting the success or failure of local programs. An educational campaign of high intensity designed to convey the difficulties experienced by Soviet immigrants in the socialization process might break down some of the barriers to acceptance in the native community. There also must be a concerted effort to remove some of the stereotyping about Soviet newcomers and to make it clear that they are not any less Jewish than native St. Paul Jews.

That many St. Paul Jews did not come in contact with Soviet immigrants may not be the fault of the community but may be linked to reclusive social tendencies of the immigrants themselves. While a normal state of things cannot be established overnight, community sponsorship of events that make efforts to bring immigrants and local community members together should be enhanced. Quite clearly, some arrangements should be made for younger community members to meet with immigrants on a more frequent basis. Synagogue involvement in resettlement also needs improvement, especially in the area of establishing linkages with newcomers.

In short, the survey indicated that the Jewish community of St. Paul was aware of the Soviet Jewry issue and of the problems faced by the new immigrants. Nonetheless, it also is clear that more effort needs to be expended by the community—and by the newcomers—to make the integration of the Soviet-Jewish immigrants into the St. Paul community a more successful one.

9. Adaptation and Acculturation of Soviet Jews in the United States: A Preliminary Analysis

Ilya I. Levkov

During the 1960s and early 1970s American Jews were preoccupied with Soviet anti-Semiitism and the effort to help Soviet Jews leave the USSR. When the emigrating Soviet Jews chose increasingly to come to the United States instead of Israel, however, American Jews were ill-prepared for their absorption, particularly since no studies had been made about the attitudes and perceptions of the emigrating Soviet Jews. This analysis, based on an extensive computer-coded survey of Soviet-Jewish émigrés living throughout the United States, is a first step toward understanding the émigrés. Given the length of the study, only a section of it is presented here.[1]

Methodology, Scope, and Structure of the Sample

This analysis of Soviet-Jewish acculturation in the United States is based upon a field survey conducted among Soviet émigrés by use of a questionnaire. A questionnaire was used in lieu of personal interviews for three reasons: it achieved anonymity, which is a highly important element in surveying former Soviet citizens; it eliminated subjective interpretations by the interviewer; and it made possible a national sample within a limited budget.[2]

From a total of approximately twenty thousand Soviet-Jewish immigrant households, a pool of five thousand households was compiled from the mailing lists of several Russian-language newspapers and journals. From this list, five hundred households were selected at random and mailed a detailed questionnaire containing 216 questions.

The primary goal was to analyze the impact of the American environment upon a group of individuals whose ideas, values, and perceptions about the United States had developed in the environment of a closed society, the Soviet Union.

Demographic and Professional Structure of the Group

The response rate to the questionnaire was 26 percent (130 out of 500). This comparatively high degree of response refutes the common assumption that Soviet émigrés are deeply suspicious of authority when it comes to replying

Table 9.1. Ages of the emigrants

Age group	19-30	31-40	41-50	51-65	66-83
Men	11	24	22	33	40
Women	11	17	20	33	25

to a detailed questionnaire. Responses from men numbered 105; from women, twenty-one. The bulk of the respondents (eighty-eight) resided in five major cities: New York (fifty), Chicago (thirteen), Los Angeles (eleven), San Francisco (nine), and Boston (five). The remaining forty-two resided in thirty-eight cities from twenty-nine states. This broad geographical base constitutes a national sample of newly arrived émigrés.

Of the respondents, 110 were married, ten were single, four were divorced, one was engaged, two were widows, and two widowers. The age groups of the respondents are given in table 9.1.

Cities of Origin

A majority of respondents (seventy-seven) came from cities in the Ukraine: Kiev (thirty-four), Kharkov (seven), Odessa (thirty-one), and Lvov (five). The second largest group came from cities in the Russian Republic of the USSR: Leningrad (fifteen) and Moscow (thirteen). Seven came from Baltic cities: Riga (five), Tallin (one), and Vilnius (one). Minsk and Tashkent accounted for four immigrants each; Kishinev and Chernovtsy for three each. There were 119 respondents from heartland Russia, including Minsk and the Ukraine. Thus, the sample represents that part of Soviet Jewry which bore the brunt of the repression of the Soviet regime from its beginning in 1917.

The educational level of the respondents was as follows:

University (with degree)	71.5%
University (without degree)	3.7
High School	2.8
Vocational high school	12.8
Elementary	8.2

This corresponds to the generally high level of education among Soviet Jews.

Professional Structure

A similar trend is apparent in the distribution of the professions. The majority of the male respondents (sixty-seven) were technically skilled, forty-five were engineers, eight technicians, and fourteen vocational workers. Among the others were seven economists, six bookkeepers, five physicians, three watch repairmen, two lawyers, one chemistry professor, three Russian-language teachers, and two photographers. The professional structure of women paralleled that of men:

Table 9.2. Amount of the emigrants' salary and the number of people working under their supervision

Monthly earnings in rubles	99	100–150	151–200	201–250	251–350	350+
Percentage of respondents	8.3	30.2	23.9	25.6	8.3	3.7
Number of people under their supervision	—	6	12	25	180	—

four engineers, four bookkeepers, three teachers, two economists, two technicians, one nurse, one worker, one chemist, and one designer.

The professions—and therefore the social structure—comprised in this sample represent a microcosm of Soviet Jewry. The only under-represented professions were musicians (there was only one) and journalists.

The respective lengths of time that the respondents have lived in the United States are as follows:

Up to 1 year	6.2%
2 years	39.8
3 years	21.2
4 years	14.2
5 years	7.1
6 years	7.1
7 to 9 years	4.4

Thus, 85 percent of the households have lived from two to four years in the United States.

Only 38.5 percent of the respondents earned 150 rubles or less (which is average for Soviet citizens) while living in the USSR, while 61.5 percent earned more (see table 9.2). There was a clear difference between the earning capacity of men and women. Only 15.8 percent of women respondents earned about 170 rubles per month. They were mechanical engineers from Moscow and Minsk with thirty years of experience. The majority of women earned an average of 128 rubles per month, whereas the average for men was 195. It is interesting to note that women, for the most part professionals, were not in supervisory or management positions, which partly explains the disparity in earning power.

Socioeconomic Status of the Émigrés

The socioeconomic aspects of the emigrants' background have a significant effect on their problems of expectation and adaptation to their new environment. To place this group within the Soviet scale of "achievers," the goods they acquired with their earnings must be described. There are three standard consumer goals in the Soviet Union: a spacious apartment, urban (rather than suburban) residence, and an automobile.

Forty-two families lived in the USSR in apartments of 300 square feet or less; fifty in apartments of less than 500 square feet, and only twelve in apartments of 500–620 square feet. The majority of the families (one hundred) resided in city centers, and only thirty families lived in the suburbs. The average size of their apartments was above the standard for an average Soviet family residing in such central cities as Moscow, Leningrad, and Kiev. However, the group that lived in the suburbs does not differ from the rest in terms of occupational structure or income, which averaged 170 rubles per month.

Of 130 respondents 20.8 percent owned a car in the Soviet Union. This is an unusually high percentage of car owners for any Soviet social/professional group other than the high-ranking party elite. It is interesting to consider the car models that the respondents owned. Over 55 percent owned a Zhiguly (Fiat) or a Volga, the best Soviet cars. The concentration of car owners was 22.2 percent in Odessa and Kiev, 14.8 percent in Leningrad, and 7.4 percent in Moscow, Minsk, and Tashkent.

These data illustrate that Soviet Jews belong to the Soviet upper-middle class. Had respondents also belonged to the Communist party, their standard of living would have been much higher. In any case it is safe to conclude that the immigration of the Soviet upper-middle class to the United States cannot be explained only in terms of physical survival. What then were the forces that compelled this group to uproot itself and embark upon a journey to an unfamiliar country?

Political/Social Setting Surrounding the Decision to Emigrate

In response to the question of which person initiated the move to emigrate, we received the following answers:

Husband	24.0%
Wife	16.3
Husband and wife	11.6
Children	22.4
All	10.8
Children and grandparents	1.6
Grandparents	0.8
Husband and children	6.2
Wife and children	3.1
Husband and grandparents	0.8
Wife and grandparents	1.6
Relatives in United States	0.8

The data reveal that the number of husbands and wives who initiated emigration (51.9 percent) is more than double the number of offspring initiators (22.4 percent). Thus, the middle generation, born in the Soviet Union and carrying the major burden of emigration, decided to undertake the challenge. Since the average age of the parents whose offspring initiated the emigration process was 65.6 years, the offspring were 35 to 40 years old when they chose to move. Four elements characterize the older group of parents: (1) Almost 50 percent had completed high school or vocational school. (2) They appeared to have heeded their university-educated children who deemed the risk to be acceptable. (3) They were leaving their position as retired people and were familiar with the U.S. social-welfare system. (4) None of them were from Moscow.

The average age of husbands who initiated emigration was 45 years and of wives, 48 years. It is important to note that the earning capacity of those husbands who initiated emigration was very high—326 rubles per month. The average income of men in our sample was 195 rubles per month. Although they had achieved the upper limits of socioeconomic status in the USSR, and thus had the most to lose, initiator husbands were achievers and, consequently, probably assumed they also would be effective providers in America.

Eighty-seven percent of respondents received permission to emigrate on their first application. The longest waiting period for a visa (eleven years, from 1969 to 1980) occurred not in the case of an expert who possessed state secrets, but of a simple worker from Riga.

The respondents were asked the length of time they had to wait for an exit visa. Their answers broke down in this fashion:

1 month	3.9%
2	16.5
3	22.8
4	15.7
5	11.0
6	10.2
7	5.5
8	4.7
9	1.6
10	3.1
11	1.6
12	0.8
15	0.8
18	0.8
20	0.8

Close to 60 percent of respondents received visas within four months, 80 percent within six months, and 90 percent within eight months. Compared with early stages of Jewish emigration from the Soviet Union, when this process took years, these time periods constitute relatively rapid responses.

One measure employed by Soviet authorities to dissuade people from applying for an emigration visa is to deny their incomes by instantly firing them from their jobs. In our sample the total percentage of those who were fired was 43.4 percent. The percentage of people who did not undergo this process was 43.5 percent (including the forcibly retired and demoted).

When asked whether they were fired from their jobs upon submitting a visa application, our sample responded in the following percentages:

Fired	24.8%
Left myself	13.1
Wife fired	11.0
Children fired	7.6
Was retired	4.8
Not fired	35.9
Demoted or asked to retire	2.8

It is nearly impossible to discern the dominant factor in the decision to fire someone under these circumstances. Although, at this point, the Soviet executives did not have to furnish the applicant with the infamous character list, a political/social/professional evaluation of the individual that can be used against him or her, the immediate superiors still preferred to have fewer dropouts from the ranks of their workers. Therefore, many were fired as a result of a decision undertaken by their immediate superiors. This condition also made it possible for applicants to make their own calculations, in the light of their familiarity with superiors and previous decisions in similar cases. The decision of 13.1 percent was to leave their jobs prior to filing an application for an exit visa.

Let us now turn to the social environment of the applicants and examine the role it played in the development of their decision to emigrate.

The respondents were asked about the level of support from friends on the decision to emigrate, resulting in these percentages:

Supported	63.8%
Divided	33.1
Opposed	1.5
Did not tell friends	0.8
Only told Jews	0.8

It seems that the majority of the respondents had cultivated a circle of friends who shared their views concerning the Soviet regime, the Soviet quality of life, and the prospects of life in the United States, and that these people wholeheartedly supported the decision to emigrate. Thus, it seems that the social environment was not hostile to the idea of leaving the Soviet homeland for a Western nation. This outlook would have been highly unusual as recently as twelve years ago, which means there was only a limited risk to the respondents of being ostracized by their social circle for undertaking this political decision.

The final element that sheds light on the pattern of the decision-making process to emigrate was the availability of information about the hazards of life abroad that was received from immediate family members who already lived abroad. Forty percent of the entire sample had relatives in the United States and Canada and thus probably had direct, although self-censored, information concerning the hazards and rewards of life in the West. The 16.2 percent whose relatives had recently emigrated to Israel chose nonetheless to go to the United States.

Of the total sample, 50 percent of the respondents had relatives living abroad at the time of their visa application. These were the percentages for the various countries where their relatives resided:

United States	31.5%
Israel	10.0
Both the U.S. and Israel	6.2
Canada	2.3

"Push" and "Pull" Factors Involved in the Decision to Emigrate

The major reasons for the respondents' immigration to the United States were these:

Provide children with a higher (college) education	20.8%
Professional advancement	5.4
To live in a free country	88.5
To be reunited with relatives	23.1
To improve standard of living	43.8
Freedom to travel abroad	36.9
Soviet anti-Semitism	86.9
Provide children with Jewish education	23.8

Respondents listed two major reasons that drove them from the Soviet Union: the desire to live in a free country (88.5 percent) and anti-Semitism (86.9 percent). Other reasons included economic improvement (43.8 percent) and freedom to travel abroad (36.9 percent).

Although 50 percent of the sample had relatives abroad, less than half of these (23.1 percent) stated that their primary reason for emigrating was to be reunited with their families. The relatively low number of people who stated that their emigration was motivated by a desire to assure their children a higher education (20.8 percent) perhaps may be explained by the fact that some had children over the age of twenty-two. Otherwise the low figure would be surprising since it has become more and more difficult for Jewish youngsters to enter universities in the Soviet Union. This low number was surpassed by the group who desired to provide their children with a Jewish education (23.8 percent), which is prohibited in the Soviet Union. The reason least often cited for emigrating (5.4 percent) was to promote professional careers. Respondents in this category included a salesperson, a photographer, a chemical engineer, an electrician, a physician, a violinist, and a bookkeeper.

Table 9.3 offers an overall map of the reasons for emigration. The lowest percentage of the respondents who emigrated because of Soviet anti-Semitism was registered in Riga (60 percent), the second lowest in Leningrad (80 percent). This may be the result of greater contact with Western tourists and businessmen in these cities. However, it is more difficult to come up with an explanation as to why all of the respondents from Tashkent and Lvov cited anti-Semitism, but only 83.3 percent in Odessa and Kharkov did so.

A desire for an increased standard of living was cited as a reason for emigration by 75 percent of the respondents from Minsk and Tashkent. This figure was twice the national average. Those from Minsk, Riga, and Tashkent stated that they had no motivating goal to expand their professional careers. The second lowest motivational factor in emigration to the United States (5.7 percent) was the desire to establish a successful business. Most of those who were motivated to emigrate for this reason came from Moscow (16.7 percent) and Kiev (9.4 percent). People from Leningrad, Minsk, Lvov, Riga, and Tashkent expressed no such desire at all.

Only 3.1 percent of the respondents expressed the desire to live an American style of life (from Lvov, Kiev, and Leningrad only). The most common motivation for emigration to the United States was the desire to live in a free country (82.3 percent) and to feel free as a Jew (79.2 percent). These reasons, however, are not unique to Soviet emigrants going to the United States. Therefore, these replies are somewhat vague about the primary motivations of Soviet Jews who chose to emigrate to the United States. After all, there are several free countries that would be ready to receive such a highly skilled labor force. Should the desire to "feel free as a Jew" be accepted at face value, it would also leave an important question unanswered. Why, with such a desire, didn't respondents choose Israel as a haven from Soviet anti-Semitism? Their limited association with Jewish life in America (whether institutionally or in another form once having settled in the United States), as their responses indicate, adds additional weight to this question.

To further analyze the respondents' motivations for emigrating to the United States, it is necessary to analyze numerous facets of their cultural and political adaptation to actual life in the United States.

The Process of Employment in the United States

The working pool of the 130 families breaks down into these categories:

Working	58.3%
Retired with supplemental security income	27.5
Unemployed	5.8
Study (language and professional)	6.7
Welfare	1.7

Table 9.3. Reasons given for emigration, by national sample and cities (in percentages)

	Provide a higher education for children	Professional advancement	Live in a free country	Reunited with relatives	Improve standard of living	Freedom to travel abroad	Soviet anti-Semitism	Provide a Jewish education for children
National sample	20.8	5.4	88.5	23.1	43.8	36.9	86.9	23.8
Moscow	8.3	8.3	83.3	8.3	25.0	33.3	100.0	8.3
Leningrad	40.0	6.7	86.7	40.0	26.7	6.7	80.0	46.7
Minsk	25.0	—	100.0	—	25.0	50.0	100.0	25.0
Kiev	28.1	9.4	87.5	25.0	34.4	28.1	96.9	28.1
Lvov	20.0	—	80.0	20.0	80.0	40.0	100.0	20.0
Odessa	20.0	3.3	90.0	23.3	30.0	33.3	83.3	26.7
Kharkov	16.7	—	100.0	—	50.0	33.3	83.3	16.7
Riga	—	—	100.0	20.0	60.0	60.0	60.0	—
Tashkent	—	—	80.0	50.0	75.0	—	100.0	25.0

The process of finding employment demonstrates a pattern of adaptation and the ability to function in the new environment. Immigrants in our sample have found employment through the following channels:

Themselves:
   (*a*) directly   44.3%
   (*b*) via newspaper 12.9
Community   21.4
Business school   5.7
Union   1.4
Relatives/friends   11.4
Employment agency   2.9

The results point out that the overwhelming majority of the immigrants (78.6 percent) found their present employment independently, without the assistance of resettlement organizations such as the New York Association for New Americans (NYANA).

It is difficult to evaluate the quality of the professional referral systems of local Jewish organizations. However, some indication of their effectiveness can be determined by comparing the immigrants' previous professions with those found in the United States, although, given the different standards for a number of professionals in the United States, this can be only a very limited indicator.

Before analyzing this particular aspect of employment patterns, let us examine the overall picture. Out of the total working pool of respondents, 25.7 percent worked in the United States in a field different from their previous profession. The shift to another vocation occurred for a variety of reasons, including an inability to pass required examinations, limited possibilities for employment in certain professions in the United States (such as Russian-language teachers), and a shift to a lower level of a related profession.

The average income of those who work outside their profession was $9,750; the average of those working in their profession was $16,931. The average income of those referred by Jewish organizations was $11,119, 34.3 percent lower than the average income of those latter professionals who found employment without outside assistance. Over 45 percent of the respondents were satisfied with their present employment, while 54.7 percent were dissatisfied. Naturally, the general mood was higher among those who were satisfied. The highest average mood was registered among those who planned to leave their jobs to become self-employed. (The lowest mood was expressed by a physician who was employed as a sanitation man.)

Soviet immigrants have made a successful entrance into the American job market. Their average income surpasses the U.S. national average. However, they occupy the lower end of the income-level spectrum within their professions in the United States. From the upper-middle class of the USSR, the respondents, as a whole, have slid into the lower-middle class of the United States.

Table 9.4. Number of evenings per week spent by the emigrants with friends

	Number of evenings				
	1	2	3	4-6	None
Percentage of participants	27.6	27.6	16.4	8.6	19.8
Years in the United States	2.4	2.1	1.8	2.6	2.0

Social Environment and Patterns of Socializing

Socializing among the Soviet immigrants occupies the greater part of their leisure time (see table 9.4). This phenomenon continues the traditional pattern of new immigrants to America and is facilitated by a high concentration of immigrants in specific areas of major cities. As will be shown later, this "Russified" milieu reinforces itself by promoting more publications, radio and television programs, and live entertainment in the Russian language.

Over 93 percent of the friends of Soviet Jews are Soviet Jews. They frequent each other's houses. Thus, it is possible to make the claim that Soviet Jews constitute the most tightly knit sector in American Jewry. Of the remainder, 5.4 percent associate primarily with American Jews and 1.5 percent with non-Jewish Americans. This last group states that it associates with non-Jews because there are no Jews in its towns (Dover, Missouri; Appleton, Wisconsin). As we shall see later, this lack of connection to Americans in general and American Jews in particular is perceived by the immigrants as a major shortcoming in their new life.

Patterns of Absorption

The process of absorption encompasses such factors as English-language acquisition, institutional absorption, acquiring specific household items, and individual awareness of changes that have taken place in cultural, professional, and financial status, as well as in opinions about the decision to emigrate to the United States.

Extent of Previous Exposure to the English Language

Previous knowledge of the English language is a major factor facilitating the entrance of new immigrants into the American environment. It enables the immigrant to regain his status within his profession and to select his social circle. To correctly ascertain the émigrés' command of English, the following questions were asked: In the USSR did you study English in high school, university, or in special courses? How long did you formally study English in the USSR? The respondents listed these places of study:

Did not study	64.7%
High school	10.0
High school and university	14.6
University	3.8
Special courses	3.1

An absolute majority did not study English prior to their emigration, and only 21.5 percent had some exposure to the English language. The knowledge of English required at the university level in the USSR is lower than that gained through compulsory study of Spanish or French at American colleges. The respondents gave these answers for their length of study:

1–2 months	16.5%
3 months	18.3
4 months	3.7
5 months	1.8
6 months	8.3
Up to 12 months	13.7
18 months	2.8
24 months	2.8
Continuing at the time	14.6
By myself	2.8
None	14.7

The bulk of the respondents studied English from one to three months (34.8 percent) and together with the groups that studied at home by themselves (17.4 percent) and those that did not study at all (14.7 percent), they constitute the absolute majority of 66.9 percent of the entire sample.

From these results it can be deduced that the respondents' knowledge of English is limited and hinders their cultural and social integration, thus slowing the process of adaptation to the American environment. However, the most effective method of measuring their knowledge of English is by evaluating the reading materials available to them in English. Out of the entire sample 63.1 percent do not read English newspapers. The rest read local newspapers. This high percentage of nonreaders cannot be explained by a short period of settlement in the United States, since respondents averaged two and one-half years in the United States at the time of the survey.

When asked about their reading of journals, the respondents gave the following answers:

Read only Russian	39.7%
Russian and English	10.3

Table 9.5. Role of Jewish organizations in assisting the emigrants' absorption into American life (in percentages)

	Yes	No	Not sure
Understood your specific needs	80.7	15.6	3.7
Helpful	92.2	6.8	0.9
Understood your professional status	52.1	41.5	6.4
Cared enough about your family's needs	82.6	15.6	1.8
The case worker accepted and trusted your background	85.6	9.6	4.8
Should the services of these organizations be improved?	89.3	10.7	—

| Only English | 17.2 |
| None | 32.8 |

The absolute majority of respondents (72.5 percent) read either Russian journals only or no journals at all. We shall discuss the content of these materials in the section that analyzes the patterns of émigré perceptions. Here, we note that the very small segment of readers of English-language newspapers and journals suggests the existence of a gap between the respondents' previous cultural experience and their present, which hinders their acculturation and reverberates through the entire scope of their social intercourse with members of the new society.

Institutional-Organizational Dimension of Integration

A high degree of dissatisfaction concerning professional incompatibility could be expected in culturally bound professions such as law, teaching, writing, and journalism. However, 47.9 percent of those who encountered a lack of appreciation for their professional status were engineers and technicians, who actually had expected the fewest such problems (see table 9.5). Although this mood of expectation could be the source of their disappointment, other more substantive factors might be the cause. In the Soviet Union most of these engineers were already in supervisory, executive positions and consequently removed from intimate knowledge of operating industrial installations themselves. This background created high expectations of successful integration on the professional level while lowering the chances of finding an intermediate level of entry in the profession. This response demonstrates the difficulty they have encountered in recovering their previous professional status and the extent of this dissatisfaction with the institutions in charge of their absorption.

The other significant aspect relates to the statement made by the absolute majority of the respondents (89.3 percent) that the services of the institutions in charge of absorption should be improved. This high percentage who call for improvements in the functioning of the absorption institutions is almost identical with the percentage of their opinions of how understanding, helpful, caring, and kind those institutions were to them. It is obvious that this aspect sheds new light on their previous four responses concerning the degree to which assisting organizations were in fact helpful.

In the light of this finding, it is possible to conclude that the respondents' replies concerning the effectiveness of the absorption institutions were inflated. Otherwise, it is difficult to explain why almost 90 percent of them would like the services of these organizations to be improved.

Acquiring Material Things

The new immigrants within the labor market had average annual earnings of $12,500. Immigrants' patterns of material acquisition will now be examined with the intention of pinpointing the focus of their interests and desires. Judging from the high number of respondents who owned a car in the Soviet Union (20.8 percent), it was expected that they would make a car one of their first purchases. Indeed, the absolute majority of the respondents (58.5 percent) bought at least one car. This percentage was even more impressive considering that most of the respondents resided in urban centers that had large public transportation systems. This can be explained partly by the fact that ownership of a car constitutes an unquestionable symbol of success among new Soviet immigrants, not to mention the impact created when a picture of the car is sent to friends in the Soviet Union.

The type of car selected also can indicate a certain degree of identity. Therefore, a question was posed: is the car you own American-made, European, or Japanese? It was believed that if respondents looked for the most economical car, it would be Japanese. If they chose a European car, it would be a sign of familiarity (Fiats and Volkswagens were seen in the USSR), dependability, and perhaps even identification with European culture and technology and craftsmanship in particular. If they chose American-made cars, it would indicate their identification with American products. An overwhelming majority (88.9 percent) owned American-made cars, mostly Oldsmobiles, Chevrolets, and Fords. All of the respondents who owned two cars (4.2 percent) owned one made in America and one made in Japan; just 6.9 percent of the total sample owned only a Japanese car. According to our hypothesis it would appear that Soviet Jews identify with American technology even more than Americans do.

An additional effort to locate the focal point of respondents' material interests was made by asking which of the following appliances the emigrants had purchased in the United States: color television, stereo system, washing machine, dishwater, or furniture. The answers were as follows:

Color TV	69.2%
Stereo system	32.3
Washing machine	13.1
Dishwasher	7.7

Table 9.6. Comparison of the emigrants' perceptions of status in the United States and the USSR (in percentages)

Status	Higher	Equal	Lower
Professional	2.4	17.8	58.8
Cultural	19.3	25.2	55.5
Financial	70.2	17.7	12.1

Furniture	43.1
None	13.1

The absolute majority (69.2 percent) purchased a color television. The second most popular item was furniture (43.1 percent). As their responses testified, the respondents listened to the radio only in their cars. Televisions allowed them to comprehend more easily and to absorb more information. It is difficult to guess why 13.1 percent of the respondents purchased none of the listed items. Their average income ($9,700), however, was below the sample's average, as was their average time in the United States (one and one-half years).

To summarize the degree of absorption, the following question was used: How do you compare your present social, cultural, and financial status to the one you had in the USSR? Respondents were asked to mark their current status as higher, equal to, or lower than the status they enjoyed in the USSR (see table 9.6). The absolute majority of émigrés considered their present professional status and cultural position to be lower (59.8 percent and 55.5 percent, respectively) and their financial position higher (70.2 percent). With these figures about shifts in profession, cultural, and financial status in mind, we are in a better position to trace more precisely the cumulative effect of these shifts on the émigrés' total evaluation of their American experience. This seeming paradox is explained by the much higher salaries in the United States where a draftsman earns more than an engineer in the Soviet Union.

The sample of respondents offered these answers to the question, Are you pleased with your decision to emigrate to the United States?

Yes	83.3%
Very much	5.6
Not sure	3.9
No	4.8
Yes, with reservations	2.4

The absolute majority of respondents (91.3 percent) replied that they were either pleased, very pleased, or pleased with some reservations about their decision to settle in the United States. There is an additional dimension that reflects the degree of the respondents' evaluation of their move to the United States. They were asked to grade their present mood on a relative scale (of very bad, medium, good, and excellent). The responses were divided as follows: 37 percent were in an excellent mood, 31.9 percent in a good mood, 30.3 percent in a satisfactory mood, and only 0.8 percent in a very bad mood. Again, the overwhelming majority (68.9 percent) was in an excellent or good mood. This may support the conclusion that negative shifts in professional and cultural life are of secondary importance to emotional well-being, while the dominant factor is the financial situation, or it also may reflect the émigrés' happiness that they are living in a free society.

The following additional questions were asked to complete the process of determining the emigrants' feelings of well-being in the United States: Do you wish that your remaining relatives would emigrate from the Soviet Union? Would you like them to emigrate to the United States? Where the first question tries to elicit an indirect notion about the respondents' evaluation of the entire process of emigrating from the Soviet Union to the United States, the second question poses a direct inquiry that could reflect again their own evaluation of their move.

When asked whether they would recommend emigration from the USSR to their relatives, the respondents answered:

Yes	86.1%
No	3.5
Up to them	4.3
Don't know	3.5
It is impossible	2.6

An absolute majority of 86.1 percent of the respondents said they would advise their relatives to emigrate from the Soviet Union, whereas only 3.5 percent would not. Thus, it can be said that only 3.5 percent were disappointed in the change of their life-style in the United States to the degree that they would not recommend emigration to their friends and relatives.

As for recommending emigration to the United States, these answers were given:

Yes	89.5%
No	2.9
Not sure	4.8
If they decide so	1.9
Should go to Israel	0.9

As can be seen, the absolute majority of respondents (89.5 percent) said that they would advise their relatives to emigrate to the United States, a response that appears to further support the general level of their satisfaction in spite of the negative shifts and changes that took place in certain aspects of their lifestyles as a result of their own move.

Jewish Family Formation in the USSR and Its Responses to Stress in America

To shed light upon the behavior of emigrants, it is necessary to present relevant data concerning patterns of Jewish family formation in the Soviet Union, since intrafamily relations have a direct impact upon family cohesiveness and upon the ability to withstand stress. Some current hypotheses contend that parents, in order to prevent accidental intermarriage, take the initiative in introducing their children and other relatives to Jewish youngsters; and the young Jewish urban student, as a result of being denied the right to study in the major university in his native city due to anti-Semitism, is forced to apply to a less prominent university in a remote locale where he or she is enticed by local Jews to marry their daughters or sons.

The data from the questionnaire negated the first hypothesis: only 1.8 percent of couples married in the USSR were introduced by relatives; almost 31 percent were introduced by friends; and the absolute majority, 67.3 percent, found their spouses through their own initiative. No correlation was found between various regions or ages.

Almost 32 percent of the respondents who wed in the USSR were married in the city where they went for their higher education. The dominance of this pattern is higher if we include only those with higher education—63 persons, or 48.5 percent. In that group the percentage of those married in "educational exile" is 44.4 percent. This points out a definite marriage pattern. However, since there is insufficient information about the spouse's family, the credibility of this hypothesis can be tested by three questions: Is the duration of dating prior to marriage substantially different from the rest of the sample? Did newlyweds live with the wife's or husband's parents after marriage? What part of their leisure time did they spend with the wife's or husband's parents?

The following lengths of courtship were given by the respondents:

1–3 months of dating	18.9%
4–5 months	—
6–8 monthhs	18.9
9–12 months	22.6
15 months	36.0
3–5 years	3.6

The group that married far from their hometown dated their spouses an average of nine months, which is close to the average of the entire sample and therefore does not constitute a dominant factor that would support the second hypothesis about marriages arranged by relatives. After the wedding 56 percent lived with parents of the bride or groom, and 44 percent moved away from their parents

Table 9.7. Length of the emigrants' leisure time spent with their parents (in percentages)

	Hours per week spent with one or both parents				
	5–20	30	40	50	60–100	once a year
The entire sample	37.3	5.1	6.8	18.6	18.6	13.6
Those who married outside their cities	35.7	—	—	—	14.3	42.9

to live alone. Both groups continued to be in close touch with parents. The data shown in table 9.7 support the notion that those couples who stayed and married in their cities had closer contact with their parents.

Let us now analyze the impact of stress caused by emigration. In the new country the father's authority declines, both as the provider and as a carrier of knowledge and experience. The new environment functions as a leveler that puts greater value on adaptability. New shifts take place in husband/wife relations. From field observation it appears that women are able to learn the English language more quickly and are more flexible in their adaptation to new professions.

The extent of divorce among the new immigrants is low; only one young couple (age 26) from Moscow replied that they were divorced. However, two additional couples answered the question about divorce with "not yet."

There is a clear tendency of family and in-laws to cluster together. Almost two-thirds, 62.5 percent, reside close to parents and in-laws; 37.5 percent reside beyond a walking or short ride distance. The frequency of visiting those relatives points to an additional dimension of family cohesion. Over three-quarters of the entire sample visit each other on a daily or weekly basis, as can be seen from these responses:

Daily	26.0%
Weekly	50.6
Monthly	19.5
Less than monthly	3.9

To clarify this pattern of behavior, which could have been purely traditional or conditioned by lack of other acquaintances, a specific question was posed: How do you compare the closeness of your relations with your family now in the United States with the way it was in the USSR? The symmetry of the answers is surprising as 19.8 percent of the respondents felt closer to their families, while the exact percentage felt more distant. Another 60.4 percent felt no change in their degree of intimacy.

Two similar questions were asked about the specific change of relations between the spouses and between parents and children. Almost three-quarters of the parents said that the quality of their relations with their children was

9. Adaptation and Acculturation in the U.S.

unchanged. This is remarkable in any immigrant group (not to mention the average American family). Only one person (a woman) cited her divorce prior to emigration as a reason for the worsening of her relationships. The rest of the group fell into two categories of equal size: those who were unemployed and received SSI; and those who came from financially established families in which the average income was $15,692, which is very close to the income of those who are employed in their professions.

Perceptions and Images of Vienna, Rome, and the United States

Turning now to an examination of the émigrés' background, it is necessary to classify the respondents' knowledge and information about the West. On the basis of the material they read in the Soviet Union, they were asked to state three things that impressed them most in Vienna and Rome (which were their first two stops in the West en route to the United States) and in the United States. Their answers about Vienna were as follows:

Abundance of goods	44.8%
Beauty of Vienna	35.2
Cleanliness	29.6
Culture	24.8
People: polite & pleasant	14.4
Order	12.8
Tranquility	8.8
Freedom	6.4

The number of people who were overwhelmed by the abundance of goods was seven times the number who were impressed by freedom, or as one of them stated, the absence of the Soviet regime. Only one (age 43, Tashkent) stated he was impressed by the first big synagogue he saw, and another (age 75, Odessa) was impressed by the religious culture in general. Others cited Viennese poodles, and one the rudeness of the representative of the Jewish Agency. A majority was overwhelmed by the cleanliness, order, and tranquility of the city. Since this was an open-ended question, the number of similar responses again stresses the uniformity of Soviet cultural values. Next come their impressions of Rome, where they spent four to six months:

Architecture, museums, monuments	86.4%
Dirt, disorder, noise	15.2
Italians: friendliness, warmth	21.6
Abundance of goods	15.2
Freedom	6.4
Bolshevism, strikers	4.0
Nature, sea	3.2
Tranquility	0.8

The longer duration of the respondents' stay (from four to six months there vs. about three weeks in Vienna) brought different aspects of life to their attention. Only one-tenth of those who considered Vienna tranquil said the same of Rome. The absolute majority was completely overwhelmed by the beauty of Rome, its architecture, historical monuments, and museums. An additional 4 percent were most impressed by the Vatican and an equal percentage by Italian Bolshevism. Some 15 percent were impressed by the dirt, disorder, and noise of Rome. Never having encountered a Mediterranean people, 21.6 percent were most impressed by the friendliness, openness, gaiety, and energy of the Italians. The abundance of material goods and food impressed only 15.2 percent, and freedom impressed an equal percentage of respondents as in Vienna—6.4 percent. Only one person stated that he was impressed by the reception of the local Jewish community.

Again, in spite of the open-ended questions, the responses frequently were rather unanimous and definitive, as if they were students of the same class.

As for the United States, respondents were most impressed by the following things:

Abundance	30.6%
America	16.7
Freedom and democracy	21.7
Standard of living	10.0
Higher class cars	8.3
Way of life	6.7
Razmakh Mashtaby (broad scope)	5.8
Greenery	5.0
Dirt	5.8
Crime	4.2
Religion	2.5

As a result of the respondents' longer residence in the United States, the number of things that impressed them is almost double those in Vienna and Rome. However, the quantitative shifts in values mentioned in Vienna and Rome are significant in understanding the respondents' portrait of the United States, on the one hand, and their cultural center of gravity, on the other. Only 1.7 percent were impressed by American culture compared with 24.8 percent in Vienna. The beauty of New York City and its architecture impressed 13.3 percent compared with 35.2 percent in Vienna and 86.4 percent in Rome. Similarly, 16.7 percent were impressed, rather negatively, by the dirt on the streets and in public areas, as opposed to 29.6 percent who were impressed by the cleanliness of Vienna.

There were specific values that impressed respondents only in the United States. *Razmakh*—which can be translated as scope, wide-ranging enterprise (an adjective generally reserved for Americans)—was one such value cited by 5.8 percent of the respondents. Crime was mentioned by 4.2 percent, religion, service, and technology by 2.5 percent each. A group of 4.2 percent was impressed by the status and number of Jews in American society, the annual parade in support of Israel in New York City, and the absence of anti-Semitism. This is the only element of perception that reflects the ethnic self-awareness of the respondents. The common denominator among members of this group is their average age of 55. Half of them had graduated from high school, and the other half have university degrees. One was impressed by the warm welcome of community representatives, one by the withering of spiritual life, and one by the stupidity of Americans.

In general, America appeared less predictable and more alien to respondents than did European cities. The extent of Soviet-Jewish affinity to several aspects of cultural and social life in the United States will be examined below.

Sources and Content of Information Obtained about the United States, Israel, and Judaism

To evaluate the motivations of Soviet Jews to emigrate to the United States, one must isolate and trace the sources and content of their information about American cultural and political systems. To this end, respondents were asked to provide the names of books about America that they had read in the USSR, in Rome, and in the United States.

The responses indicated that 43.1 percent had not read a single book or journal about the United States in the Soviet Union, in Rome, or even after arriving in the United States. This is astonishing, for it means that within this group the decision to emigrate was undertaken on the basis of oral information. No less striking were the kinds of books about life in the United States that the remaining 56.9 percent did read. Almost 8 percent had read Theodore Dreiser, Mark Twain, James Fenimore Cooper, Jack London, or Ernest Hemingway. An equal number had read *One-Floor America*, one of the first Soviet books about the United States written by Ilf and Petrov, the two most prominent Soviet satirists. They wrote the book after traveling coast to coast in the United States in 1929. Ten percent stated that they had read "some" and "numerous" books, but it is safe to assume that they could have read books by the most popular authors mentioned above.

Four and one-half percent had read the journal *America*, a glossy monthly resembling *Life* magazine, published in Russian by the U.S. Information Agency. Another 5.4 percent had read *Businesslike America* by Soviet journalist Smeliakov, which is a vivid, if propagandistic, Soviet portrait of workaday America. Additional books of this type, for example *From Washington to Washington* by Peskov and Strelnikov, or *The Land Over the Ocean* by Strelnikov, had been read by 1.5 percent of the respondents. Although containing the standard type of criticism about exploitation of one man by another, these works stunned Soviet readers with the sheer amount of information they contained about daily life in the United States. Nonetheless, these books were about as helpful in providing objective information to those intending to emigrate as *Gulliver's Travels* would have been. The average Soviet citizen's lack of understanding about life in the United States is astonishing. (Thus, I witnessed a Soviet university dean shocked to discover that black Americans speak English.)

Of the émigrés polled, 5.4 percent stated that they read the monthly publication of the Soviet Union of Writers, *Foreign Literature*, and books published by the Progress Publishing Company. This journal carried excerpts from the American authors Kurt Vonnegut and John Updike. The Progress Publishing Company published several books about United States foreign policy. A majority of the respondents read books that described the United States at the turn of the century and in the 1920s.

The responses of 29.2 percent who said they chose to emigrate because of their desire to read without censorship is ironic, since only 15.4 percent of the entire sample stated that they read something about the United States after leaving the USSR. Thus, only half of them actually exercised their freedom to read when no censorship existed. Of that 15.4 percent, the majority stated that it read just some material. In Rome 3.8 percent read a pamphlet, *Entering a New Life*, prepared by David Harris under the auspices of HIAS. In the United States 3.1 percent read *The History of the United States*. Although this sudden drop in active reading can be explained by difficulties encountered by the new immigrants adjusting to their new environment (they had more pressing tasks than reading), there also are other reasons rooted in the general political culture and intellectual immobility of the average Soviet citizen.

To delimit this hypothesis, it is advisable to survey the respondents' reading about Israel and Judaism. Soviet Jews are denied the right to study and to obtain books about Judaism in the USSR. However, Soviet authorities saturate bookstores with extremely vicious anti-Semitic publications, which go beyond the official struggle against religion and its adherents. Anti-Semitic publications are used by Soviet authorities to both rekindle and regulate the desired level of anti-Semitism and anti-Zionism within the population. Since close to 90 percent of the sample stated that anti-Semitism was the main reason for their decision to emigrate, it would be safe to assume that they, at least, were sensitized to this oppression and therefore would be moved to find the truth about Judaism.

In the light of the above, the replies are puzzling. Only a minority of the respondents (15.4) read anything about Judaism in the Soviet Union or in Rome, whereas this figure rose to 31.5 percent in the United States. The material they read in the Soviet Union included Soviet anti-Semitic publications, the Bible, Simon Dubnov's *The History of the Jews, The Jewish Encyclopedia*, Leon Feuchtwanger, and the works of Zeev Jabotinsky. (Each respondent read only one or two books, at the most.) Their knowledge about contemporary trends in Judaism was thus limited. During their period in Rome they read such books as the Bible, Herman Wouk's *This is My God*, and the works of the Jewish historian Gratz. It was expected that the amount of their reading in Rome would increase over what it had been in the Soviet Union, but it actually decreased, possibly because they were concentrating on learning English. Books read in the United States fell into three groups. One-third read the Bible, one-third read booklets concerning Jewish holidays and traditions published in Israel and disseminated by FREE (Friends of Refugees from Eastern Europe), and one-third read books published in Israel by the Aliya Library, including Ettinger's *The History of the Jewish People*, Dimont's *Jews, God and Reality*, Margolin's *A Tale of a Thousand Years*, and Fast's *My Glorious Brothers*, all of which were translated into Russian. Again, the respondents' limited efforts to uncover their historical roots for intellectual-academic purposes and not religious ones remains yet to be explained.

Similarly, their reading about Israel was limited. In the Soviet Union, 20.8 percent had read about Israel, while only 10 percent more had done so in Rome, and an additional 6.9 percent in the United States. This growth does not correspond to the availability of numerous materials in the Russian language.

The book that the respondents read in the Soviet Union about Israel were vehemently anti-Zionist (as the majority described them). One outstanding exception is *Exodus* by Leon Uris, which was translated by numerous Zionist groups and circulated in the Jewish samizdat. The majority of those who read some material about Israel during their stay in Rome read *Exodus*. Some read two books by Menachem Begin, *The Revolt* and *White Nights*. Two people read books by Randolph Churchill, *The Six Day War* and *Entebbe*, for which Russian translations were published by the Aliya Library in Israel. The majority of the 37.7 percent who read some publication about Israel after arriving in the United States said that they read *Israel Today*, a monthly digest of the Israeli press promoted in the United States by the Russian Department of the Israel Aliyah Center. *Exodus* retained its popularity with Soviet-Jewish immigrants. Additional books read in the United States include books by Begin and Churchill's *The Entebbe Operation*. Although the number of selected books was small, Soviet Jews were most attracted to those that revolved around a heroic-romantic figure or dealt with nationalism and patriotism. This preference is generated by Soviet culture in general and self-awareness in particular. This can be explained by one central factor: Soviet Jews, being a nonentity at best, or a negative entity at worst, as presented by Soviet propaganda, can most easily identify with national aspects of Judaism—i.e., with the State of Israel and mostly with its heroic deeds as recounted in *Exodus*, *The Six Day War*, and *Entebbe*. It is much more difficult for them to identify with religious or ethnic social aspects of Judaism, whether in Israel or the United States.

The process of acquiring information about Jewish life, therefore, which was limited while in the Soviet Union, was surprisingly slow and limited in content. It was expected that such omnivorous readers as Soviet Jews would seize the first opportunity to read the books they could have been imprisoned for reading in the USSR. An explanation for this lack of interest can be found in the other uses of leisure time in nonreading activities and in their choosing to read other things.

Adaptation of Soviet Jews to the U.S. Jewish Community

The reluctance of Soviet Jews to take part in Jewish institutions in America has received wide attention. To examine this situation and to trace its origins, the unique relationship between Soviet Jews and Judaism in the United States will be analyzed on the following levels: their official association with religious institutions (active participation); their indirect or passive participation (for example, sending children to Jewish schools); their direct-passive participation (for example, acquainting themselves with Jewish holidays and history); their general outlook on Jewish heritage and on Israel in particular.

The following question was posed to determine the respondents' affiliation with institutions: do you belong to a Jewish Community Center, a Jewish social club, a Jewish sports organization, or a synagogue (Orthodox, Conservative, or Reform)? The word "belong" was used instead of "member" to allow for any form of affiliation, formal or informal. The question elicited these data:

JCC	49.2%
Social club	5.4
Sports organization	3.8
Synagogue (total)	43.2
Orthodox	10.1
Conservative	16.9
Reform	16.2
None	26.2

Membership in a local Jewish community center (JCC) was usually extended automatically to each new immigrant without charge. Since the JCC was often the first and in many instances the only place in which Soviet Jews could meet American Jews, this explains, in part, the popularity of JCCs (49.2 percent of respondents were members). Affiliation with other institutions required more initiative than joining a JCC. Affiliation with synagogues totaled 43.2 percent and broke down almost evenly among Orthodox, Conservative, and Reform congregations. Two major conclusions can be drawn from the data concerning synagogue affiliation. First, there is a clear difference in the average age among those groups. Orthodox synagogue members averaged 64.5 years of age, Conservative 48.1, and Reform 57.3. Second, the majority of those affiliated with synagogues did not reside in the major urban centers where the bulk of Soviet Jews were concentrated, but in suburbia where synagogues are predominantly Reform and Conservative. The percentages of Soviet Jews affiliated with synagogues in major urban centers were as follows:

New York	10.0%
Chicago	4.6

Boston	2.3
Los Angeles	0.8
San Francisco	0.8
St. Louis	0.8
Philadelphia	2.3

This disproportionate dispersal of the synagogue-affiliated among smaller communities partially explains their high percentage as well as the symmetry of their association with the three branches.

Let us now consider the frequency of synagogue attendance. On the high holidays Jews traditionally attend synagogue services. The behavior of Soviet Jews follows this pattern. A small fraction attended synagogues only on Rosh Hashana (3.2 percent) or on Yom Kippur (3.8 percent), and almost one-third of them (32.3 percent) attended on both holidays. An additional 10.8 percent attended Shabbat services as well. About one-fifth (19.2 percent) did not attend services.

Let us now survey the second level, the indirect-passive form of identity with Judaism, i.e., those who send their children or grandchildren to Jewish day schools. Of the 23.8 percent of the respondents who sent their children to Jewish day and afternoon schools, 16.7 percent received financial support from these schools. They were asked to select three reasons for sending their children to religious schools. The following were the results:

Acquiring Judaism	35.5%
Better schooling and education	35.5
Discipline	22.6
Better environment and family	12.9
Jewish identity, solidarity	29.0
Jewish history and language	16.1
Belief in God and laws	9.7
High morals	9.7
Respect for parents	12.9
Respect for the United States	3.2
Don't know yet	9.7

These reasons put forth by parents can be grouped under three sets of values: religious (45.2 percent), Jewish-nationalistic (45.1 percent), and general (93.6 percent). It is evident that the religious factor (belief in God and Jewish law) was among the least important in the decision to send children to religious schools. The dominant factor in such decisions was related to a desire for a better education; most respondents considered public schools to be of inferior quality.

Let us now inquire into the third direct-passive dimension of approaching Judaism by acquainting oneself with Jewish holidays, Jewish history, the history of Russian Jewry, the history of American Jewry, and the history of Israel. The percentage of respondents seeking acquaintance with the Jewish holidays

Table 9.8. Acquaintance of the emigrants with Jewish history and customs (in percentages)

	Yes	Partly	No
Jewish holidays	82.3	9.2	8.5
Jewish history	53.8	9.2	37.0
History of Russian Jewry	33.1	5.4	61.5
History of American Jewry	17.7	6.9	75.4
History of Israel	49.2	13.8	36.9

Table 9.9. Interest of the respondents in books and courses (in percentages)

	Some	Many	None	Specific
Read books	26.9	10.8	50.0	12.3
Took courses	3.1	11.5	83.5	2.3

paralleled the percentage of synagogue attendance on the high holidays (see table 9.8). The rest of the data showed that 53.8 percent familiarized themselves with Jewish history, 33.1 percent with the history of Russian Jewry, 17.7 percent with the history of American Jewry, and 49.2 percent with the history of Israel. These data contradicted the data concerning the size of the group that read any material about Judaism, Jewish history, or Israel. To restate those data: in the Soviet Union 15.4 percent read something related to the above-mentioned issues, in Rome 15.4 percent, and in the United States 31.5 percent.

To estimate the extent of the respondents' acquaintance with Judaism and its history, we shall use the responses to two questions: What books related to these topics did you read? What courses related to those topics did you attend? In order to create some scale of credibility, the data obtained (see table 9.9) were grouped into four categories: specific books by name, many books or courses, some books or courses, and none of these.

The same categories used in regard to courses were provided by the respondents themselves. Regrettably, these data do not help us understand and accept the respondents' acquaintance with the Jewish holidays (82.3 percent), Jewish history (53.8 percent), and the history of Israel (49.2 percent), since only a small percentage stated specific names of books they read (12.3 percent) and specific courses they attended (2.3 percent). This leads to the conclusion that the figures given on acquaintance with Judaism and Jewish history after arrival in the United States are highly inflated, unless the respondents obtained a general view of these issues during their orientation programs in Rome and in the United States.

Since this point is of great value in determining the credibility of their answers on religion, it is important to test it again. Let us trace the extent to which persons who stated that one of their reasons for emigrating to the United States was "to assure Jewish education to their children" also claimed to read any

Table 9.10. Possibilities of combining a deep Jewish religious conviction with contemporary values (in percentages)

	Yes	No	Not Sure
National sample	71.3	19.4	9.3
Elementary education	70.0	20.0	10.0
Average age	64.1	35.5	6.9
High school education	60.9	30.4	8.7
Average age	48.1	56.4	19.0
Vocational education	63.4	21.4	14.3
Average age	57.0	48.7	46.5
University education	76.1	15.5	8.4
Average age	55.0	45.0	61.0
Average age	54.8	50.3	50.5

specific material related to Jewish holidays, Jewish history, or the history of Russian, American, or Israeli Jewry. The results were these: 19.1 percent read specific books about Judaism, 23.8 percent read some materials without naming them, and 51.7 percent did not read any materials.

Parents desiring Jewish education for their children did not actively engage in expanding their own knowledge of the Jewish religious and cultural heritage. Although 79.2 percent stated that their reason for emigrating was to feel free as Jews, perhaps a more realistic indicator of fulfilling this desire is seen in the statistics on books read about Judaism (19.1 percent).

Let us now consider the fourth level of the respondents' Jewish identity: their evaluation of the Jewish heritage in general and that of Israel in particular. The first question was intended to obtain their outlook on the compatibility of a conviction about Judaism on the one hand with the values of contemporary civilization on the other.

The majority of the respondents (71.3 percent) considered these values to be compatible (see table 9.10). As expected, the average age of the respondents who accepted such a compatibility was higher than that of those who did not (45.8–50.3). An inexplicable case is that of the high school–educated respondents who find these values compatible and whose average age (48.1) is lower than those who deny this compatibility (56.4). The responses to this question point out only a general awareness of the compatibility that "deep religious conviction" has with the values of contemporary civilization since the émigrés' other responses neither portrayed them as very knowledgeable about Judaism nor as avid practitioners of it. Their unique Soviet-Jewish experience, however, creates a basis for the development of the ethnic and national dimension of their consciousness.

Let us now see how ethnic and national consciousness is reflected in their choices of three of the most respected American and Israeli leaders. The question was posed to detect the essence of the émigrés' identity, which in turn reflects the degree of their familiarity with those leaders and the countries they represent. The answers were these:

Don't know	17.1%
Begin	36.9
Ben Gurion	38.7
Golda Meir	49.5
Dayan	26.1
Herzl	14.4
Jabotinsky	15.3
Weizman	12.6
Lubavicher Rebe	9.0

In addition to the group that could name not even one Jewish leader (17.1 percent), the rest named a variety of thirty historical people, while one respondent added the unique category, "leaders of Histadrut" (the Israeli Trade Unions). The rest of the replies are meaningful as well.

The following group of non-Jewish leaders were named as Jewish leaders: Abraham Lincoln (3.6 percent), Franklin Roosevelt (1.8 percent), Harry Truman (0.9 percent), Richard Nixon (0.9 percent), John F. Kennedy (0.9 percent), Jimmy Carter (1.8 percent), Woodrow Wilson (0.9 percent), George Washington (0.9 percent), and Henry Jackson (2.7 percent). Abraham Lincoln received twice the recognition of Joseph Trumpeldor, equal to that given to Israeli Defense Minister Ariel Sharon, and more than that of Henry Kissinger (2.7 percent). The total of those identifying American leaders as Jewish amounted to 14.4 percent of the respondents. They, together with those who could not name a single Jewish leader (17.1 percent), constitute almost one-third (31.5 percent) of the entire sample.

Within the group of responses, three categories could be detected: ancient military leaders (such as Bar Kochba and Judah Ha-Macabee, 0.9 percent each), Jewish political figures (Jacob Javits, 1.8 percent, Henry Kissinger, 2.7 percent, and Nachum Goldman, 0.9 percent), Israeli political figures (Shimon Peres, 2.7 percent, Yitzhak Rabin, 0.9 percent, Yitzhak Navon, Abba Eban, and Rabbi Kahane, 1.8 percent each).

However, the most revealing results come from the majority of responses that fall into two distinct categories: Zionist and Israeli leaders and leaders of the American religious community. The first category consists of three groups: founders of political Zionism Theodore Herzl, Vladimir Jabotinsky, and Chaim Weizman received a similar degree of recognition; Israeli leaders who were deceased or no longer active (Golda Meir had the highest recognition, 49.5 percent, followed by Ben Gurion, 38.7 percent, and Moshe Dayan, 26.1 percent); and Menachem Begin who had a 36.9 percent recognition rate.

Summarizing these data, it is safe to state that they support the notion that the Soviet-Jewish identity with Jewish heritage is built around nationalistic pictures, images, and personalities.

9. Adaptation and Acculturation in the U.S. 137

Use of Leisure Time

The use of leisure time is an important analytic factor of social change and adaptation in a nonmigrating society. Its importance is amplified when we analyze a migrant group. What occupies people in their free time is indicative of their background, ability, and determination to become an integral part of society.

As could have been expected, a major part of the respondents' free time was occupied by television, since 70.9 percent of the respondents owned a color television and 29.1 percent a black and white set. Forty-three percent watched more than twenty hours of television per week. These are the numbers of hours per week that the respondents spend watching television:

Watched 6–10 hours   15.9%
Watched 11–15 hours   21.8
Watched 16–20 hours   19.3
Watched 21–30 hours   11.8
Watched 31–45 hours   31.2

The respondents were asked to rate the following types of television shows they preferred on a scale of 1 to 5: comedy, news, sports, movies, game shows, and soap operas. The absolute majority watched each type of program. However, they were mostly impressed with the daytime television game shows and soap operas, which they perceived as representative of the colorful, dramatic, suburban America they rarely experienced. The younger age group tended to watch more sports shows and movies.

A separate question was posed: What are your children's favorite programs? The overwhelming majority replied cartoons for children and soap operas for teenagers. To summarize, the respondents were asked to compare American television with Soviet television. Over 95 percent found American television superior. Their evaluation of American television was as follows: 58 percent gave American television the highest rating; 23.2 percent considered it to be good; and 18.8 percent quite acceptable.

Based on their familiarity with television and the amount of hours spent viewing it, we can state that television images are a major influence upon the Soviet-Jewish immigrants' perceptions of contemporary American life.

Radio plays a minor role in obtaining information and shaping opinions. There are three major reasons: respondents listened only a few hours per week to radio, mostly in a car; many of them listened to the shortwave programs of Voice of America broadcast in Russian to listeners in the Soviet Union; the rest preferred American mellow popular music.

Now we shall trace the impact of the written word upon their post-emigration development. By measuring this impact, we can locate the core of their intellectual understanding of American life. As noted, only 17.2 percent read only English-language journals, and an additional 10.3 percent read English-language and Russian journals. Half of the respondents (50 percent) depended on journals in Russian and 32.8 percent did not read at all. The following is a breakdown of American journals and magazines read by the respondents:

Time	57.4%
Newsweek	10.8
U.S. News and World Report	10.8
Cosmopolitan	2.7
National Geographic	5.4
People	5.4
National Enquirer	2.7
Family Circle	5.4
Playboy	5.4

It is very puzzling that the number of *Time* readers was five times greater than the number of readers of *Newsweek*. In any event those who read magazines (73 percent) read *Time, Newsweek,* and *U.S. News and World Report.* Many respondents read local newspapers (42.9 percent); however, the majority (57.1 percent) did not read newspapers in English at all.

Soviet Jews' Perception of American Jews

There is a unique relationship between Soviet and American Jews. On the one hand, American Jews fought for the freedom of emigration of Soviet Jews and, upon their arrival in the United States, assisted them generously in the process of absorption. However, in spite of this involvement there is limited contact between Soviet and American Jews: only 5.4 percent of Soviet Jews have some kind of social contact with American Jews. Nonetheless, the historic and geographic ravine of images and perceptions, on both sides, plays a major role in the process of self-esteem and social adaptation of Soviet Jews in the new social setting.

The images, on both sides, are constructed mostly of unrealistic clichés derived from nostalgic memories about grandparents and from some reading of the authors Eli Wiesel and Isaac Babel. This kaleidoscope of romantic-tragic figures does not help to promote understanding between American and Soviet Jews. The images held by Soviet Jews are more fragmented and distorted. To obtain a structural picture these perceptions will be analyzed in two separate categories: social images and personal images.

Social Images

The question underlying the entire set of social images and perceptions was this one: In your opinion, were the American Jews happy to receive you here? Positive answers were given by 29.5 percent of the respondents, while 10.7

percent responded negatively. The majority (59.8 percent) of Soviet Jews were not sure whether or not American Jews were happy to receive them. Several respondents stated that American Jews envied the assistance given to immigrants. Beyond the assertion, itself, we have no detailed data as the basis for this perception. Such conclusions could not have been based on a broad personal social experience, since such an experience does not exist. Since 93 percent of the respondents stated that they socialize only with Soviet Jews, the absence of social relations between Soviet and American Jews can be both the cause and the result of a perception of dislike. This perception also could have been gathered within the framework of functional relations, i.e., when émigrés encountered the officials of various American-Jewish organizations.

To expose the origins of this social gap, a special question was posed: Do you feel a special identity with those American Jews whose grandparents came from Russia? The answers were "yes" for 69.2 percent, "just a little" for 8.6 percent, and "no" for 22.2 percent. These results testify that the majority of Soviet Jews (77.8 percent) felt some extra affinity with American Jews of Russian background. This response testifies that Soviet Jews would be interested in establishing closer links with American Jews. Therefore, the opinion of the Soviet Jews who are not sure whether or not American Jews were happy to receive them in the United States is of paramount importance. After all, who else could be happy to see them in American society?

In an effort to uncover more of the social interrelationship between American and Soviet Jews, two additional questions were asked. The first one, although unrelated to the social interrelationship in its content, brought out an important element of Soviet-Jewish trust in American Jews. The question read: "Were American Jews sensitive to your needs and location of residence?" Over 54 percent felt that American Jews were not sensitive enough about their needs. Regardless of the degree of the objective credibility of this statement, the mere size of the group that held this belief reflects the major elements of estrangement between these two groups. Such alienation breeds unrealistic images of American Jewry, which consequently promotes this process of alienation.

One major characteristic of Soviet Jews in general and the respondents of this sample in particular was the high percentage of university graduates. Therefore, it was interesting to analyze this particular segment of their intellectual self-awareness in comparison with American Jews, especially against the underlying perception of being unwanted. The respondents were asked to state their opinion about the intellectual level of an average American Jew in relation to that of the average Soviet Jew. Half of the respondents (50.4 percent) considered the intellectual level of American Jews to be equal to that of Soviet Jews. The remaining 50 percent broke down into two groups: 16.8 percent considered American Jews to be more intellectual than Soviet Jews, and 32.8 percent considered Soviet Jews to be more intellectual. The ratio is almost 1:2 in favor of those who consider their intellectual experience and their schooling superior to that of American Jews. Although the question asked them to make a comparison

Table 9.11. Soviet Jews' self-perception of their intellectual levels (in percentages)

	Educational level			
	Elementary	High school	Technical-vocational	University
American Jews intellectually above Soviet Jews	10.1	20.0	10.0	60.0
American Jews intellectually below Soviet Jews	5.9	23.5	8.8	61.8

between an average American and Soviet Jew, it is assumed that each respondent compared himself to American Jews with whom he was acquainted.

Let us check the educational backgrounds of those who considered their intellectual levels to be above or below those of the American Jews. Consistent with common sociological assumptions, we would expect that the higher the level of education, the more realistic would be the Soviet Jew's perception of the intellectual training of his American counterpart. To our great surprise the educational level of these Soviet Jews who disagreed concerning their American counterparts was almost identical (see table 9.11). No matter how relatively educated or uneducated the Soviet Jews, the same percentage in each level of education regarded American Jews as more educated and the same percentage regarded them as less so. Other variables—age, city of origin, and profession—did not provide guiding clues sufficient to explain this phenomenon. Indeed, this perception is in need of additional research.

Personal Images

In order to obtain a clear picture of the perceptions and opinions of Soviet Jews about their American counterparts, thirteen pairs of adjectives describing American Jews were presented (see table 9.12). Soviet Jews were asked to choose on a scale of 1 to 5 (1 being lowest, 5 the highest) about American Jews. The adjectives presented were: (1) sincere—insincere, (2) generous—stingy, (3) likable—disagreeable, (4) interesting—boring, (5) talkative—quiet, (6) intelligent—dull, (7) cultured—uncultured, (8) educated—uneducated, (9) polite—impolite, (10) honest—dishonest, (11) understanding toward Soviet Jews—not understanding, (12) naive in politics—astute in politics, (13) naive in business—astute in business.

As this topic by itself deserves a special study, I shall refrain from a cross-factor analysis and report only the basic responses.

The sincerity of Americans is an underlying image. So let us see (table 9.12) how sincere American Jews are in the eyes of Soviet Jews. Of the respondents, 46.6 percent considered American Jews to be sincere or very sincere, whereas 36.6 percent viewed them only as acceptable. A minority of 14.8 percent considered American Jews to be insincere. That is, the overwhelming majority of 83.2 percent viewed American Jews as sincere.

9. Adaptation and Acculturation in the U.S. 141

Table 9.12. Overall perceptions by Soviet Jews of their American counterparts (in percentages)

Categories	Grades				
	1	2	3	4	5
Sincere	2.3	12.5	36.6	26.1	20.5
Polite	—	—	6.3	29.2	63.5
Honest	—	6.1	20.0	30.8	43.1
Likable	—	16.3	29.3	28.3	26.1
Generous	4.9	18.3	36.5	24.4	15.9
Interesting	8.5	19.7	36.6	29.6	5.6
Talkative	11.4	16.4	36.1	24.6	11.5
Intelligent	—	12.9	26.9	42.3	17.9
Cultured	—	10.2	34.2	37.9	17.7
Educated	1.3	6.5	20.8	57.1	14.3
Naive in politics	21.6	17.3	33.3	13.9	13.9
Naive in business	—	8.3	13.9	19.4	58.3
Understanding toward Soviet Jews	7.9	23.8	41.6	15.8	10.9

The highest marks were awarded for the politeness of American Jews: 63.5 percent thought American Jews highly polite; 29.2 percent, very polite; and 6.3 percent, acceptable; while 1 percent found them rude. Apart from the politeness of American Jews, it has to be stated that the general level of politeness in the West is one of the greatest surprises to the majority of Soviet immigrants.

A similar trend was visible in the evaluation of the honesty of American Jews. Over 43 percent thought American Jews highly honest, 30.8 percent very honest, and 20 percent honest. Only 6.1 percent held the opinion that American Jews were dishonest.

The majority of the respondents found American Jews to be highly likable (26.1 percent), very likable (28.3 percent), or acceptable (29.3 percent), while 16.3 percent found them disagreeable. A different breakdown occurred when the generosity of American Jews was evaluated: only 15.9 percent of the respondents considered them very generous; 24.4 percent saw them as generous; and 36.5 percent answered acceptably generous; while 23.2 percent considered them stingy. Since the majority of Soviet Jews received an equal amount of assistance, the discrepancy of this perception could be attributed to the specific clusters of their expectations of American Jews. That is, those who expected to be pampered by their American counterparts were the disappointed ones.

Only a minority of respondents found American Jews very interesting (5.6 percent) or interesting (29.6 percent), while 26.6 percent found them acceptable and 28.2 percent boring. On the other hand, the picture of talkativeness in American Jews is more balanced: 11.1 percent of the respondents considered American Jews loquacious, whereas 11.5 percent considered them the opposite, and most (36.1 percent) found them normal. Again, it is very difficult to explain the discrepancy between the perceptions of American Jews as interesting and as talkative. It is possible that these perceptions were based on very limited personal experience or were the result of a remote perception.

Most Soviet Jews found American Jews very intelligent (17.9 percent) or intelligent (42.3 percent), and only 12.9 percent found them unintelligent. The respondents also found American Jews very cultured and well educated. Almost forty percent of the respondents considered American Jews naive in politics, while 27.8 percent thought them astute in politics. In business, only 8.3 percent regarded American Jews as naive and 77.7 percent as astute. Again, these images are still based upon remote perception. Is it the extension of an ethnic pride or a continuation of positive elements of the Soviet anti-Semitic propaganda? (Soviet propaganda frequently asserts that the American economy is controlled by Jews.)

It is interesting to analyze the degree to which Soviet Jews feel understood by American Jews. Only 10.9 percent of the respondents thought that American Jews understand Soviet Jews very well, and 15.8 percent thought they were well understood. That is, 26.7 percent thought they were understood by American Jews. On the opposite side, 31.7 percent felt they were not understood at all by American Jews. The bulk, 41.4 percent, considered the level of understanding of American Jews toward Soviet Jews to be average.

This notion of being misunderstood constitutes an element of mistrust and isolation. The issue becomes more significant when the immigrant's total perception of American Jews is seen as positive. To be misunderstood by someone negative would matter much less. The end result is an underlying social loneliness and isolation.

Conclusion

The major goal of this study was to draw an initial picture of Soviet Jews who arrived in the United States during the last decade. The study analyzed several aspects of immigrants' adaptation, acculturation, and perceptions of the new social, economic, and political environment that so drastically differed from the one they knew in the Soviet Union.

On the personal level the following changes occurred as a result of immigration of Soviet Jews in our sample: the majority (70.2 percent) felt that it had improved its financial position (annual incomes averaged $15,000 and 58.5 percent owned cars). However, in the realm of professional and cultural expectations they felt that their present status was lower than what they had attained in the Soviet Union. In addition, 58.8 percent felt a lower professional status and 55.5 percent a lower cultural status. This specific culmination of changes harbors a hidden stress that may well affect the future development of the Soviet-Jewish community in the United States. On the other hand, however, the happiness of Soviet Jews in living in a free society may well compensate for lowered professional and cultural status.

An effort was made to locate the center of gravity of the identification of Soviet Jews after their arrival in the United States. The results pointed out that the dominant element of their identity is nationalistic. The origin of this element stems from the political culture in which the immigrants matured: the totalitarian Soviet society that demanded an active expression of patriotism and nationalism. Soviet Jews retained the values of this political culture but changed its object from the USSR to their own national symbol, Israel. The absence of deep roots in cultural and religious sectors makes the nationalistic elements of immigrant identity highly dominant.

These immigrants, 75 percent of whom were university graduates, differed radically in professional status from the Russian-Jewish immigrants of the nineteenth century. Their modern professions exposed them immediately to the outside environment without any period of incubation within the Jewish community, as was usually the case with the first Russian group. However, they remained unable to establish a broad circle of American friends. Thus, professional integration, while generally considered to be positive, also can serve to stress awareness of social isolation. Whether this social isolation will continue into the future is a very open question.

Epilogue: From the Inauguration of Reagan to the Death of Brezhnev

In the two-year period between the election of President Reagan and the death of Soviet leader Leonid Brezhnev, the position of Soviet Jewry took a sharp turn for the worse. Emigration dropped precipitously from its high of 51,320 in 1979 to only 2,688 in 1982. At the same time harassment of Soviet refuseniks increased in intensity, and anti-Semitism in the USSR grew more severe. Meanwhile the "detente" between the U.S. and the USSR had ended with the Soviet invasion of Afghanistan in December 1979, and by 1983 relations had deteriorated so badly that many observers felt that a new Cold War between the superpowers had come into being—a development that had very negative effects on the Soviet Jewish emigration movement.

In the past two years, as emigration has plummeted, the Soviet authorities have placed a number of new barriers in the path of would-be emigrants. These obstacles have included the failure to deliver visa affidavits sent from Israel; the refusal to accept visa applications from people with refusenik relatives; the military conscription of children of emigration activists in order to delay the family's emigration; the demand for parental permission—even when the emigrating couple are adults; the requirement to obtain new clearances from places of employment and residence after an initial refusal; and finally, a reduction in the hours when emigration offices are open for business. The end result of these actions by the Soviet government was that many Soviet Jews who had been thinking of emigration put off actually applying, both because they felt it would not do any good and because of the increasingly severe difficulties faced by refuseniks. Despite this pressure there remain in the USSR some 400,000 Soviet Jews who have requested visa affidavits and approximately 10,000 refuseniks.

The plight of the refuseniks became even more desperate in the 1981–82 period. A number were physically attacked by KGB thugs, while Western tourists who visited them were similarly harassed. Perhaps even worse, a number of refusenik scientists, in addition to losing their jobs, were stripped of their scientific degrees and were prohibited even from meeting in informal scientific seminars as the Soviet authorities, perhaps hoping thereby to deter other Jewish scientists from emigrating, tried to prevent the refuseniks from keeping up with the latest scientific developments in their fields. Adding to the psychological pressure on the refuseniks, which in some cases was causing such health problems as ulcers and hypertension, were statements by some Soviet officials that the refuseniks would never be allowed to go to Israel.

While the refuseniks were encountering increasing harassment, anti-Semitism in the USSR was increasing in intensity. There was a marked upsurge in anti-Semitic propaganda, especially in the Soviet armed forces, and the limitations on admission of Jews to Soviet universities increased sharply. Indeed, two Jewish scholars, Boris Kanevsky and Valery Senderov, who documented the anti-Semitic admissions procedures that were designed to keep Jews out of such schools as Leningrad University and Moscow State University, were arrested for their efforts. Also arrested was Felix Kochubievsky, a refusenik, whose "crime" was the attempt to re-establish the USSR-Israel Friendship Society. In the 1981–82 period the Soviet authorities also cracked down on the few autonomous elements of Jewish culture that had precariously existed in the USSR for the past decade. Thus, classes in Hebrew and Judaica were disrupted, teaching materials confiscated, and teachers warned that they faced arrest if they continued to teach. At the same time college students attending these classes were threatened with expulsion from their Soviet universities. Indeed, an *Izvestia* article on October 23, 1981, went so far as to allege that the Hebrew seminars were a "cover" for "illegal activities instigated by Zionist organizations."

Nonetheless, despite the barriers to emigration, the harassment of refuseniks, and the rising tide of anti-Semitism, Soviet-Jewish activists did not give up. Mikhail Tsivin chained himself to a fence in Moscow's Red Square and displayed a sign that read, "Let me go to Israel." An undaunted Ida Nudel, released after four years in Siberian exile, again demanded to go to Israel—and was again refused. In perhaps the most significant action of all, refusenik Anatoly Shcharansky began a hunger strike—an action that drew international support to his cause. Still, despite an increasing outcry from the West, the pressure that was successful in obtaining the release of hundreds of thousands of Jews in the 1970s proved ineffective in the first two years of the Reagan administration. This was particularly unfortunate, because at least at the start of his administration President Reagan had a considerable amount of leverage he could have used on behalf of Soviet Jewry.

When the Reagan administration took office, the Soviet government evidently feared that the president, elected with a large popular mandate and pledged to increase defense spending and to a harder line toward the USSR, would escalate the arms race at a time of serious economic difficulty in the USSR. Therefore, Moscow sent a series of signals to the United States in quest of an improved relationship. Speaking at the Twenty-sixth CPSU Party Congress in February 1981, Brezhnev devoted a great deal of space to the need for a new strategic arms agreement with the United States; he also appealed for improvement in Soviet-American relations as a whole. The Soviet leader followed up this appeal by offering to meet Reagan in a summit conference—a marked Soviet departure from the Carter period when the former American president had appealed—in vain—to Moscow for a summit during his first two years in office. In another move to improve Soviet-American relations, the USSR sent a series of signals to the American-Jewish community in an effort to have American Jews exert influence on the Reagan administration to take a softer line. Thus, the Soviet representative at the Helsinki follow-up meeting in Madrid, S. A. Kondrachev, in November 1980 stated, "the more detente prospers, the more Basket Three (which deals with emigration among other human rights issues) prospers. Thus those circles who do not want detente also limit the implementation of Basket Three." A second signal to the American-Jewish community came in the unusual (for the CPSU) denunciation of anti-Semitism, in Brezhnev's Twenty-sixth Party Congress address. The fact that a high-ranking member of the Soviet Embassy, Sergei Rogov, made a special point of informing major American-Jewish organizations such as B'nai B'rith of Brezhnev's denunciation of anti-Semitism clearly indicated that Moscow wished to highlight this point. Yet another Soviet signal was the release of Yosif Mendelevich, the last of the Jewish participants in the alleged 1970 airplane hijacking, from jail and the granting of permission for him to emigrate to Israel.

It seems clear why Moscow was sending these signals. With the Soviet economy, and particularly its agricultural sector, weak, with a popular U.S. president now in office pledging sharply increased defense spending, and with the USSR continuing to fear a closer Sino-U.S. tie, the Soviet leaders wanted to improve Soviet-American relations. Yet, while at the beginning of his administration Reagan appeared thereby to have a certain amount of leverage in dealing with the USSR—at least in the area of obtaining an increase in the Soviet-Jewish exodus—such was not to be the case. This was particularly unfortunate because President Reagan, at least rhetorically, seemed committed to the cause of Soviet Jewry. At a Holocaust ceremony early in his presidency, Reagan stated:

> Never shall it be forgotten for a moment that wherever it is taking place in the world, the persecution of people for whatever reason—persecution of people for their religious belief—that is a matter to be on [the] negotiating table or the United States does not belong at that negotiating table.

The cause of Soviet Jewry also received oral support from Vice President Bush who met twice with leaders of the National Conference on Soviet Jewry and other Western Jewish leaders, from Secretaries of State Haig and Shultz who raised the issue during their talks with Soviet Foreign Minister Gromyko, and, especially, from Max Kampelman, chairman of the U.S. delegation to the Madrid meeting of the conference on Security and Cooperation in Europe who eloquently kept the issue of Soviet Jewry at the forefront of the discussions.

Nonetheless, despite the administration's rhetorical support, there was some question, at least until George Shultz became Secretary of State, as to just how high a priority human rights in general, and the cause of Soviet Jewry in particular, was for the Reagan administration. In any case, Reagan soon dissipated much of the leverage he might have used on behalf of Soviet Jews. As far as the Sino-Soviet-U.S. triangle was concerned, despite U.S. offers to sell Peking arms, Sino-American relations were clearly troubled during the first two years of the Reagan presidency over the administration's handling of the Taiwan issue. As might be expected, Moscow repeatedly sought to exploit this situation to improve relations with China, and Peking made some gestures to Moscow in return, thereby distancing itself somewhat from Washington, and thus reducing the leverage Reagan might have had by a prospective Sino-American alignment.

In the area of nuclear armaments Reagan's generally bellicose statements (and those of his advisors) helped lead to the growth of the nuclear freeze movement in the U.S., as well as to opposition in Western Europe to the planned deployment of U.S. Pershing II and Cruise missiles. As this political opposition grew, Reagan found himself pressured into a more rapid agreement to resuming the strategic arms limitation talks (he called them START talks) than he might have wanted. As far as the Carter-imposed partial grain embargo was concerned, Reagan unilaterally lifted it (primarily under pressure from U.S. farmers), apparently without asking any quid pro quo in return, and then, in October 1982, offered to guarantee the sale of 23 million tons of grain to the USSR. Indeed, U.S. actions toward Moscow in both the strategic arms and grain areas, in which the U.S. apparently did not seek any quid pro quo on Soviet Jewry, placed in question the public commitment Reagan made to the cause of Soviet Jewry at the Holocaust ceremony.

If the issue of Soviet Jewry received little, if any, emphasis during discussions of either strategic arms or the sale of grain where the United States had leverage, the continuing deterioration of Soviet-American relations in other spheres was not conducive to improving the chances for Soviet Jews to leave the country. Whether on petty issues, such as the denial of Soviet Ambassador Dobrynin the right to park in the State Department garage, or on more serious ones such as the refusal to renew the U.S.-USSR agreements on science and technology, energy, and the use of outer space for peaceful purposes, as well as the Reagan campaign against the gas pipeline that the West Europeans were building for the USSR, the United States gave Moscow little hope that Soviet-American relations would improve. To be sure, by remaining in Afghanistan, by engineering the martial law crackdown in Poland, and by sending increased amounts of sophisticated military equipment to Cuba, Moscow was doing more than its share to maintain the Cold War atmosphere between the two countries. In such an atmosphere the chances of a significant number of Soviet Jews being allowed to leave the USSR were not great, and the end result was that the Soviet-Jewish exodus declined precipitously.

As the Soviet-Jewish exodus diminished, a dispute arose in the world Jewish community as to the cause of the decline. Israeli figures such as Aryeh Dulzin, chairman of the Jewish Agency, and Prime Minister Begin asserted that the reason for the decline in the emigration of Soviet Jews was the fact that a high proportion were dropping out—not going to Israel—and that the Soviet government was angered by the dropout phenomenon because the visas that it issued were for Israel. Many others (including contributors to this book) strongly disputed the assertion of the Israeli leaders, pointing out that the decline in the Jewish exodus from the USSR reflected the deterioration in

Soviet-American relations and noting that the emigration of both Germans and Armenians had been equally severely restricted, though in neither of these cases was dropping out a factor.

Nonetheless, the Israeli government succeeded in persuading the Hebrew Immigrant Aid Society (HIAS) to withhold assistance to émigrés choosing not to go to Israel unless they had a first-degree relative (spouse, parent, child) elsewhere. While HIAS went along with the plan in mid-December 1981, there were clearly mixed feelings in the organization, and, as a result, HIAS agreed only to withhold support for a three-month trial basis, beginning in 1982, to see whether the decline in emigration would be reversed, as the Israeli government had asserted. In fact, the monthly total of emigrants continued to drop, from 434 in December 1981 to only 288 in April 1982. The end result was that HIAS, in early May 1982, seeing that the Israeli officials were incorrect, returned to its traditional policy of aiding all Soviet Jews who, upon arriving in Vienna, opted to go to countries other than Israel.

Another Soviet-Jewish issue that proved divisive in the world Jewish community during this period was the postponement of the Third International Conference on Soviet Jewry, originally scheduled for Paris in October 1982. The lingering impact of the Israeli invasion of Lebanon and diplomatic difficulties between Israel and France (particularly between Prime Minister Begin and French President Mitterand) led the Israeli government to urge a rescheduling and relocating of the conference to Jerusalem in March 1983. While Jewish leaders from other countries acquiesced, they were clearly unhappy both because a number of prominent world leaders had already agreed to address the Paris meeting and because they perceived that the scheduling of the conference in a European capital would have given the appearance of more universal support for the cause of Soviet Jewry.

In any case, soon after the formal cancellation of the Paris meeting, Soviet Communist Party boss Leonid Brezhnev died. Whether the status of Soviet Jewry would be improved once his successor, Yuri Andropov, had consolidated his position was a question only the future could answer.

Annex 1: Jewish Emigration from the USSR, 1965 to 1981

1965–June 1967	4,498	1974	20,628
October 1968–1970	4,235	1975	13,221
1971	13,022	1976	14,261
1972	31,681	1977	16,736
1973	34,733	1978	28,864

	1979		1980		1981	
January	3,722	(39.4)*	2,803	(39.6)*	850	(24.9)*
February	3,837	(35.9)	3,023	(42.1)	1,407	(15.8)
March	4,418	(34.7)	3,049	(40.9)	1,249	(14.3)
April	4,296	(29.9)	2,469	(37.3)	1,155	(15.5)
May	4,163	(35.4)	1,976	(37.3)	1,141	(15.8)
June	4,358	(35.7)	1,767	(31.8)	866	(14.5)
July	4,068	(30.0)	1,205	(23.8)	779	(22.2)
August	4,711	(32.3)	770	(28.1)	430	(22.3)
September	4,663	(29.1)	1,307	(24.3)	405	(28.6)
October	4,746	(33.8)	1,424	(22.0)	368	(24.2)
November	4,193	(34.7)	789	(26.4)	363	(25.0)
December	4,145	(34.3)	889	(23.1)	434	(22.8)
	51,320	(33.7)	21,471	(34.4)	9,447	(18.6)

*Figures represent the percentage of those who proceeded to Israel. From October 1968–December 1981, 259,619 persons left the Soviet Union with Israeli visas. Approximately 161,750 of them went to Israel.

Source: Soviet Jewry Research Bureau, National Conference on Soviet Jewry, New York City.

Annex 2: Soviet-American Trade and Soviet-Jewish Emigration, 1969–80 (trade in millions of rubles)

Year	Soviet exports to the United States	Soviet imports from the United States	Total trade	Soviet-Jewish emigrants
1969	54.5	105.1	159.6	2,902
1970	57.8	103.1	160.9	1,044
1971	54.4	76.4	130.8	13,022
1972	129.2	461.4	590.6	31,681
1973	137.8	1,023.2	1,161.0	34,733
1974	177.3	564.9	742.2	20,628
1975	137.4	1,462.1	1,599.5	13,221
1976	198.7	2,006.8	2,205.5	14,261
1977	271.6	1,256.3	1,527.9	16,736
1978	253.1	1,599.3	1,852.4	28,864
1979	350.2	2,486.9	2,837.1	51,320
1980	151.0	1,351.5	1,502.5	21,471

Sources: On Soviet trade: *Vneshniaia Torgovlia SSSR* Za 1970, 1972, 1974, 1976, 1978, and supplement to *Soviet Foreign Trade*, 1981. On Soviet Jewish Emigrants: For 1969 and 1970: Paula Stern, *Water's Edge: Domestic Politics and the Making of American Foreign Policy*. (Westport, Conn.: Greenwood Press, 1979) p. 217. For 1971–80: Soviet Jewry Research Bureau of the National Conference on Soviet Jewry, New York City.

Notes

1. Soviet-Jewish Emigration, 1971-80: An Overview

1. The emigration of ethnic Germans and Armenians is similar in terms of national repatriation, but the numbers involved in these cases are smaller, and consequently the internal and international impact has been less.
2. Primarily the International Covenant on Civil and Political Rights (adopted by the UN General Assembly on December 16, 1966) and the Helsinki Agreement (1975).
3. Larisa Bogoraz, "Do I Feel I Belong to the Jewish People?" in Alexander Voronel and Viktor Yakhot, eds., *I Am a Jew: Essays on Jewish Identity in the Soviet Union* (New York: Academic Committee on Soviet Jewry and A.D.L. of B'nai B'rith, 1973), p. 63.
4. Edward Kuznetsov, *Prison Diaries* (New York: Stein & Day, 1975), p. 63.
5. *Izvestia*, Nov. 10, 1976. The more than fifty thousand ethnic Germans who have emigrated to West Germany are the single significant exception to this rule.
6. *Sovetskaya kultura*, Dec. 10, 1976.
7. Ibid.
8. There are a few hundred exceptions to this each year, but the path of least bureaucratic resistance is still officially to Israel.
9. For a discussion of this literature, see Zvi Gitelman, "Moscow and the Soviet Jews: A Parting of the Ways," *Problems of Communism* 39, no. 1 (Jan.-Feb. 1980): 25-29.
10. The term used by Roy Medvedev in *On Socialist Democracy* (New York: Knopf, 1975).
11. Vladimir Osipov, "Three Attitudes Toward the Homeland," in Michael Meerson-Aksenov and Boris Shragin, eds., *The Political, Social and Religious Thought of Russian Samizdat: An Anthology* (Belmont, Mass.: Nordland, 1977), p. 399.
12. Ibid. According to Alexander Voronel, Osipov later underwent a conversion to fundamentalist Christianity and dropped his anti-Semitism. See Alexander Voronel, "The Search for Jewish Identity in Russia," *Soviet Jewish Affairs* 5, no. 2 (1975): 73.
13. HIAS Statistical Abstract, vol. 29, no. 4 (1979).
14. Theodore Friedgut, p. 70 of this volume.
15. The extent of this relation is indicated by the positive 0.62 correlation coefficient between the annual U.S.-USSR trade volume and annual number of Jewish emigrants in the 1969-80 period. Of course, this correlation does not demonstrate a causal relationship, but it does show that trade and emigration tend to vary together—both good barometers of the state of Soviet-American relations. Data taken from Annex II of this volume.
16. This and following figures are compiled from relevant Statistical Abstracts issued by HIAS (New York).

2. The Jews in the Soviet Union: Emigration and Its Difficulties

1. Much of the information in the chapter, including statistics, comes from persons in the Soviet Union and Vienna who cannot be identified, from documents sent to the West from the Soviet Union through private channels, and from official and private sources in Austria, Israel, and the Netherlands (which represents Israel's interests in the USSR). These data cannot be referenced and have been incorporated in the text. I am aware that this will not satisfy many serious students, but it does reflect some of the problems in dealing with the sensitive matter of Jews in the Soviet Union, especially in terms of emigration and other matters of Jewish interest.
2. The seeming inconsistencies in the table reflect the unique conditions of compiling data from within the USSR. For example, it is virtually impossible to determine how many people actually arrive in Vienna, the primary entry site. A few persons arriving by train are immediately taken by friends and relatives and do not register with the private agencies, such as the Jewish Agency or HIAS. They are then lost for tallying purposes and are not entered in the statistics. Yet they are reflected in the data on those given exit permission. Some people receive exit visas in December and are tallied in that year, but they actually depart in January of the following year. They are then tallied into the next year's

figure for arrivals. Finally, there are people who receive exit permits, despite difficulties, but for reasons, generally personal, choose not to leave within the normal time after permission is granted and before the documents expire. There is no precise method for determining who they are and when or if they actually leave. In many instances such persons, or their relatives in Israel or the United States, do not report the final outcome. In any case, figures in a specific category are reasonably accurate even if all columns do not tally.

3. Brezhnev and Soviet Anti-Semitism

1. *Pravda*, Feb. 23, 1981; *FBIS* 3, no. 036, supp. 001 (Feb. 24, 1981): 38.
2. *Los Angeles Times*, May 23, 1979. The disclosure was made by the newspaper's correspondent in Moscow, Dan Fisher.
3. *Vremia i my*, no. 44 (Aug. 1979), pp. 134–56.
4. *New York Times*, June 27, 1979. The article was written by its Moscow correspondent, Craig Whitney.
5. Ibid.
6. *Anti-Semitism in the Soviet Union: Its Roots and Consequences*, vol. 2 (Jerusalem, 1980), 190.
7. This was made available in samizdat by Okuneva. A copy is in the author's possession.
8. Roy Medvedev, *Blizhnevostochnyi Konflikt i Yevreiskii Vopros* (May 1970). This document was a samizdat paper, a copy of which the author obtained.
9. *Novye Knigi SSR*, no. 15 (April 11, 1980).

4. Soviet Jewry and Soviet-American Relations: A Historical Analysis

1. Stalin is known to have commented, in reference to the large percentage of Jews in the Menshevik Faction at the Russian Social Democratic Party Congress of 1907 (as compared with the Bolshevik Faction that was primarily Russian): "It would not be a bad idea for us, the Bolsheviks, to organize a pogrom in the Party." Cited in William W. Orbach, *The American Movement to Aid Soviet Jews* (Amherst, Mass.: University of Massachusetts Press, 1979), p. 14.
2. For an excellent discussion of the rise and fall of the Evsektsiia, see Zvi Y. Gitelman, *Jewish Nationality and Soviet Politics: The Jewish Sections of the CPSU 1917–1930* (Princeton: Princeton University Press, 1972).
3. The best discussion of the origin and development of the Jewish Anti-Fascist Committee is found in Yehoshua Gilboa, *The Black Years of Soviet Jewry* (Boston: Little, Brown, 1971), chapter 2.
4. Ibid., p. 42.
5. Ibid., p. 51.
6. Zionist Archives, (Jerusalem) Documents No. S25/486/17/7/1941; S25/486/13/10/41; S25/6600/4/5/47—Skira I; S25/6660/5/47—Skira II; S25/6600/5-6/47—Skira III; and especially S25/9299/7/31/47 (report of a conversation between a high-ranking Yishuv official, Eliahu Epstein, and the first secretary of the Soviet Embassy in Washington).
7. The story is told in Gilboa, *Black Years*, chapters 7–10.
8. Ibid., p. 295.
9. *Jerusalem Post*, Feb. 3, 1961. Cited in William Korey, *The Soviet Cage* (New York: Viking Press, 1973), p. 35.
10. For a description of the matzo ban, see Korey, *The Soviet Cage*, pp. 46–47, and Joshua Rothenberg, *The Jewish Religion in the Soviet Union* (New York: Ktav, 1971), pp. 85–88. The Brezhnev regime lifted the ban in 1969, although Soviet Jews still have difficulty getting sufficient matzoth.
11. It should be noted that the book was published at a time when many Jews were being given the death penalty for alleged "economic crimes." For a description of these "crimes," see Korey, *The Soviet Cage*, pp. 80–81.
12. For a description of Sino-Soviet relations at this time, see William Griffith, *Sino-Soviet Relations, 1964–1965* (Cambridge, Mass.: MIT Press, 1967), chapter 2.
13. Cited in Korey, *The Soviet Cage*, p. 81.
14. See the description by Elie Wiesel, *The Jews of Silence*, (New York: Holt, Rinehart and Winston, 1966).

15. A description of the Leningrad trial is found in Korey, *The Soviet Cage*, chapter 11, and Leonard Schroeter, *The Last Exodus* (New York: Universe Books, 1974), chapters 10 and 11.

16. For a description of the events in Poland, see A. Ross Johnson, "Polish Perspectives, Past and Present," *Problems of Communism* 20, no. 4 (July – Aug. 1971): 59–72. Ironically, Gomulka had blamed the student demonstrations of 1968 on "Zionists" and as a result had expelled the vast majority of Poland's Jews by 1970 so that they were no longer available to be blamed for the December 1970 riots. For an analysis of Gomulka's policies toward Jews, see Paul Lendvai, *Anti-Semitism Without Jews* (Garden City, N.Y.: Doubleday, 1971), part 2.

17. Marvin Kalb and Bernard Kalb, *Kissinger* (New York: Dell, 1975), p. 245.

18. Leonid Brezhnev, "Report of the Central Committee of the Communist Party of the Soviet Union to the 24th Congress of the CPSU," *The 24th Congress of the Communist Party of the Soviet Union, March 30–April 19, 1971* (Moscow: Moscow Press Agency Publishing House, 1971), p. 50.

19. For a detailed description of Soviet policy at this point, see John Newhouse, *Cold Dawn: The Story of SALT* (New York: Holt, Rinehart and Winston, 1973), p. 215.

20. For a description of the sit-in, see Korey, *The Soviet Cage*, pp. 179–82.

21. Ibid., pp. 293–294.

22. Perhaps due to poor American intelligence, or possibly because of Kissinger's desire to encourage trade as a means of ensuring detente, the Russians were able to buy up a great deal of American grain at a very low price. For an excellent analysis of the grain deal, and other Soviet-American economic agreements, see Marshall Goldman, *Detente and Dollars* (New York: Basic Books, 1975), especially chapter 7.

23. For a description of the background of Sadat's expulsion decision, see Robert O. Freedman, *Soviet Policy Toward the Middle East Since 1970* (New York: Praeger, 1978), chapter 3.

24. Ibid., p. 73.

25. For a description of the head tax, see Korey, *The Soviet Cage*, pp. 315–20.

26. Marquis Childs, *Washington Post*, March 13, 1973. Cited in Paula Stern, *Water's Edge: Domestic Politics and the Making of American Foreign Policy* (Westport: Greenwood Press, 1979), p. 65.

27. For studies of the development of American opposition to the head tax into the Jackson-Vanik Amendment, see Stern, *Water's Edge*, and Orbach, *The American Movement*. Stern, a former legislative assistant to Senator Gaylord Nelson, is unsympathetic to the role played by Senator Jackson. Orbach takes a more balanced approach. For earlier studies, see Morris Brafman and David Schimel, *Trade for Freedom: Détente, Trade and Soviet Jews* (New York: Shengold, 1975) and William Korey, "The Story of the Jackson Amendment," *Midstream* 21, no. 3 (March 1975): 7–36.

28. Cf. *Vneshniaia Torgovlia SSSR ZA 1970*, p. 12, and *Vneshniaia Torgovlia SSSR ZA 1979*, p. 10.

29. Anyone interested in participating in this research project is invited to contact Dr. Heitman, Department of History, Colorado State University, Fort Collins, Colorado 80523; or myself, Office of the Dean, Peggy Meyerhoff Pearlstone School of Graduate Studies, Baltimore Hebrew College, 5800 Park Heights Avenue, Baltimore, Maryland 21215.

30. Korey, "The Story of the Jackson Amendment," pp. 9–10.

31. Cited in Korey, *The Soviet Cage*, p. 320.

32. *American Jewish Yearbook*, 1974–1975, p. 211. Cited in Brafman and Schimel, *Trade for Freedom*, p. 41. For a description of Viktor Louis, see Freedman, *Soviet Policy*, p. 57.

33. For an excellent analysis of the Soviet leadership's interest in Western trade at this time, see *Foreign Broadcast Information Service Special Report: Pressures for Change in Soviet Foreign Economic Policy* (Washington, D.C.: FBIS, April 5, 1974), report no. 306.

34. For a description of Soviet policy during the Yom Kippur War, see Freedman, *Soviet Policy*, chapter 5.

35. Korey, "The Story of the Jackson Amendment," p. 30.

36. For a description of some of the natural gas and oil projects for which the Soviet leadership was seeking American assistance, see John P. Hardt, "West Siberia: The Quest for Energy," *Problems of Communism* 22, no. 3 (May–June 1973): 25–36.

37. Korey, "The Story of the Jackson Amendment," p. 30.

38. Stern argues, not entirely convincingly, that Jackson's quest for publicity and Kissinger's secretiveness doomed the agreement (*Water's Edge*, pp. 162–93).

39. Marjorie Hunter, *New York Times*, Aug. 16, 1974. See also the report by Wolf Blitzer, *Jerusalem Post*, Aug. 16, 1974.

40. For a description of Soviet policy on emigration since the signing of the Helsinki Agreement, see Elizabeth C. Sheetz, "Emigration from the USSR in the Post-Helsinki Period," *Radio Liberty Research Bulletin,* RL (Jan. 7, 1977), pp. 1-11.

41. Dmitry Proektor, "Problems of Military Detente in Europe," *International Affairs* (Moscow), Dec. 1975, p. 33; and Morton Schwartz, *Soviet Perceptions of the United States* (Berkeley: University of California Press, 1978).

42. Seymour E. Goodman, "Soviet Computing and Technology Transfer," *World Politics* 31, no. 4 (July 1979): 539-70. See also Philip Hanson, "Western Technology in the Soviet Economy," *Problems of Communism* 27, no. 6 (Nov.-Dec. 1978): 20-30.

43. For a study of the development of the SALT talks, see Thomas W. Wolfe, *The SALT Experience* (Cambridge, Mass.: Ballinger, 1979).

44. Bernard Gwertzman, *New York Times,* Jan. 31, 1976.

45. Freedman, *Soviet Policy,* chapters 6 and 7.

46. *Pravda,* Dec. 1, 1976.

47. *Pravda,* Dec. 11, 1976.

48. *National Conference on Soviet Jewry News Bulletin No. 131* (Nov. 15, 1978), p. 2.

49. *Pravda,* Jan. 19, 1977.

50. Carter's telegram to Soviet dissident Jew Vladimir Slepak (who had been refused an exit visa) reportedly expressed "great concern about the treatment" that Jewish dissidents had suffered at the hands of the Soviet secret police and stated that Carter had a "deep personal interest" in their cases. See the report by Peter Osnos, *Washington Post,* Oct. 26, 1976.

51. Cited in Orbach, *The American Movement,* p. 153.

52. For a good analysis of the human rights controversy, see Jeremy Azrael, "Soviet-American Relations: Notes on Detente," *Current History,* (Oct. 1978): 117-20.

53. Adam Ulam, "U.S.-Soviet Relations: Unhappy Coexistence," *Foreign Affairs—America and the World 1978* (New York: Council on Foreign Relations, 1979), p. 559.

54. *Izvestia,* Jan. 22, 1977.

55. *New York Times,* Jan. 28, 1977.

56. Radio Moscow, in English, Jan. 29, 1977.

57. Cited in report by Peter Osnos, *Washington Post,* Feb. 5, 1977.

58. The text of the press conference is printed in Congressional Quarterly, *Presidency, 1977* (Washington, D.C.: Congressional Quarterly, 1978), p. 124.

59. Ford later said he was sorry he did not meet with Solzhenitsyn (*Christian Science Monitor,* March 3, 1977).

60. *Pravda,* March 22, 1977. For a comparative analysis of the various Soviet peace plans, see Robert O. Freedman, "The Soviet Conception of a Middle East Peace Settlement," in Yaacov Ro'i, ed., *The Limits to Power: Soviet Policy in the Middle East* (London: Croom Helm, 1979), pp. 282-327.

61. Congressional Quarterly, *Presidency, 1977,* p. 133-A.

62. For a discussion of the "back channel," see Newhouse, *Cold Dawn,* pp. 203-5.

63. Cf. *Pravda* and *Izvestia,* April 3, 1977.

64. *Pravda,* April 1, 1977 (translated in *Current Digest of the Soviet Press* 29, no. 13: 5-9).

65. Congressional Quarterly, *Presidency, 1977,* p. 146-A.

66. *Pravda* on June 11 had called the meeting "the infamous White House reception of the criminal Bukovsky."

67. Congressional Quarterly, *Presidency, 1977,* p. 152-A. Sharansky had been arrested in March.

68. *Documents and Resolutions, 25th Congress of the CPSU* (Moscow: Novosti, 1976), pp. 16, 39.

69. For President Carter's justification for not using the B-1 as a bargaining chip, see his news conference of June 30, reprinted in Congressional Quarterly, *Presidency, 1977,* p. 153-A.

70. *Pravda,* July 17, 1977.

71. The text of the speech is found in the *Department of State Bulletin,* August 15, 1977, pp. 193-198.

72. Cf. *Pravda,* July 24, 1977.

73. *Pravda,* Aug. 3, 1977.

74. Cited in the report by Don Oberdorfer, *Washington Post,* July 30, 1977.

75. For a description of Soviet policy during this period, see Freedman, *Soviet Policy,* pp. 295-98.

76. Cited in an Associated Press report from Beirut, *Baltimore Evening Sun,* Sept. 14, 1977.

77. For the text of the joint statement and an analysis of its implications, see Freedman, *Soviet Policy,* pp. 303-6.

78. Ibid., chapters 6–8.
79. *Pravda*, Sept. 25, 1977.
80. *Pravda*, Oct. 4, 1977.
81. Orbach, *The American Movement*, pp. 153–54.
82. For a monthly breakdown of Soviet-Jewish emigration in 1977, see *National Conference on Soviet Jewry News Bulletin No. 131* (Nov. 15, 1978), p. 2.
83. Soviet strategy in the Middle East during this period is discussed in Robert O. Freedman, "Soviet Policy Toward the Middle East from the Sinai II Accord to the Egyptian-Israeli Peace Agreement," in W. Raymond Duncan, ed., *Soviet Policy in the Third World* (New York: Pergamon, 1980), pp. 155–95.
84. For a detailed study of Soviet intervention in the Ethiopian-Somali war, see Richard Remnek, *Soviet Policy in the Horn of Africa: The Decision to Intervene* (Alexandria, Va.: Center for Naval Analyses, 1980). See also David Albright, "The Horn of Africa and the Arab-Israeli Conflict," in Robert O. Freedman, ed., *World Politics and the Arab-Israeli Conflict* (New York: Pergamon, 1979), pp. 147–91.
85. Robert O. Freedman, "The Soviet Union and the Arab-Israeli Conflict," in *World Politics*, pp. 84–85, n. 58.
86. Cited in Congressional Quarterly, *President Carter: 1978* (Washington, D.C.: Congressional Quarterly, 1979), p. 85-A.
87. Ibid., p. 84-A.
88. Ibid., p. 85-A.
89. *Pravda*, March 5, 1978.
90. The text of the speech is in Congressional Quarterly, *President Carter: 1978*, pp. 139-A–41-A.
91. Translated in *Current Digest of the Soviet Press*, 30, no. 12: 4.
92. *Pravda*, April 26, 1980.
93. Carter's press conference on May 25, 1978, in Congressional Quarterly, *President Carter: 1978*, p. 101-A.
94. Cited in Congressional Quarterly, *President Carter: 1978*, p. 101-A.
95. For a study of the evolution of Chinese economic policy to this point, see Robert F. Dernberger, "Prospects for the Chinese Economy," *Problems of Communism* 28, no. 5–6 (Sept.–Dec. 1979): 1–15.
96. The text of the speech is in Congressional Quarterly, *President Carter: 1978*, 148-A–51-A.
97. Translated in *Current Digest of the Soviet Press*, 30, no. 24: 1. Interestingly enough, a former speechwriter of Carter's, James Fallows, claimed that the speech was essentially a "stapling" of a Vance memorandum to a Brzezinski memorandum. See James Fallows, "The Passionless Presidency," *Atlantic Monthly* (May 1979), p. 43.
98. *Pravda*, June 26, 1978.
99. Congressional Quarterly, *President Carter: 1978*, p. 109-A.
100. Cited in National Conference on Soviet Jewry Press Service Release, May 30, 1980.
101. *Izvestia*, July 14, 1978.
102. For Moscow's reaction, see *Izvestia*, July 28, 1978.
103. *Pravda*, July 15, 1978.
104. *President Carter: 1978*, p. 116-A.
105. *Pravda*, Aug. 13, 1978.
106. Congressional Quarterly, *President Carter: 1978*, p. 45.
107. *Pravda*, Oct. 29, 1978.
108. By the end of 1978 no less than 28,864 Jews had been permitted to emigrate, the highest number since the record 33,500 in 1973.
109. For an excellent study of these events and the subsequent Sino-Vietnamese war, see Sheldon W. Simon, "The Soviet Union and Southeast Asia," a paper prepared for the Council on Foreign Relations Conference, "The Soviet Union in Asia," New York City, Dec. 1979.
110. For the text of the joint announcement and Carter's comments on it, see Congressional Quarterly, *President Carter: 1978*, p. 161-A.
111. Radio Moscow, in English in North America, Dec. 22, 1978, and *Pravda*, Dec. 22, 1978.
112. Radio Moscow, in English to North America, Dec. 21, 1978.
113. *Izvestia*, Jan. 14, 1979.
114. *Pravda*, Feb. 4, 1979.
115. *Izvestia*, March 21, 1979.
116. Dernberger, "Prospects for the Chinese Economy," pp. 10–11.

156 Soviet Jewry in the Decisive Decade

117. An editorial in the *New York Times* on April 6, 1979, reflected this viewpoint. It was rebutted in a letter to the editor by Eugene Gold, chairman of the National Conference on Soviet Jewry, which was published on April 26, 1979.
118. Report by Kevin Klose, *Washington Post*, April 21, 1979.
119. For analyses of the increasing tide of anti-Semitism in the Soviet Union at this time, see World Conference on Soviet Jewry, *The Position of Soviet Jewry 1977–1980: Report on the Implementation of the Helsinki Final Act Since the Belgrade Follow-up Conference* (Surrey, England: World Conference on Soviet Jewry, 1980); William Korey, "The Future of Soviet Jewry: Emigration and Assimilation," *Foreign Affairs* 58, no. 1 (Fall 1979): 67–81; and Zvi Gitelman, "Moscow and the Soviet Jews: A Parting of the Ways," *Problems of Communism* 29, no. 1 (Jan.–Feb. 1980): 18–34.
120. *Pravda*, June 17, 1979 (translated in *Current Digest of the Soviet Press* 31, no. 24:2).
121. The text of the communique was printed in *Pravda*, June 19, 1979.
122. For an analysis of the dilemmas facing Moscow in Afghanistan prior to the invasion, see Freedman, "Soviet Policy Toward the Middle East from the Sinai II Accord to the Egyptian-Israeli Peace Agreement," pp. 181–82.
123. Cited in a report by Hedrick Smith, *New York Times*, Aug. 3, 1979. State Department spokesman Hodding Carter was subsequently to relate the warning specifically to Afghanistan.
124. See the report in the *Washington Post*, Aug. 7, 1979.
125. *Pravda*, Sept. 28, 1979.
126. *Izvestia*, Aug. 17, 1979.
127. *Pravda*, June 20, 1979, and July 1, 1979.
128. *Pravda*, Sept. 16, 1979.
129. This is documented in World Conference on Soviet Jewry, *The Position of Soviet Jewry, 1977–1980*.

5. The Welcome Home: Absorption of Soviet Jews in Israel

1. Virtually all European Jews speak Russian, with a minority knowing Yiddish and even fewer Hebrew. The Georgian Jews are generally fluent in Georgian with varying command of Russian. Bukharan Jews have as their mother tongue a Judeo-Persian dialect, and many do not speak good Russian. Dagestani (Mountain) Jews speak Russian or the Judeo-Tat dialect.
2. While no complete analysis of the educational and occupational makeup of Soviet-Jewish immigrants is available, a survey taken for the period from January 1, 1974, to June 30, 1979, shows 39.4 percent "professionals" and an additional 9.8 percent "semiprofessionals." Of the professionals arriving in the period from January 1, 1977, to June 20, 1979, 25.2 percent were in medicine and 36.5 percent in engineering and architecture. See N. Magor, *Immigrants from the USSR and Dropouts Arriving in America: A Comparative Demographic Survey* (Jerusalem: Ministry of Immigrant Absorption, Research and Planning Division, 1980), tables 4.7.1–4.8, 4.9, pp. 52–54. A perhaps apocryphal story has it that one aircraft landing at Lydda brought with it nine Soviet-Jewish concert violinists. An analysis of the Soviet-Jewish minority's elite status in education based largely on the 1970 census will be found in Thomas E. Sawyer, *The Jewish Minority in the Soviet Union* (Boulder: Westview Press, 1979), pp. 42–50. A broader and more detailed historical survey will be found in M. Altshuler, *Soviet Jewry Today* (Jerusalem: Magnes Press, 1979), chapter 4 (in Hebrew).
3. All figures for annual emigration from the USSR to Israel are from Zvi Alexander, "The Emigration Policy of the USSR 1968–1978," *Behinot* (Jerusalem, 1970), p. 42 (in Hebrew). An earlier version in English may be found in the *Israel Yearbook on Human Rights* (Tel Aviv, 1977), pp. 268–335.
4. See *Izvestia*, Dec. 5, 1966.
5. See Khrushchev's statement in Vienna in 1960 and Gromyko's statement in July 1953, cited in Alexander, "Emigration Policy," p. 12. The bases in international law for the right of emigration are the UN Universal Declaration of Human Rights to which the USSR is a signatory, and the more recent Helsinki Final Act.
6. See Hadassa Adar, *Israel Public Attitudes Towards Immigrant Absorption* (Jerusalem: Ministry of Immigrant Absorption, 1973). Though this attitude has become much less of a problem, it was expressed at a political demonstration in March 1981 by M. K. Charlie Biton of the Communist-led "Peace and Democracy List" at a Knesset reception for former Prisoner of Zion Joseph Mendelevich.

7. A detailed description of such problems is given in Leonard Schroeter, "Anxious in Arad," *Jerusalem Post*, March 7, 1972. Numerous similar pieces can be found in all the Israeli newspapers of the period.

8. See Yitzhak Elam, *Transfer of Georgian Immigrants from Ashkelon to Shaderot* (Jerusalem: Ministry of Immigrant Absorption, 1976), for a full report on this problem and recommendations for corrective procedures.

9. A brief survey of the development of Israel's immigration absorption services will be found in Arthur Saul Super, *Absorption of Immigrants* (Jerusalem, 1967).

10. Ibid., p. 34. Ulpan experience was found to have an important effect on social and linguistic absorption in N. Carmon and B. Manheim, *Achieving Social Goals Through Housing Policy* (Haifa: Technion, 1976).

11. A survey made in the end of 1972 found the dependence of elderly Soviet-Jewish immigrants on National Insurance payments to be "a new and awkward situation." See Shlomo Cohen, *Old Age Pensions for New Immigrants* (Jerusalem: National Insurance Institute, 1974).

12. Super, *Absorption of Immigrants*, pp. 32–33.

13. See, for example, M. Checinski, *Engineering in the Soviet Union* (Jerusalem: Ministry of Immigrant Absorption, 1975); Yosef Litvak, *Jewish Scientists in the Soviet Union* (Jerusalem: Ministry of Absorption, 1976); Arnold Schwartz, *Medicine in the USSR* (Jerusalem: Ministry of Absorption, 1975).

14. R. Bar Yosef and J. Varsher, *A Follow-up Study on the Professional Absorption of Engineers* (Jerusalem: Hebrew University, 1977).

15. *Ha'aretz*, weekly supplement, Dec. 19, 1980, p. 8.

16. R. Bergman et al., *The Absorption of Immigrant Nurses from the Soviet Union* (Tel Aviv: University of Tel Aviv, 1974).

17. T. Horowitz and C. Frenkel, *Absorption of Immigrant Teachers Within the Educational System* (Jerusalem: Henrietta Szold Institute, 1977).

18. J. Shuval and A. Schwartz, *Absorption Processes of Soviet Immigrant Doctors* (Jerusalem: Institute of Applied Social Research, 1976).

19. A broad survey of the subject will be found in H. Graff, *Absorption of Immigrant Students from the Soviet Union* (Jerusalem: Ministry of Immigrant Absorption, 1977).

20. The figure, taken from a 1966 Soviet source, is cited in A. Nove and J. A. Newth, "The Jewish Population: Demographic Trends and Occupational Patterns," in L. Kochan, ed., *The Jews in Soviet Russia Since 1917* (London: Oxford University Press, 1978), p. 157.

21. Articles on the growing Russian-language cultural life in Israel appear regularly in the *Jerusalem Post Weekly*.

22. Leonard Schroeter, "Anxious in Arad," *Jerusalem Post*, March 7, 1972.

23. See Hadassa Adar, *Israeli Public Attitudes Toward Immigrant Absorption* (Jerusalem: Ministry of Immigrant Absorption, 1973). This is corroborated by David Katz, *Public Attitudes on Immigrant Absorption in Israel* (Jerusalem: Institute of Applied Social Research, 1971), who finds that one-half of the survey population has never discussed absorption problems with a new immigrant and one-third has done so at least three times.

24. Schroeter, "Anxious in Arad."

25. R. Bar Yosef, Gili Schild, and Judith Varsher, *University Graduates Seeking Employment* (Jerusalem: Hebrew University, 1975), found that among Soviet and Romanian immigrants, friends and family are one of the chief channels of information for job seekers. Americans and Europeans turn to newspaper advertisements and to personal initiative to a greater extent.

26. J. Shuval, Y. Marcus, and Y. Dotan, *Adjustment of Patterns of Immigrants from the USSR* (Jerusalem: Institute of Applied Social Research, 1974), pp. 36–37, in particular, deal with the complex connections of assistance in finding work and development of identification with Israel.

27. See the discussion of this point in Y. Branover, *About Russian Immigrants in Israel* (Jerusalem: World Zionist Organization, 1980).

28. Gur Ofer, Aaron Vinokur, and Yehiel Bar Haim, *Absorption and Economic Contribution of Soviet Immigrants in Israel* (Jerusalem: Falk Foundation for Economic Research, 1980).

29. Shuval, Marcus, and Dotan, *Patterns of Immigrants*, p. 41.

30. Figures cited by E. Lesham of the Ministry of Immigrant Absorption at the annual meeting of the Israel Slavic Association, Beersheva, May 1980.

6. A New Soviet Jewry Plan

1. See Annex 1 for a table listing the annual emigration of Soviet Jews and their countries of resettlement.
2. My forthcoming book, *The Development of the Soviet Jewry Movement: Observations of a Participant Observer*, will deal with these "signals."
3. On Kosygin's statement, see above p. 69.
4. For analyses of the impact of the Six Day War, see chapters 2 and 4 of this volume.
5. For an excellent analysis of the Leningrad Trials, see William Korey, *The Soviet Cage* (New York: Viking, 1973), pp. 201-75.
6. For an analysis of the politics of the emigration movement, see chapter 4 of this volume.
7. For analyses of Soviet anti-Semitism that prompted emigration, see chapters 2 and 3 of this volume.
8. The legal status of new immigrants is discussed in the Israeli government publication *Guide for the Oleh*.
9. The period of twelve months minus one day has been selected to satisfy American legal requirements.
10. This point is emphasized in chapter 5 of this volume.
11. See chapter 5 of this volume.

7. Soviet-Jewish Immigrants to the United States: Profile, Problems, Prospects

1. See Nuna Magor, *Haolim miBrihm vehanoshrim shehigiu leArhab—Skira demografit hasvaatit* (Jerusalem: Ministry of Immigrant Absorption, 1980), p. 18.
2. Data on immigration to the United States and other Western countries are culled from various issues of the HIAS quarterly, *Statistical Abstracts*; data on immigration to Israel are taken from annual reports of the Israeli Ministry of Immigrant Absorption, *Klitat Ha'Aliyah*, and from Magor, *Haolim miBrihm*.
3. Magor, *Haolim miBrihm*, p. 27.
4. See Mordechai Altshuler, *Haikbutz hayehudi biBrihm beyamainu* (Jerusalem: Magnes Press, 1979), p. 59.
5. See HIAS, *Statistical Abstract* 21, no. 4 (1980): 220.
6. Israelis have charged that some Soviet émigrés have sent their aged parents to Israel so as not to be responsible for their support, but have themselves immigrated to North America.
7. Jerome M. Gilison, *Summary Report of the Survey of Soviet Jewish Émigrés in Baltimore* (Baltimore: Center for the Study of Jewish Emigration and Resettlement, 1979). Another version is "The Resettlement of Soviet Jewish Emigres: Results of a Survey in Baltimore," in Dan Jacobs and Ellen Frankel Paul, eds., *Studies of the Third Wave: Recent Migration of Soviet Jews to the United States* (Boulder: Westview Press, 1981), pp. 29-56.
8. Jacobs and Paul, *Studies of the Third Wave*, pp. 57-75.
9. "The New Soviet Migration in Cincinnati," in Jacobs and Paul, *Studies of the Third Wave*, chap. 4.
10. Zvi Gitelman, "Soviet Immigrants and American Absorption Efforts: A Case Study in Detroit," *Journal of Jewish Communal Service* 55, no. 1 (1978): 11-28.
11. Funding for the project was generously provided by the Ford Foundation and the National Council for Soviet and East European Research.
12. See my "Soviet Political Culture: Insights from Recent Jewish Émigrés," *Soviet Studies* 29, no. 4 (Oct. 1977): 543-64, and the study cited in note 10.
13. V. Gerasimov, "Na vashikh ekranakh," *Novyi Amerikanets*, Feb. 3-9, 1981, p. 34.
14. Georgii Vil'dgrube, "Eti Amerikantsy," in ibid., p. 26.
15. According to figures I was shown in Baltimore, of the 160 Soviet-Jewish children in school in 1980-81, 130 were getting some Jewish education and more than 90 percent were in school. This is a far higher proportion than in New York, Chicago, or Detroit.
16. See *Narodnoe obrazovanie, nauka i kultura v SSSR: Statisticheskii sbornik* (Moscow: Statistika, 1977), p. 313.

8. Aspects of Integrating Soviet-Jewish Immigrants in America: Attitudes of American Jewry Toward the Recent Immigration

1. For an analysis of the cultural outlook of Soviet-Jewish immigrants to the United States, see Dan N. Jacobs and Ellen Frankel Paul, eds., *Studies of the Third Wave: Recent Migration of Soviet Jews to the United States* (Boulder: Westview Press, 1981), especially chapters 1–4.

9. Adaptation and Acculturation of Soviet Jews in the United States: A Preliminary Analysis

1. The research for this study was made possible by a grant from the Center for Soviet Jewry, Baltimore, Maryland. I am especially indebted to Mr. Fabian Kolker who supported this project from its inception. I would also like to express my sincere thanks to Howard Marks for his invaluable assistance in providing computer facilities and assisting with the analysis.

2. This problem is often voiced by community people who deal with Soviet émigrés on a functional level. For additional information concerning this aspect of surveying, see: Michael F. Weeks and R. Paul Moore, "Ethnicity-of-Interviewer Effects on Ethnic Respondents," *Public Opinion Quarterly* 45, no. 2 (Summer 1981): 245–49.

Bibliography

Statistical Collections

Hebrew Immigrant Aid Society, *Statistical Abstracts*.
Israeli Ministry of Immigrant Absorption, *Klitat Ha'Aliyah*.
Narodnoe obrazovanie, nauka i kultura v SSSR: Statisticheskii sbornik Moscow: Statistika, 1977.
Vneshniaia Torgovlia SSSR Za 1970, 1972, 1974, 1976, 1978, and supplement to *Soviet Foreign Trade*, 1981.

Books, Monographs, and Samizdat Publications

Adar, Hadassa. *Israeli Public Attitudes Toward Immigrant Absorption*. Jerusalem: Ministry of Immigrant Absorption, 1973.
Altschuler, Mordechai. *Soviet Jewry Today*. Jerusalem: Magnes Press, 1979.
Anti-Semitism in the Soviet Union: Its Roots and Consequences. Jerusalem: 1980.
Bar Yosef, R., Gili Schild, and Judith Varsher. *University Graduates Seeking Employment*. Jerusalem: Hebrew University, 1975.
Bar Yosef, R. and J. Varsher. *A Follow-up Study on the Professional Absorption of Engineers*. Jerusalem: Hebrew University, 1977.
Bergman, R., L. Graif, et al. *The Absorption of Immigrant Nurses From the Soviet Union*. Tel Aviv: University of Tel Aviv, 1974.
Brafman, Morris and David Schimel. *Trade for Freedom: Detente, Trade and Soviet Jews*. New York: Shengold, 1975.
Branover, Y. *About Russian Immigrants in Israel*. Jerusalem: World Zionist Organization, 1980.
Carmon, N. and B. Manheim. *Achieving Social Goals Through Housing Policy*. Haifa: Technion, 1976.
Cohen, Shlomo. *Old Age Pensions for New Immigrants*. Jerusalem: National Insurance Institute, April 1974.
Documents and Resolutions of The 24th Congress of the Communist Party of the Soviet Union. Moscow: Moscow Press Agency Publishing House, 1971.
Documents and Resolutions, 25th Congress of the Communist Party of the Soviet Union 1976. Moscow: Novosti, 1976.
Elam, Yitzhak. *Transfer of Georgian Immigrants from Ashkelon to Shaderot*. Jerusalem: Ministry of Immigration Absorption, 1976.
Foreign Broadcast Information Service Special Report No. 306: Pressures for Change in Soviet Foreign Economic Policy. Washington, D.C.: Foreign Broadcast Information Service, 1974.
Freedman, Robert O. *Soviet Policy Toward the Middle East Since 1970*. New York: Praeger, 1978.
Gilboa, Yehoshua. *The Black Years of Soviet Jewry*. Boston: Little, Brown, 1971.
Gitelman, Zvi Y. *Jewish Nationality and Soviet Politics: The Jewish Sections of the CPSU 1917–1930*. Princeton: Princeton University Press, 1972.

Goldman, Marshall. *Detente and Dollars.* New York: Basic Books, 1975.
Graff, H. *Absorption of Immigrant Students from the Soviet Union.* Jerusalem: Ministry of Immigrant Absorption, 1977.
Griffith, William. *Sino-Soviet Relations, 1964-1965.* Cambridge, Mass.: MIT Press, 1967.
Horowitz, T. and C. Frenkel. *Absorption of Immigrant Teachers Within the Educational System.* Jerusalem: Henrietta Szold Institute, 1977.
Jacobs, Dan, and Ellen Frankel Paul, eds. *Studies of the Third Wave: Recent Migration of Soviet Jews to the United States.* Boulder: Westview Press, 1981.
Kalb, Marvin, and Bernard Kalb. *Kissinger.* New York: Dell, 1975.
Korey, William. *The Soviet Cage.* New York: Viking Press, 1973.
Kuznetsov, Edward. *Prison Diaries.* New York: Stein & Day, 1975.
Lendvai, Paul. *Anti-Semitism Without Jews.* Garden City, N.Y.: Doubleday, 1971.
Magor, Nuna. *Immigrants from the USSR and Dropouts Arriving in America: A Comparative Demographic Survey.* Jerusalem: Ministry of Immigrant Absorption, Research and Planning Division, 1980.
Medvedev, Roy. *On Socialist Democracy.* New York: Knopf, 1975.
―――. *Blizhnevostochnyi Konflikt i Yevreiskii Vopros.* Samizdat 1970.
Meerson-Aksenov, Michael, and Boris Shragin, eds. *The Political, Social and Religious Thought of Russian Samizdat: An Anthology.* Belmont, Mass.: Nordland, 1977.
Newhouse, John. *Cold Dawn: The Story of SALT.* New York: Holt, Rinehart and Winston, 1973.
Ofer, Gur, Aaron Vinokur, and Yehiel Bar Haim. *Absorption and Economic Contribution of Soviet Immigrants in Israel.* Jerusalem: Falk Foundation for Economic Research, 1980.
Orbach, William W. *The American Movement to Aid Soviet Jews.* Amherst, Mass.: University of Massachusetts Press, 1979.
Remnek, Richard. *Soviet Policy in the Horn of Africa: The Decision to Intervene.* Alexandria, Va.: Center for Naval Analysis, 1980.
Rothenberg, Joshua. *The Jewish Religion in the Soviet Union.* New York: Ktav, 1971.
Sawyer, Thomas E. *The Jewish Minority in the Soviet Union.* Boulder: Westview Press, 1979.
Schroeter, Leonard. *The Last Exodus.* New York: Universe Books, 1974.
Schwartz, Arnold. *Medicine in the USSR.* Jerusalem: Ministry of Absorption, 1975.
Schwartz, Morton. *Soviet Perceptions of the United States.* Berkeley: University of California Press, 1978.
Shuval, J., Y. Marcus, and Y. Dotan. *Adjustment of Patterns of Immigrants from the USSR.* Jerusalem: Institute of Applied Social Research, 1974.
Shuval, J., and A. Schwartz. *Absorption Processes of Soviet Immigrant Doctors.* Jerusalem: Institute of Applied Social Research, 1976.
Stern, Paula. *Water's Edge: Domestic Politics and the Making of American Foreign Policy.* Westport: Greenwood Press, 1979.
Super, Arthur Saul. *Absorption of Immigrants.* Jerusalem, 1967.
Voronel, Alexander, and Viktor Yakhot, eds. *I Am a Jew: Essays on Jewish Identity in the Soviet Union.* New York Academic Committee on Soviet Jewry and ADL of B'nai B'rith, 1973.
Wiesel, Elie. *The Jews of Silence.* New York: Holt, Rinehart and Winston, 1966.
Wolfe, Thomas W. *The SALT Experience.* Cambridge, Mass.: Ballinger, 1979.

Articles and Chapters in Books

Alexander, Zvi. "Immigration to Israel from the USSR." *Israel Yearbook on Human Rights* 7 (1977): 268-335.

Azrael, Jeremy. "Soviet-American Relations: Notes on Detente." *Current History* (October 1978): 117-20.

Dernberger, Robert F. "Prospects for the Chinese Economy." *Problems of Communism* 28, nos. 5-6 (1979): 1-15.

Freedman, Robert O. "The Soviet Conception of a Middle East Peace Settlement." In Yaacov Ro'i, editor, *The Limits to Power: Soviet Policy in the Middle East*. London: Croom Helm, 1979. Pp. 282-327.

———. "Soviet Policy Toward the Middle East from the Sinai II Accord to the Egyptian-Israeli Peace Agreement." In W. Raymond Duncan, editor, *Soviet Policy in the Third World*. New York: Pergamon, 1980. Pp. 155-95.

Gerasimov, V. "Na vashikh ekranakh." *Novyi Amerikanets* (February 3-9, 1981).

Gitelman, Zvi. "Moscow and the Soviet Jews: A Parting of the Ways." *Problems of Communism* 39, no. 1 (1980): 18-34.

———. "Soviet Political Culture: Insights from Recent Jewish Émigrés." *Soviet Studies* 29, no. 4 (October 1977): 543-64.

Goodman, Seymour E. "Soviet Computing and Technology Transfer." *World Politics* 31, no. 4 (July 1979): 539-70.

Hanson, Philip. "Western Technology in the Soviet Economy." *Problems of Communism* 27, no. 6 (1978): 20-30.

Hardt, John P. "West Siberia: The Quest for Energy." *Problems of Communism* 22, no. 3 (1973): 25-36.

Johnson, A. Ross. "Polish Perspectives, Past and Present." *Problems of Communism* 20, no. 4 (1971): 59-72.

Korey, William. "The Future of Soviet Jewry: Emigration and Assimilation." *Foreign Affairs* 58, no. 1 (Fall 1979): 67-81.

———. "The Story of the Jackson Ammendment." *Midstream* 21, no. 3 (March 1975): 7-36.

Nove, A., and J. A. Newth. "The Jewish Population: Demographic Trends and Occupational Patterns." In L. Kochan, editor, *The Jews in Soviet Russia Since 1917*. London: Oxford University Press. Pp. 132-67.

Sheetz, Elizabeth C. "Emigration from the USSR in the Post-Helsinki Period." *Radio Liberty Research Bulletin* 2 (1977): 1-11.

Ulam, Adam. "U.S.-Soviet Relations: Unhappy Coexistence." In *Foreign Affairs: America and the World: 1978*. New York: Council on Foreign Relations, 1979. Pp. 555-71.

Index

Afghanistan, 13, 51, 64, 66, 89, 144, 147
Akhimov, V. S., 45
Altman, Anatoly, 63
Amalrik, Andrei, 9
Amin, Hafiz, 64
Andropov, Yuri, 148
Angola, 48, 57
Anti-Semitism in the USSR, 5, 11, 12, 13, 14, 16, 17, 22, 26, 29, 30–31, 32–34, 35, 36, 37, 38, 39–40, 41, 63, 66, 99, 144
Arbatov, Georgi, 45, 53, 56
Averbuch, Yisroel, 86
Azbel, Mark, 86
Azerbaidzhan, 14

Baltic Republics of the USSR, 90
Barabanov, Evgenii, 27
Begin, Menachem, 131, 136, 147, 148
Begun, Vladimir, 33, 35, 36
Belgrade conference, 54
Ben Gurion, David, 86, 136
Beria, Lavrenti, 32
Biden, Senator Joseph, 65
B'nai B'rith, 30, 146
Bogoraz, Larisa, 4, 5
Brailovsky, Irina, 28
Brailovsky, Viktor, 27–28
Brandt, Willy, 44
Branover, Herman, 86
Brezhnev, Leonid, 3, 5, 7, 10, 29, 30, 31, 33, 34, 35, 37, 42, 44, 46, 48, 49, 51, 53, 56, 57, 59, 62, 63, 66, 144, 145, 146, 148
Brzezinski, Zbigniew, 55, 58, 64
Bukovsky, Vladimir, 50
Bush, George, 146
Butman, Hillel, 63
Byelorussia, 14, 20, 22, 23, 35, 91
Byrd, Senator Robert, 65

Cambodia, 42, 61, 62
Camp David agreements, 54
Carter, Jimmy, 10, 38, 47–48, 51, 52, 53–67 passim, 136, 145
Chernovstsky, 23
China, 40, 41, 42, 43, 47, 48, 57, 58, 59, 60, 61, 62, 146, 147
Corvalan, Louis, 50
Crawford, Francis, 59, 60
Cuba, 55, 57, 63, 64, 65, 147
Czechoslovakia, 42

Dayan, Moshe, 136
"Democratic Movement" in USSR, 4, 12
Detente, 7, 34, 45–46, 51, 53. *See also* Soviet-American relations
Dobrynin, Anatoly, 147
"Doctors' Plot," 35, 36, 40
Dropouts. See *Noshrim*
Dulles, John Foster, 66
Dulzin, Aryah, 147
Dymshitz, Mark, 6, 63

Eban, Abba, 136
Egypt, 43–44, 45
Estonia, 22
Ethiopia, 55, 63
Evsektsiia, 39

Fain, Benjamin, 86
Feffer, Yitchak, 39
Ford, Gerald, 41, 46, 47
Fridman, Kim, 28
Furtseva, Yekatarina, 40

"Gang of Four, The," 47
Geneva Peace Conference, 48, 53
Georgia (Soviet), 14, 22, 90, 91
Georgian Jews in Israel, 72–73
Germany, Federal Republic of, 44–45, 92
Gierek, Edward, 42
Gilboa, Joshua, 39
Gilen, Sister Ann, 81
Ginsburg, Aleksandr, 50, 60, 63
Glazunov, Ilya, 12
Gomulka, Wladyslaw, 42
Gorky (city), 66
Gromyko, Andrei, 51, 52, 146

Haig, Alexander, 66, 146
Head tax, 7, 45, 66, 67
Helsinki Agreement, 10, 24, 28, 30, 47, 49, 50, 59
Herzl, Theodore, 136
HIAS (Hebrew Immigrant Aid Society), 9, 79, 84, 90, 130, 148
Hofstein, David, 39
Hua Kuofong, 57

Israel, 7, 10, 13, 18, 19, 21, 23, 24, 26, 31, 41–42, 43–44, 65, 68–78, 79, 80, 81–88, 90, 94, 100, 101, 115, 131, 132, 136, 145, 148

Israeli Ministry of Immigrant Absorption, 68, 70, 72, 75; absorption of Soviet professionals, 73–75, 77; absorption of students, 73

Jabotinsky, Vladimir, 136
Jackson, Senator Henry, 7, 17, 44, 46, 81, 136
Jackson-Vanik Amendment, 7, 38, 45, 46, 49, 54, 63
Japan, 61–62
Javits, Senator Jacob, 46
Jewish Agency (of the World Zionist Organization), 9, 68, 72, 75, 79, 84, 85, 147
Jewish Anti-Fascist Committee, 39, 66
Jews in the USSR, 27–28
Joint Distribution Committee, American-Jewish, 35–36, 40, 84
Judaism Without Embellishment, 36–37, 41

Kahane, Myer, 136
Kamenev, Lev, 38
Kampelman, Max, 146
Kanersky, Boris, 145
Katz, Natalia, 61
Kefrov, B., 32
Kennedy, John F., 64, 80, 136
Kharkov, 19, 28, 110, 116
Khrushchev, Nikita, 3, 11, 36, 38, 40, 41, 64, 66, 69
Kichko, Trofim K., 36–37, 41
Kiev, 19, 23, 28, 110, 112, 116
Kirilenko, A. P., 31
Kishinev, 19, 23
Kislik, Vladimir, 28
Kissinger, Henry, 43, 46, 48, 51, 54, 67, 136
Klepikova, Elena, 31
Knokh, Arieh, 63
Kochubievsky, Felix, 150
Kolker Plan, 82–88
Kondrachev, S. A., 151
Korneyev, Lev, 33, 34–35
Kosygin, Aleksei, 29, 31, 41, 43, 69, 80, 81
Krimsky, George, 50
Kuznetsov, 4–5, 6, 63

Latvia, 14, 22
Lenin, Vladimir, 11, 29
Leningrad, 19, 28, 31, 110, 112, 116
Leningrad Trials, 6, 42, 43, 81
Leningrad University, 150
Levich, Benyamin, 61, 86
Lithuania, 22
Louis, Viktor, 45
Lugar, Senator Richard, 65
Luntz, Alexander, 86
Lvov, 110, 116

Madrid Conference on Security and Cooperation in Europe, 24, 28, 30

Medvedev, Roy, 34
Meir, Golda, 86, 136
METAR, 86
Mikhoels, Solomon, 39, 40
Minsk, 18, 35, 59, 110, 111, 112
Mitin, Mark B., 32
Mitterand, François, 153
Mohsen, Zuheir, 54
Moldavia, 14, 22, 90
Mondale, Walter, 49, 62
Moroz, Valentin, 63
Moscow (city), 19, 31, 66, 110, 111, 112, 113, 116
Moscow Helsinki Monitoring Group, 26, 50
Moscow State University, 26, 145

National Conference on Soviet Jewry, 17, 146
Narovchatov, Sergei, 32
Navon, Yitzhak, 136
Nixon, Richard, 43, 44, 45, 46, 47, 136
Noshrim (dropouts), 9, 23–24, 77–78, 79–80
Novaia Gazeta, 95
Novoe Russkoe Slovo, 95
Novosibirsk, 28
Novy Amerikanetz, 95
Novy Mir, 4, 32
Nudel, Ida, 59, 60

Odessa, 14, 19, 23, 110, 112, 116
Okuneva, Ruth, 33, 34
Orlov, Yuri, 50, 57
Osipov, Vladimir, 12
OVIR (Soviet emigration office), 6, 13

Palestine Liberation Organization (PLO), 54, 65
Panis, René, 30
Penson, Boris, 63
Peres, Shimon, 136
Pikul, Valentin, 33
Piper, Hal, 59
Podgorny, Nikolai, 31
Poland, 32, 42, 147
Pol Pot, 62
Polsky, Victor, 86
Press, Frank, 60

Rabin, Yitzhak, 136
Reagan, Ronald, 31, 66, 144, 145, 146, 147
Refuseniks, 16, 20, 24, 25, 27, 28, 33, 57, 66, 144, 145
Ribicoff, Senator Abraham, 46
Riga, 19, 23, 28, 29, 110, 113, 116
Rogov, Sergei, 30–31, 146
Romania, 32
Romanov, Gregory, 31
Roosevelt, Franklin D., 136
RSFSR (Russian Soviet Federated Socialist Republic), 14, 23, 90
Ryazanov, Vasily (pseud.), 32–33

Sadat, Anwar, 43, 44, 54, 55
Sakharov, Andrei, 27, 45, 50, 66
Salt I, 38, 42, 43, 49, 54
Salt II, 38, 47, 51, 53, 54, 55, 58, 63, 64, 65, 67, 89
Samizdat, 4, 12, 27
Sazonov, Anatoly, 33, 34
Schroeter, Leonard, 76
Senderov, Valery, 145
Shcharansky, 52, 60
Shifrin, Avrum, 86
Shultz, George, 45, 146
Sino-American relations. See China
Sino-Soviet relations. See China
Sinyavsky-Daniel trial, 4
Six Day War (1967), 4, 5, 41, 70
Slepak, Vladimir, 49, 59, 60
Society of Immigrants from the USSR, 76
Solovyev, Vladimir, 31
Solzhenitsyn, Alexander, 5, 50
Somalia, 55
Soviet-American relations, 7, 10, 16, 19, 28, 38, 40, 41, 42, 43, 44–45, 46–64 passim, 66
Soviet-Germans, 44–45
Soviet Jewry Movement, 80, 81
Sovietische Heimland, 18, 40, 80
Soviet Jews: absorption in Israel, 68–78; adaptation and acculturation in the United States, 109–43; reasons for leaving the USSR, 6, 9, 10, 11, 12, 13, 21, 23–24, 66, 112–16
Stalin, Joseph, 3, 11, 29, 31, 32, 35–36, 38, 39, 40, 66
Stevenson Amendment, 7, 46
Suslov, Mikhail, 31
Sverdlovsk, 28
Syria, 45

Tadzhikistan, 22
Tallin, 110
Taraki, Noor Mohammed, 64
Tashkent, 19, 110, 112, 116
Teng Hsiao Ping, 57, 62
Tibilisi, 14

Time and We, 31
Toon, Malcolm, 59
Trotsky, Leon, 38
Truman, Harry S., 136
Tsivin, Mikhail, 150
Tvardovsky, Alexander, 3–4

Ukraine, 10, 13, 14, 18, 20, 24, 26, 28, 37, 90, 91, 110
Ulam, Adam, 49
USSR-Israel Friendship Society, 145
Uzbekistan, 14, 22

Vance, Cyrus, 51, 54, 55, 57, 58, 60
Vanik, Representative Charles, 63, 81. *See also* Jackson-Vanik Amendment
Veche, 12
Vietnam, 47, 61, 62
Vilnius, 23, 28, 110
Vins, Georgi, 63
Vladivostok Accord, 49
Voronel, Alexander, 27, 86
Vyzovs (invitations to emigrate to Israel), 5, 18, 19, 21, 22, 23–25

Watson, Thomas, 65
Weizman, Chaim, 136
Whitney, Craig, 59

Yakhot, Viktor, 27
Yemelyanov, Valery, 33
Yevseev, Yevgeny, 32, 33
Yom Kippur War (1973), 7, 23, 45–46, 75
Young, Andrew, 55, 65

Zaire, 57
Zalmanson, Wolf, 63
Zinoviev, Grigory, 38
Zionism, 11, 12, 13, 23, 30, 31, 32, 33, 34–35, 36, 37, 40, 71, 89, 131
Zorin, Valentin, 62
Zotov, Konstantin, 18

Contributors

Dr. Stephen C. Feinstein is professor of Russian and Middle Eastern history at the University of Wisconsin at River Falls. Among his publications is "Soviet Jewish Immigrants in Minneapolis and St. Paul: Attitudes and Reactions to Life in America," in Dan Jacobs and Ellen Paul, eds., *Studies of the Third Wave* (Boulder: Westview Press, 1981).

Dr. Robert O. Freedman is dean and professor of political science at the Peggy Meyerhoff Pearlstone School of Graduate Studies of the Baltimore Hebrew College. Among his publications is *Soviet Policy Toward the Middle East Since 1970* (New York: Praeger, 1982), which is now in its third edition.

Dr. Theodore Friedgut is senior lecturer in Russian studies and chairman of the department of Russian and Slavic studies at the Hebrew University of Jerusalem. He has published *Political Participation in the USSR* (Princeton: Princeton University Press, 1979) among other works.

Dr. Jerome E. Gilison is professor of political science at the Baltimore Hebrew College. Among his publications is *The Soviet Jewish Émigré* (Baltimore: Baltimore Hebrew College, 1977).

Dr. Zvi Gitelman is professor of political science at the University of Michigan. Among his publications is *Jewish Nationality and Soviet Politics: The Jewish Sections of the CPSU 1917–1930* (Princeton: Princeton University Press, 1972).

Jerry Goodman is executive director of the National Conference on Soviet Jewry.

Fabian Kolker is a Baltimore attorney and cofounder of the American Conference on Soviet Jewry.

Dr. William Korey is director of international policy research for B'nai B'rith. Among his publications is *The Soviet Cage: Anti-Semitism in Russia* (New York: Viking Press, 1973).

Ilya Levkov is a consultant in New York City. He published the article "USSR vs. Anatoly Sharansky" in *Midstream* (May 1978).